Neanderthals at Work

How People and Politics Can Drive You Crazy . . . And What You Can Do About Them

Albert J. Bernstein
Sydney Craft Rozen

John Wiley & Sons, Inc.

New York / Chichester / Brisbane
Toronto / Singapore

To Lee

In recognition of the importance of preserving what has been written, it is a policy of John Wiley & Sons, Inc., to have books of enduring value published in the United States printed on acid-free paper, and we exert our best efforts to that end.

This publication is designed to provide accurate and authoritative information in regard to the subject matter covered. It is sold with the understanding that the publisher is not engaged in rendering legal, accounting, or other professional service. If legal advice or other expert assistance is required, the services of a competent professional person should be sought. *From a Declaration of Principles jointly adopted by a Committee of the American Bar Association and a Committee of Publishers.*

Library of Congress Cataloging-in-Publication Data

Bernstein, Albert J.
 Neanderthals at work : how people and politics can drive
you crazy . . . and what you can do about them / Albert J. Bernstein.
Sydney Craft Rozen.
  p. cm.
 Includes index.
 ISBN 0-471-52727-0 (cloth)
 1. Organizational behavior. I. Rozen, Sydney Craft. II. Title.
III. Title: Neanderthals at work.
HD58.7.B466 1992
650.1—dc20 91-25866

Printed in the United States of America

10 9 8 7 6 5 4 3 2 1

Acknowledgments

The authors thank:

John Mahaney, our editor, whose marginal notes and innocent-sounding questions drove us crazy and helped us write a much better book.

Our agent, Elizabeth Wales of Seattle, who talks like a Northwest Believer but turns into a real Competitor in New York.

Denise Bjurstrom, who was always willing to transcribe just one more "final" tape.

Al thanks:

Joyce Howell, for her support from the first hour of this project, especially for inventing the Cult of Cool.

My family, Luahna, Jessica and Joshua, for loving and helping me through even the most unlovable stages of writing this book.

My parents, Elliot (ohev shalom) and Connie Bernstein, for their love and what they taught me; and to Mort, for framing all the press clippings.

Sydney thanks:

The Sidetracked Home Executives, Pam Young and Peggy Jones, who helped me get started doing the work I love.

My family of proud press agents, Lora Pellegrini, Norma Gunning, Ken Gunning, Esther and Bill Rozen, Mary Mihovilich, Boyd Rozen, Lynn and Mark Johnson, and the late Dan Giuntoli and Roy Craft, who remained convinced we were headed for the best-seller lists.

My children, Geoffrey and Amanda, whose homework never needs as many rewrites as this manuscript did.

Above all, my husband, Lee, who is a winner by standards far deeper than any Competitor's, and who always listened and understood, no matter what.

Contents

though, they are the guys you want on your side. Why everyone, from the shop floor to the CEO, has at least a touch of the Rebel inside.

Why do some people succeed and others don't? Is it plain old dumb luck, the "Old Boy Network"—or is something else going on? Why you need to look at the things you're reluctant to do, and do them.

Why bravado and disdain help some people cover up their fear. Why your company is full of people who think they're the only ones who know what they're doing—or who are doing things the right way. Everyone else is either a sell-out or just doesn't know what's going on.

Part Three
Innocents at Work: The Believers

They do so much work so well, but if they think the secret of success is "Work hard, play by the rules, and do a good job," they'll be rewarded in heaven but disappointed on earth. Unfortunately, business doesn't work that way. The Myth of Motivation is the Catch-22 of the business world.

Believer rituals—the Sacred Goals and Objectives, the Solemn Performance Review, the Posting of Rules—measure merit and point the way toward getting ahead. Or do they? Nobody will tell you the rules for success. You have to figure them out for yourself.

8 *My Boss Is Driving Me Crazy:
What To Do about Problems with
Misguided Authority Figures*

The unspoken conflict at the heart of most businesses is
not over such petty issues as who runs the company. This
is the big one. It's about who is *right*. If you work for the
Boss from Hell, rely on strategy rather than exorcism.

9 *The Myth of the Man-Eating Job*

The Romantic Disorder—the Myth of Burnout—the only
disorder named by the people who have it. How to slay
the mythical beast and begin taking responsibility for
yourself.

Part Four
Warriors at Work: The Competitors

10 *The Cult of Winning and the Management
Mystique: The Secrets of Competitors' Power*

The beliefs that have stirred the hearts of Competitors
from Alexander the Great to your boss. They understand
that it's not how hard you work; it's what you work hard *at*
that counts. They know that the way to get things done is
through politics. If that fails, armed combat will do nicely.

11 *Founders, Warriors, and Entrepreneurs:
Corporate Heroes and Mythical Tales*

From the entrepreneur who started The Greatest Company
in The World to the sales rep whose biggest pitch is his
own legend, every company is rich with stories about its
own breed of hero. There's a message in these myths, but if
you take them literally, you may miss it.

12 *Warriors' Codes of Combat*

Ritual behavior among the Competitors. Never mind that a
lot of these things could be done more cheaply and effi-
ciently by cooperating. For Competitors to buy in, every
deal has to look like personal combat. No quarter asked or
given.

Part Five
The Rules of the Game

It's almost part of the American way to hate your boss. Analyzing a national pastime.

When Competitor managers see themselves as the only ones in the department who know anything, subordinates seldom see them as a class act; but when their bosses act like royalty, employees think about revolution.

You and your boss may be speaking different languages. A handy phrase-book for trips to management country.

The only real cure for the Believer Blues is discovering what's really going on. In this chapter, we reveal the mysteries. How to learn the hard lessons of the Eleventh Commandment . . . and begin figuring out your company's first ten.

In the world of work, if you have to ask, then somebody is probably going to tell you, "No." To be a Competitor, you have to live by your own decisions and abandon the need for permission. Other trials by fire include Learning to Read the Writing That's *Not* on the Wall, Facing Down the Fear of Failure, and Giving Up the Need for Praise. With initiation requirements like this, it's easy to see why some people choose not to join and those who do attain the ceremonial pinstripes sometimes lose perspective.

How our characters fare a few years down the road. What might happen if they take our advice instead of hanging on to their outmoded beliefs. People listen and cooperate. Best of all, business doesn't seem so crazy any more. It could happen for you, too. It's worth a try.

Introduction

Dinosaur Brains, our first book, showed how to deal with impossible people and the irrational, primitive behavior programmed into the oldest part of their brains: the hyperaggressive boss whose highest compliment is "You're an idiot"; the office bully, and the fellow worker who defends turf like a primeval lizard guarding its territory.

In this book, we're still in the jungle, but we've climbed up a few rungs on the corporate evolutionary ladder, moving from the primordial swamp of dinosaurs and blatantly irrational behavior to more subtle difficulties with other people—the snares and traps that can make you wonder whether your co-workers have evolved beyond the Neanderthal Age.

How else can you explain the fact that the rules people play by are never the ones written down, or that the most savage competitors get all the big raises and promotions, while other people never seem to get ahead, no matter how hard or how conscientiously they work? Why do some of the most creative people feel like outsiders, even though they're the ones called in to lead the rescue when a crisis comes up in their department?

Why does the thinking around your office seem so rigid? Why does conflict flare so easily and cooperation seem so difficult? Why do the people you work with sometimes seem like a clan of cave-dwellers, with tiny brains and uncivilized approaches to the job? Who are these primitive blockheads who never do things in ways that make sense to a reasonable, intelligent person?

Who are they? They're *Neanderthals at Work*—and they drive you crazy, don't they?

Maybe it isn't the people themselves who make you want to

tear your hair out, but their attitudes and personalities that drive you crazy. Either you don't understand *them*, or they don't understand *you*. Or both. (Usually both.)

The problem centers on dividing the world into "Us" versus "Them." That's *really* Neanderthal thinking. When people do things we don't understand or agree with, we tend to assume there's something wrong with them. We call them "Neanderthals" (or whatever other pet name we reserve for people who are not like us.) They don't do what we do; they don't believe what we do; they don't think as we do. We wonder whether they even think at all. Neanderthals!

We huddle together with members of our own tribe and complain about the Neanderthals down the hall . . . or joke about them . . . or plot against them. We invent stories and myths to explain the things and people who drive us crazy at work.

Why You Need This Book

This book identifies the three basic types of people in every company: those who *know* what the real rules are and play politics by those rules, those who *think* they know what the right rules are but are missing something important, and those who refuse to play by anybody else's rules at all.

The three personality types are our own invention, but they have a firm psychological base. We call them "Rebels," "Believers," and "Competitors." Each group wants and expects different rewards from the job. Each is motivated by different myths, and each is willing to defend its beliefs against attacks from the others. Each sees the others as the Neanderthals who drive them crazy.

- *Rebels'* imagination, creativity, and smarts make them indispensable to most companies, but they drive their bosses crazy with their disdain for authority. (Their bosses drive Rebels crazy with their office politics and stuffed-shirt mentality.)

- *Believers*, the original corporate innocents, stand firm in their faith that hard work and playing by the rules will pay off. It drives them crazy when the rewards don't come. Believers' naïvete and obsession with rules drives their bosses crazy—but most bosses know that, without Believers, American business would flat-out collapse.
- *Competitors* play to win. They are the warriors who make the deals, chair the meetings, and keep their eyes on the bottom line. They play the corporate game as if they were born knowing all the rules. It drives Competitors crazy when people don't understand The System as well as they do. To Rebels and Believers, Competitors may seem to be the ultimate Neanderthals—brutish and insensitive beneath their pinstripes.

The Purpose of This Book

In *Neanderthals at Work,* we use the continuing stories of several characters to illustrate and explain our three personality types and the problems they have getting along with each other—the misunderstandings that make for too much conflict and too little cooperation.

This is a book for understanding the way things are at work. Nothing will change in the corporate world until we acknowledge the way people actually behave and explore the ways they really see each other. Then we can learn to do something to reach each other, instead of labeling people as "Neanderthals" and using the label as a reason either to fight with them or ignore them.

Why do you need to know about people like these? Because you work with them every day. Until you learn to figure them out, *you're not doing your job.* No matter who you are or where you stand in the company, you cannot be effective (sometimes you can't even survive) in corporate life without understanding and learning to deal with these patterns of thought and behavior in the people you work with—and in yourself.

We all have elements of the Rebel, Believer, and Competitor personalities within us, but most of us identify more with one type than with the others. When you evaluate your score in the self-insight quiz, which follows Chapter 1, you may be surprised to discover that you are more similar to "those other people" than you thought.

The groups are states of mind, and they don't always exactly correspond with levels in a company's hierarchy. Each company has its own peculiar game and its share of Rebels, Believers, and Competitors. We all go to work with our own psychological baggage, our own Neanderthal-like way of thinking and behaving, convinced that our point of view is right and true, and that the other groups must be lazy, naïve, or just plain sleazy. We get caught up in our rigid thought patterns about what's right and heroic, and the way to get things done at the office.

Everyone at work has value, but your own viewpoint can prevent you from seeing that people don't have to be just like you to have worth. Through stories and archetypes, we analyze the problems and explain the myths and rituals of characters who, we think, will remind you of the people you work with every day. By understanding these different ways of thinking, you can make sense not only of the people you may think are Neanderthals, but of yourself as well. That is the purpose of this book.

How to Use This Book

In Chapter 1, you'll find an overview discussion of the Rebels, Believers, and Competitors and an introduction to some of our characters, whose situations throughout the book will illustrate the attitudes, problems, and strengths of the three groups.

To help you begin to identify where you fit within these personality types, we have provided you with a multiple-choice quiz at the end of Chapter 1. We call it "Just Who Do You Think You Are? A Rebel, a Believer, or a Competitor?" Answer each question with the response that most closely matches your own, and count up your points in each category: Rebel, Believer, or Competitor.

(After you've taken the quiz for yourself, we suggest that you take it again—this time answering each question as you think your boss or the coworker who drives you craziest would respond. Odds are that the scores will be different from your own—which is another reason why you need this book!)

Chapter 2 follows our characters through the rituals and ceremonies associated with "Joining the Tribe," many of which you've sweated through yourself.

The book then divides into three sections that focus on each of our three personality types and the myths and rituals that affect them, brought to life by the characters who appear throughout. Later, we offer practical advice and strategies for working more successfully with the people at your company whom you may think of as Neanderthals.

In Part Two, "The Rebels: Corporate Mavericks," you'll meet Luke, our computer troubleshooter, and other members of what we call the "Cult of Cool." Their stories will help you understand the "corporate teenager" you work with (or the one who may still be a part of your own personality.)

In Part Three, "Innocents at Work: The Believers," you'll follow the professional ups and downs of Lesley, Carl, and other hard-working employees who don't understand why they're not moving up. They're trapped by their belief in "The Myth of Motivation." What they learn (or fail to learn) about the _real_ rules of office life may help give your own career a jump-start, or help you understand what motivates and frustrates the people you manage.

In Part Four, "Warriors at Work: The Competitors," you'll get a new view of the pressures, myths, and motivations that engage Dana, Bronson, and Jack (our Competitor characters), and many real-life managers within the Cult of Winning. As you read, you can evaluate which of our characters' approaches is closest to your own—or your boss's.

At the end of each of these sections, we include a short quiz that will help you identify the Rebel, Believer, or Competitor within yourself. Following the questions is an analysis of the strengths, weaknesses, and choices that your answers reveal, as well as suggestions for managing or working with each personality type.

Part Five is called "The Rules of the Game." If you've decided you want to play the corporate game, this section will teach you how to play it well. We'll help you figure out the real rules of the office and give you suggestions and strategies for dealing with Competitor bosses from hell, learning the language of management, and unlocking the secrets of what it takes to get promoted.

The final chapter, "A Happy Ending for a Business Book?" illustrates the positive changes that can result when Rebels, Believers, and Competitors learn to work with, instead of against, each other.

We have organized this book around continuing characters' stories, examples, discussions, and suggestions. We strongly recommend that you read the *entire* book, not just the section that you think most closely describes your own personality. To break the patterns of Neanderthal misunderstanding and friction among the groups, you need to understand the whole picture: Rebels, Believers, and Competitors, no matter how different they are from you.

If you want to get promoted, this book will tell you how. However, you don't have to want to change jobs or play politics to find value in these pages. Our advice will work equally well toward helping you stay where you are and feel less hassled by the people you work with and the politics they play.

We believe that change is possible. You *can* learn to work more effectively with the people who drive you crazy. You can even learn to stop driving yourself crazy—and that may be the greatest change of all.

PART ONE

The Players

1

"They're Driving Me Crazy!"

All Those Neanderthals at Work

Luke stormed into the bullpen, where he and the rest of the computer guys had their cubicles. Waving a sheet of paper over his head, he shouted, "Can you believe this? A formal letter of reprimand!"

"Dear Luke," he pretended to read. "You are a bad boy because you haven't filled out your 326s *again*. Fill them out right now or go directly to Jail. Do not pass 'Go,' and do not collect $200. . . . ."

As his buddies grinned, Luke folded the letter into paper airplane wings and sailed it into the circular file. "Wasn't it just two weeks ago that the Suits and Ties were talking about giving me a 'Hero of the People' medal for working 20 hours straight to get the mainframe on line?" he asked sardonically.

He shook his head, sighed, then rolled his eyes upward and clasped his hands. "OK, OK, your worships, I'll fill out the 326s—and *you* can come down here and get the bugs out of the inventory control program!" As he rummaged through his bottom drawer for the required forms, Luke muttered, "This place is driving me crazy."

* * *

3

Don't cry, Lesley warned herself fiercely as she read the memo. Look professional.

"Congratulations to Andy Lite, who has been selected as this department's Assistant Manager."

Lesley read it three times, hoping the name would change, but there it was: Andy—and not me, she whispered. Not me. I wanted it so much, and I worked so hard to get it. I asked everybody—the Human Resources people, that political gorilla, Bronson, and especially my boss, Jack—what I should do to show I was ready for management, and they all said the same things: Be a team player; show you're motivated and that you're not afraid of a little hard work.

I did it, too, Lesley told herself, grinding her teeth as she clenched her jaw. My numbers are right at the top of the department, and I've volunteered for every job that's come along. I even manage the softball team! Team player, they say. Oh, sure. . . .

Then they give it to Andy?! That guy wouldn't recognize hard work if it came up and bit him. He spends all his time playing politics with the guys from the finance department. . . . It's not fair! I wish there was somebody I could talk to, somebody who would tell me what's really going on around here. What do I have to do to get these people to appreciate me? They're driving me crazy. . . .

* * *

The delegation filed out of Bronson's office, leaving their proposal on his desk for consideration. Bronson skimmed it quickly, then turned it face-down and snorted with contempt. So they wanted a consultant to come in and "clarify job responsibilities and authority in the department"? He knew what they were really after: a set of ironclad job descriptions that they could wave in his face whenever he asked them to do something that wasn't already spelled out. What did they think this was—the federal government?

They're always looking to pin things down and make rules about how to play the game, Bronson thought disgustedly. Well, why don't they ask their consultant to try going to Wall

Street and making a rule that our stock will keep going up, no matter how soft-headed we are around here? Man, they're driving me crazy. . . .

Luke, Lesley, and Bronson are all employees of "Neander-Tek," but they aren't feeling much esprit de corps at the moment. Each has a different idea about what work is all about and what it means to get ahead. These three characters, as well as others you'll meet later, represent the three most common attitudes people have toward work. We call these personality types the "Rebels," the "Believers," and the "Competitors." Many of the problems people have at work—why conflict comes so easily and cooperation seems so difficult—stem from what each personality type considers Neanderthal-like thinking and behavior by the other two groups. People in each group see themselves and the way they do things as "right." Everyone else is a "Neanderthal"—primitive, brutal, or stupid.

He's a Rebel

Luke, computer troubleshooter extraordinaire, is just the guy you want to get the mainframe up and running, or to uncover costly glitches in the programs—if you can find him. He keeps his own hours and verbally manhandles anybody who complains about his erratic schedule. He's there to fix computers, and that's it. Just *try* to get him to fill out the paperwork or to come to a meeting.

Luke is the best, and he knows it. He doesn't have to read the manual or take classes on computer tech; they always frustrate him because they're so elementary. He just has a feel for it. He's the picture of cool competence. A natural. While everybody else stands around, wringing their hands over the latest mainframe tantrum, Luke can just walk in and take control. A glance at the screen, a couple of typed commands, and Bingo!, it's fixed. He drives the "Suits and Ties" crazy with his allergic reaction to corporate rules and rituals. The feeling is mutual. The managers drive him crazy, too. Guys

like Luke are one in a million, but he spends most of his time just this side of probation.

Luke is a classic Rebel, the kind of guy who seems to have "Born To Be Free" tattooed on his soul. The phrase is an expression of who Luke is and how he sees himself: tough, street-smart, a lone wolf who makes his own rules. (Some people would say the tattoo reads, "Take This Job and Shove It" because guys like Luke have a knack for getting under the skin of people who take their own authority too seriously. That's not quite accurate, though. When faced with a glitch in the program, Luke will gladly work 20 hours a day, through the weekend, to fix it. He just won't come in or call in the next Monday after it's fixed because he knows there's no urgent reason for him to show up. After all, the glitch is fixed, isn't it?)

Luke knows you have to play politics to get ahead, and that's definitely not for him. He knows that people in management (the Suits and Ties) get all the perqs, but the privileges aren't worth all the hassles or the political games to him.

Luke and many other Rebels are caught up in a myth we call the "Cult of Cool." Their toughness and disdain give them a certain intriguing status. (Remember how you felt about the rebels in your high school class? Think back to fourth period history: Remember how athletes, cheerleaders, student council members, and other "popular" kids reacted to the little group whispering in the back row: the girl with the black batwings of eyeliner and the tight sweater, the guys with the hooded eyes and black leather jackets. They talked in class, and they might get into trouble, but they were so *cool*.)

In the business world, the Rebels' "cool" covers what such an attitude usually tries to hide: fear. Fear of failure. Fear of the unknown. Fear of not fitting in. Competitors and Believers know a lot of crucial information about The System that Rebels don't know; they can operate within the constraints of that System in ways that Rebels such as Luke can't tolerate or refuse to learn.

No matter how unreadable or infuriating the Rebels can be,

smart bosses won't write them off. They're too valuable. Few companies can do without the Rebels' imagination, creativity, and ability to get to the heart of a problem. Yet Luke and other Rebels could get more satisfaction from their jobs and would benefit both themselves and the company if they stopped thinking about business in such a superficial way and stopped assuming that everyone in management is a sell-out. Those promotions may not be for Luke, but the negative aspects of the Cult of Cool prevent him from even considering the offers.

Believers: Corporate Innocents

Lesley is committed to her job. Whatever she does, she does well. Even though she more than pulls her weight in her department, she never misses a chance to pitch in and help the company as a whole. Besides managing the company softball team on her own time, she's also on the recycling committee and is working on a task force to study child care. Fifty-hour weeks are typical for her, and 60-hour weeks aren't unheard of. When Jack James, her boss, needs to reorganize a project, he goes to her, and Lesley always says, "OK." Her thinking is, "You have to show you're motivated if you want to get ahead."

We call Lesley a "Believer," for her dedication and commitment to her job. She gets lots of praise from Jack, who admits that she's saved the bacon more times than he can count. Despite all this, Lesley is definitely not getting ahead. Sure, she gets great reviews, and her step-raises come in like clockwork, but she's still in the same position she was hired into four years ago. She realizes that promotions aren't that easy to come by, but now that Jack has turned her down for the assistant manager opening, Lesley is beginning to wonder.

The thing that most bothers Lesley and other Believers is that nobody in management seems to appreciate or even realize everything they do. As soon as Lesley finishes one extra project, her boss or a couple of other managers will hand her more to do, saying, "We're giving this to you, Les, because we know it will get done." It will—but there doesn't seem to be any end to it. Some days, Lesley feels downright used. Don't get her wrong, she likes working hard, but . . .

The problem came to a head when the assistant manager position came up. Here was Lesley's big chance. She went in to talk to Jack about it, but he didn't say anything close to what she had expected. There was no, "Oh, yeah, it's in the bag," the inevitable reward for all her hard work. Instead Jack just looked at her quizzically and asked, "Are you sure you're ready for a position like that?"

"Besides," he joked, "I can't let you go. I need you too much right here."

Lesley thought he meant it as a compliment, but maybe there was more than a little truth in it. Also, what was this about not being ready for management? Hadn't she always done everything she was assigned and done it well? What was Jack talking about? It was all so confusing and unfair, so crazy-making.

Lesley's case is typical of the conflict between the viewpoints of Believers and Competitors. The Believer view is that there's something terribly wrong here. Lesley is highly motivated, follows the rules, and does more than her share of the hard work. She is the epitome of Believer virtue. However, in the world where merit is supposed to count, what does she get for it? Not as much as she hoped for. Certainly no promotion. Just more hard work.

As you read this, internal conversations such as Lesley's are going on in the heads of millions of Believers all over the country. The visible conflict here may be between Believers and Competitors, but the battle is fought in the hearts and minds of Believers: "Is it me, or is it my boss?" This ambiguity is characteristic of the struggle.

So who is to blame? Let's ask Jack James, Lesley's Competitor boss.

Jack answered, "Lesley is great. No question about it. There are times when I think she runs the department single-handed. And then she volunteers for all those committees. Salt of the earth. Backbone of the company."

"So why didn't you give her the promotion, Jack? Why did you say she wasn't ready?"

Jack said firmly, "Well, she isn't ready. If you want to be a manager, you have to think like one. She should be lobbying me for projects that require more initiative and zip, instead of just taking whatever anybody puts on her desk.

"And her choice of committees. Don't get me wrong, recycling and child care are great. But she passed up the chance to work on the Founder's Day program, where she could have rubbed elbows with a lot of upper managers and the Old Man himself. Instead, she decided to manage the softball team, which is composed of mostly folks from the plant. To make matters worse, she eats lunch with secretaries."

"So why didn't you tell her?"

"I did," Jack said. "That was pretty hard for me. She took it like a slap in the face."

"Now wait a minute. All you told her was that she wasn't ready. You didn't tell her to quit the softball team and stop eating lunch with secretaries, did you?"

"Well, if I had, she wouldn't have understood." Jack shrugged. "She would have looked at me like I was crazy, and the next day the grapevine would have been full of stories about why I don't like secretaries and have a personal vendetta against softball players. Sure, I could have told her, but she wouldn't have understood."

"Jack, Lesley worked in your department for several years. Couldn't you have taken her under your wing and groomed her, become her mentor and all that?"

Jack hesitated. "Well, I will do that . . . when she's a little more . . . ready."

"That never quite happens, though. Instead of telling her she's not doing the right things, you give her praise and tell her how great she is and that you wish you had ten other employees just like her. Isn't that a little deceptive?"

"No," Jack James said, frowning. "That's true."

People who work as hard as Lesley are great for the company. Competitors couldn't do anything without them. Lesley and other Believers think that doing what's good for the company is doing what's good for them—and Competitors don't tell them otherwise (they'd be crazy to do so).

Who's right? Who's wrong? Who's to say whether Lesley would make a good manager? Lesley's problem is that she's a corporate innocent, too caught up in what we call the "Myth of Motivation." This myth says, "If you want something enough, if you believe in it and give it your best effort, you'll get it." The positive side of this myth for Believers is the willingness to work hard. However, they don't realize that hard work and motivation aren't the only things that count. You also need to know about how to make things happen within The System.

Once Lesley learns what we call the "Eleventh Commandment"—that nobody will tell you your company's first 10— she will understand what to work hard at. To get what she deserves, she needs to stop being vulnerable and to begin doing the right things for herself and her career.

Competitors: Corporate Warriors

Bronson is a high-powered management type—a Competitor archetype from the word "Go." He sees a deal, and he makes it. He spots a political weakness in a colleague, and he grabs his spear. To Bronson and many other corporate warriors, it's a jungle up there on the thirty-seventh floor. No wonder the Rebels and Believers at Neander-Tek see him as the role model for all those newly minted MBA Neanderthals who will drive them crazy in a few short years.

What really drives Bronson crazy are some of the narrow-minded people he works with. They want to pin him down on everything—why he did one thing in one situation and something different in another. Don't they realize that a manager

has to be flexible and can't be tied down by a bunch of rules that are only going to be changed anyway? They just don't buy into The System. If his subordinates say anything critical, Bronson thinks they must have an attitude problem.

Not all Competitors are as blood-thirsty as Neanderthals like Bronson, but they *do* value winning—sometimes above anything else. And they know *how* to win.

Competitors' skill comes in understanding the real rules of their company's culture well enough to know how to take action to reach their goals. They can see The System; they know how to use it to accomplish something positive. Their personal drive to win gives them the courage to take risks. Without that, there would be no expansion, no big deals, and no excellence. Believers, and even many Rebels, certainly seek to excel, but companies also need the skills of Competitors to put all the pieces of the "excellence puzzle" together.

Competitors also come to accept the great truth of the business world: Success does not depend solely on how much work you do, but also on how well you understand and deal with office politics. To the other groups, "politics" is almost a dirty word. To Competitors, politics are inevitable. They know that in any group of more than two people, it takes politics to get anything done. "Politics," said Tallyrand, "is the art of the possible." Competitors believe this with all their heart.

Needless to say, the Competitor's drive to win has its negative side. If all business is competition, then, if you're not winning, you're losing. This attitude leads Competitors to undervalue the position they occupy, wherever it may be on the corporate ladder. Promotion is their most important goal, and they keep getting neck strain from looking up to the next corporate level. Think, for example, of all the publications and training courses for entry-level personnel that include "Management" as a prominent part of the title. (Those that are headlined "Executive" are for middle managers, of course.) These courses are offered in companies whose official mottos tout "Better Than Average Excellence In All Things." But even the lowest level employees know that keeping costs down is much more important than keeping quality up. In their constant climb up the corporate ladder, Competitors can never admit that they're not number one in anything. It's against their religion.

To Competitors, coming in second is definitely losing. In their hearts, they know they can't win if they admit that losing is even a possibility. What's more, to keep a firm grasp on the will to win, Competitors will usually say that things are bigger, better, more important, or of higher quality than they really are. They see this as a necessary tactic, crucial to presenting a positive image and bolstering their motivation. From the outside, though, Competitors' tendency to exaggerate looks like wishful thinking, pretending, or out-and-out lying, and it drives Rebels and Believers crazy.

It's tough working for a Competitor. It's even tougher being one. Bronson, our heavy-duty Competitor, is a hard man to work for. He's quick to criticize and slow to praise. When a member of his staff comes up with a good idea, Bronson takes credit for it. Worst of all, he never listens. He knows it all already. The one consolation is that however demanding he is of his staff, he's twice as hard on himself.

Inside his own mind, Bronson, like other gung-ho Competitors, is caught up in what we call the "Cult of Winning." It's his greatest strength and his greatest weakness. To feel good about himself, he has to feel like the most competent person in the company. (This can also make him the loneliest person in the company.) Even though he's "a manager," he doesn't really manage. Managing involves using the skills of others to get the job done. Bronson has a hard time acknowledging that other people have any skills. He believes that if you want anything done right, you have to do it yourself, which is nearly the antithesis of real management. Bronson's subordinates see him as taking all the glory for himself and leaving the scut work for them.

Bronson has the Competitor's typical blind spot—discounting people who do not think or act as he does (in other words, people who are not Competitors. He looks at Rebels and sees only bad attitudes; in Believers, he sees hopeless naïvete. He's a "Neanderthal," all right! Bronson figures it would take too much time to bring them up to his level, so he just tells them what to do and chews them out when they mess up. What else can he do? He doesn't realize that he's clearly transmitting his own devaluating attitude, which makes it more likely that his people *will* make mistakes.

Bronson needs to learn how to lead people according to what they are, instead of assuming that if they were any good, they'd be like him.

In Their Hearts, They Know They're Right

In their hearts, each personality type—Rebels, Believers, and Competitors—thinks that their way is the right way and that they are the only ones who are doing real work. Oh, the other groups are needed—somebody has to fix the computers, keep the books, and make the deals—but *they* are what the company is all about.

The "Neanderthal-like" conflicts among Rebels, Believers, and Competitors is demoralizing at work. It is the basis for much of what companies call "communication problems" and "attitude problems," as well as for job stress and burnout. Few companies' cultures are strong enough to affect this built-in conflict. All the corporate slogans, dress codes, and employee-of-the-month awards in the world can do little to diminish it. In fact, they make it worse by trying to cover it up.

We believe that this conflict is avoidable. To avoid it, people need to know more about the three personality types—who they are, what they believe, and what their real talents are. They also need to learn more about themselves.

What does success mean to you? Being left alone to do your work in peace? Accomplishing something you can stand behind? Getting to the top? Does it mean that once you're at the top, you're the kind of leader that people willingly follow? Whatever it means to you, success depends on how well you learn the things that people never tell you at work, the things that can drive you crazy.

Come with us as we help you make sense of the "Neanderthals" you work with. Through the adventures of our characters, we'll show you the positive and negative traits of the three personality types, explain why you need to be aware of their myths and rituals, and help you deal with the Rebel, the Believer, or the Competitor inside yourself. To get you started, we offer a quiz on the next few pages, to help you figure out which group's attitudes, strengths, and weaknesses come closest to your own.

Just Who Do You Think You Are?
A Rebel, A Believer,
or A Competitor?

Take this quiz to find out how you fit within the three personality types described in this book.

Directions: For each question, choose the response that best describes you most of the time. At the end of the quiz, you will find a scoring guide for the responses you chose.

1. Choose the statement that is most true of you:
   (a) It really bothers me to have to do things that should not be part of my job.
   (b) I pride myself on doing all of my job as well as I can—including the parts I don't like.
   (c) I focus my effort on the parts of my job that my company considers important.

2. Choose the one that is most true of you:
   (a) I know how to tell where I stand with my boss.
   (b) I wish my boss would leave me alone.
   (c) I wish my boss would give me more feedback.

3. Indicate which of the following best describes your viewpoint:
   (a) I wouldn't like to be considered conceited.

    (b) I am responsible for making people aware of my skills and accomplishments.

    (c) I don't care what people think.

4. What does success mean to you?
   (a) Success is mostly a matter of luck and who you know.
   (b) Success is mostly a matter of motivation and hard work.
   (c) Success is mostly a matter of knowing The System and using it to accomplish your goals.

5. Which is most true of you?
   (a) I'd rather be right than be happy.
   (b) I'd rather be happy than right.
   (c) I don't see a connection between being happy and being right.

6. Which best describes you?
   (a) I have been reprimanded for not doing something I was supposed to do.
   (b) I make it my business to avoid being reprimanded.
   (c) If you've never been reprimanded, it means you've never taken any risks.

7. In an unfamiliar situation, you usually figure out what you're supposed to do by:
   (a) Asking someone, or reading what I can about the subject.
   (b) Watching the people in charge and doing what they do.
   (c) Figuring out the situation by myself, trying out things I think might work.

8. Which is most true of you?
   (a) I sometimes bend the rules.
   (b) I play by the rules.
   (c) It depends on what rules you mean.

9. Choose one:
   (a) I like the excitement of crisis situations.
   (b) I perform best in stable, predictable situations.

(c) I do my best work when I'm in the spotlight, when others will notice the results of my efforts.

10. With which do you most agree?
    (a) The means are as important as the ends.
    (b) The ends sometimes justify the means.
    (c) I won't think twice about breaking a stupid rule or policy if it means getting the job done better or more easily.

11. Choose the one that is most true of you:
    (a) I would like my peers to see me as my own person, different from everybody else.
    (b) I would like my peers to see me as intelligent, motivated, and hard-working.
    (c) In some situations, I have tried to have my peers underestimate me.

12. Which of the following bothers you most:
    (a) People who say one thing when they really think something else.
    (b) People who don't understand how The System really operates.
    (c) People who don't know what they're talking about.

How Did You Score?

Directions: Review your answers, and use the following scoring guide to record your points for Believer (B), Competitor (C), and Rebel (R). Following this section is a guide for tallying and interpreting your score.

For each question, you'll find that there are benefits and drawbacks to each response. Whichever answer you gave is the right answer for you. However, each answer also reveals some limitations in perspective. Competitors, Believers, and Rebels each see office life differently. The purpose of this book isn't to glorify one kind of personality at the expense of another or to change you from one kind of personality to another. Our purpose here is to show you how to build on your *own strengths while broadening your view of the "Neanderthals" you work with.*

Question 1.

If you chose (a): Rebels often have strong focus and task-centeredness, especially (but not exclusively) on the technical aspects of the job. This probably enhances your effectiveness in doing those aspects of the job, but your rebellion against doing other parts of the job may create conflict with your boss. The tasks you do not consider part of the job may actually be things you don't like, don't do well, are afraid of, or don't understand. For some of these tasks, if you try them, you may find them less irritating, difficult, and confusing than you had thought they'd be. You'll also find that you have fewer hassles with your boss. Score 1 R point.

If you chose (b): Believers demonstrate solid citizenship and reliability. ("Somebody's gotta do it" is your motto.) Your company greatly benefits by having you on the job. Unfortunately for you, however, this is not the way to get ahead at most companies. If you spend a lot of time doing tasks that nobody checks, you probably won't be appreciated or rewarded for your efforts, and you're apt to be frustrated. To get rewards (such as promotions, perquisites, or salary boosts), try doing some of the things that you know will draw attention to the valuable work you do. Watch how Competitors do it, and learn. Score 1 B point.

If you chose (c): Competitors focus on what is rewarded. This is the clear path to getting ahead at work. Unfortunately for the company that employs you, though, many of the tasks that nobody checks may still be important and necessary. Also, if you don't have an army of Believers working to fill in the gaps in your work, you may have to suffer the consequences of some of your inactions. Score 1 C point.

Question 2.

If you chose (a): Competitors' independence and self-reliance often translate into bravery on the corporate battlefield. However, they are not always right in gauging other people's opinions of them—especially the opinions held by non-Competitors. In the rare case that their boss is a non-Competitor, they could have trouble. Usually, however, this tendency to think more highly of themselves than others do makes it hard for Competitors to manage non-Competitors. Score 1 C point.

If you chose (b): Rebels' independence can be a positive force, giving you the ability to make your own decisions. As long as your decisions are effective for the company, you'll be fine. However, your independence can also lead to problems with authority, particularly if you aren't careful to make your boss look good and feel powerful. (Spurned bosses usually retaliate.) Score 1 R point.

If you chose (c): Studies show that feedback, especially positive reinforcement, is the best way to get the most from employees. If your boss (who may be a fellow Believer) enjoys giving feedback, you'll be fine. However, if your boss is a Rebel or a Competitor, your wish for feedback may be puzzling and even irritating to your boss. In fact, if your boss gives you feedback and praise, it might signal a *lower* opinion of you: Your boss may think you're too dependent. Score 1 B point.

Question 3.

If you chose (a): Believers are good team players who are concerned that others share the limelight. Your coworkers and your boss probably like having you around. However, while you may enjoy warmer relationships with your colleagues, neither modesty nor team play reap the big rewards at the office. Like it or not, self-promotion is usually the key to promotions and hefty raises. Score 1 B point.

If you chose (b): Competitors' willingness to promote themselves leads to career advancement and a greater sense of control. Unfortunately for your coworkers, this tendency makes you a bad team player and reinforces your tendency to undervalue others. Also, if your relationships with coworkers affect your ability to get the big rewards, you may have to learn some new strategies. Score 1 C point.

If you chose (c): The Rebels' response is all-American: Davy Crockett and Dan'l Boone would approve. Your immunity to other people's opinions probably also saves you from a lot of headaches, ulcers, and other stress-related illnesses. Unfortunately, however, you may also continue to irritate or hurt others by ignoring their reactions to what you do; this is not a good basis for getting along with others. The Believers you work with may be hurt by your indifference, and the Competitors you work with will find ways to make you lose if they don't think you're helping them to win. Score 1 C point.

Question 4.

If you chose (a): This may well be true. Believing it protects you from getting too upset over the things you can't control. However, don't let this attitude prevent you from realizing that you do have some control over your job. Get to know some key people if you want to get some of the rewards you deserve for the work you do. Score 1 R point.

If you chose (b): This attitude helps you to get the day-to-day work done and to do it as well as you do. Unfortunately, however, this attitude is not usually rewarded. If you want rewards, you need to learn to recognize and focus on the blue-chip tasks. Score 1 B point.

If you chose (c): You're right—This is definitely the best way to reap the big rewards. However, focusing on your personal success, rather than on the good of the group or the company, drives Believers crazy and makes Rebels even more rebellious. To encourage Believers to keep up the good work—and to minimize your hassles with the Rebels, try a little team play. Score 1 C point.

Question 5.

If you chose (a): Somebody has to stand up for principles. Unfortunately, this attitude can lead to a lot of stress-related illnesses and even to martyrdom. It's also not the way to win friends and influence people—or to get promoted. When you're sure that you're right, consider the possibility that just this once, you might be wrong. If you're still sure you're right, consider the possibility that you'll pay too high a price for being right. If you're still sure you're right, stick to your guns, and pat yourself on the back for being noble—if unrewarded and perhaps even disliked and martyred. Score 1 B point.

If you chose (b): You may get what you want, but along the way you might have to sacrifice your principles. Recognize, however, that most of the Rebels and some of the Believers around you don't appreciate your savvy and don't like your ways of getting what you want. At some point in your career, their opinions may affect your ability to get the rewards you seek. Score 1 C point.

If you chose (c): You know how to tune out the criticism of others; many of your coworkers find this to be the most distressing aspect of work life. However, if you're frequently doing things that others don't think is right—even when you know you're right—you may find yourself in hot water more often than you'd like to be. What others think of your behavior largely determines how they treat you, regardless of what you think of your behavior. Score 1 R point.

Question 6.

If you chose (a): You think for yourself, and you take chances. Good! Some of the risks you take may pay off for you and for your company. Unfortunately, however, many of the chances you take won't turn out as you would have hoped, and when that happens, you'll suffer the consequences. Not good. Score 1 R point.

If you chose (b): This attitude keeps you on the straight and narrow. You probably avoid taking chances, especially if you think you might get into trouble or be criticized for having done so, and this strategy seems to have kept you safe so far. However, when you take no risks, you also don't have much of a chance to grow or to show your ability to make independent decisions—the stuff promotions are made of. Score 1 B point.

If you chose (c): This is true; all the big management writers say so. Risk is necessary, and you're probably savvy enough to know which risks you should and shouldn't take. However, if you miscalculate, criticism still hurts. Also, you may tend to look down on those who don't take the risks you do—particularly your Believer coworkers, who avidly avoid all risks. You may want to develop a deeper appreciation of their behavior, though. If they took the risks you take, with their hard work and dedication, they might be able to climb past you on the way to the top. Score 1 C point.

Question 7.

If you chose (a): This is the best way to find out—*if* someone will tell you what to do or *if* what to do is written down somewhere. Unfortunately, when Competitors are in charge (which they usually are), they're usually careful *not* to tell you or to write it down anywhere. So the answer you get is incomplete. Score 1 B point.

If you chose (b): This is the way to learn fast and to get the real story. In most situations, this is the best approach. However, in a few situations, you may miss the chance to create an even better solution of your own. Don't blindly follow the behavior of the top Competitors if you think that your own solutions might be better sometimes. Also, recognize that Believers and Rebels don't learn the way you do. When they ask you for suggestions or for information, provide it; don't mislead them or conceal the truth out of habit. Today's advice-seeker may hold the information you need tomorrow. Score 1 C point.

If you chose (c): You're independent and creative, and you're probably often right. Unfortunately, sometimes, you're wrong in the way you size things up, so you need to develop a few other strategies for figuring things out—just for those one in a million occasions when you don't know the best way to do something. Score 1 R point.

Question 8.

If you chose (a): You're not afraid to take risks, but your rule-bending could get you into trouble if you don't know which rules don't bend. Score 1 R point.

If you chose (b): Avoiding reprimands may seem like the obvious thing to do, but not everybody does this. The behavior of Competitors and Rebels who flagrantly risk reprimands may puzzle you, but to them, these risks seem worthwhile—and often they are. Your more conforming behavior may keep you safe from reprimands, but it also keeps you from standing out from the crowd. Every once in a while, you may want to try doing something extraordinary that puts you in danger of being reprimanded. Score 1 B point.

If you chose (c): You understand the way things really are and know how to figure out the real rules. If you usually guess correctly when and where to break the rules—and which rules never to break—you'll move quickly up the corporate ladder. The down side is that you can lose sight of your own internal rules for what you should and shouldn't do. Most of the Competitors and Rebels with whom you work already may consider you untrustworthy. After a few shady transactions, some of the Believers also may learn not to trust you. If the day comes when credibility is crucial to climbing up the corporate ladder, you may find yourself unable to reach the next rung. To avoid huge credibility gaps, you may want to glance at your moral compass from time to time. Score 1 C point.

Question 9.

If you chose (a): You're great in a crisis, but work life usually is far more mundane. If you thrive only in crises, you may find your day-to-day work dull—which would make it pretty tough to show up day after day. Try to find some things of interest in the less critical aspects of work life. Score 1 R point.

If you chose (b): You get your daily work done, and you probably do it very well. Unfortunately, the route to the top is usually strewn with unpredictable events. Occasional crises help to shake things up and keep us from becoming rigid. Because there's no way to avoid crises and change, relax a little, and enjoy the spontaneity of having to take a risk or trying something new every once in a while. Score 1 B point.

If you chose (c): You definitely have the right idea for getting ahead. Unfortunately, a lot of the crucial work of a company must be done out of the limelight, where no one sees what is done or how it gets done. If you can, find some Believers or some Rebels to take care of those crucial but unrecognized tasks. If you understand the Rebels and Believers with whom you work, you will be free to focus on the high-visibility tasks. (For example, provide lots of praise to your Believers and lots of independence to your Rebels.) If you don't understand how to get Believers and Rebels to work for you, you'll end up having to do those invisible jobs yourself—or worse, having to take the highly visible negative consequences that result when those jobs aren't done. Score 1 C point.

Question 10.

If you chose (a): You're ethical, and you'll sleep well at night. However, you may also be naïve if you don't recognize that Competitors and Believers may be playing by a different set of principles. Score 1 B point.

If you chose (b): You'll get things done, but this is not the basis for conventional ethics, and the Believers and the Rebels with whom you work won't understand—or even respect— your view. Score 1 C point.

If you chose (c): Your moral compass may be set to a different set of directions than those governing your coworkers. You're going to get into trouble if you break rules that you think are ridiculous. Score 1 R point.

Question 11.

If you chose (a): Being independent is terrific a lot of the time and will sometimes even earn you the respect of your peers if it turns out that you were right and the majority (or the boss) was wrong. However, don't rebel just for the sake of being different. You could waste a lot of effort. Score 1 R point.

If you chose (b): Most of the time, it's in your best interests to have others recognize your abilities. When dealing with Competitors, however, you may lay down your cards before you have to and give them too much information about how you think. In some situations, you may be wise to remain an unknown quantity, at least for a while. Score 1 B point.

If you chose (c): You sly dog. Machiavelli would approve. However, it's hard to communicate with (or be trusted by) your peers when you play your cards this close to your vest. (*Decep-*

tive is the word that comes to mind.) Avoid gaping chasms of credibility. Score 1 C point.

Question 12.

If you chose (a): You place a high value on honesty—and, heaven knows, American business needs ethics. Unfortunately, you may find it very difficult to understand other people's messages—especially those of Competitors, and if you have to work with them, you're going to have to understand them. Score 1 B point.

If you chose (b): It's terrific for you that you understand how The System really operates. If everyone understood it, you'd face many more Competitors than you already do. Instead of dismissing your ignorant coworkers, you might occasionally clue them in. If they're true Believers or Rebels, you'll still be miles ahead of them on the fast track. Also, if you show that you understand their different perspectives and respect their intelligence, they might just help you get ahead. Score 1 C point.

If you chose (c): You focus on competence and demand a clear demonstration of ability before you respect someone. Unfortunately, you may have too narrow a view of competence. This attitude can lead you to ignore the special skills of your coworkers. The political savvy of Competitors is much to be admired, and the hard work and dedication of Believers also deserves your respect. Though they may lack the competence you particularly appreciate, they're still quite effective in their own areas of expertise. Score 1 R point.

Interpreting Your Score

Count your total number of R (Rebel), B (Believer), and C (Competitor) responses. Compare your totals, to see which of the three you most closely identify with and which of the three you would probably find the most difficult to understand.

This test and this book as a whole are designed to help you see specific situations as other people would. The ideal score for understanding your coworkers is an even balance of the three types. A balanced score indicates a high ability to see people and situations from several different points of view. The more flexible you can be, the more options you'll have, and the less likely you'll be to let other people drive you crazy—or to think of them as Neanderthals.

Most people score higher in one personality type than in the other two. Of course, no one is all Rebel, all Believer, or all Competitor, but a high score in one personality type means you tend to exhibit those strengths and weaknesses. Though we have said that the people who score at the Competitor end get the most tangible, material rewards, Believers and Rebels may find their own perspectives and work styles to be the most personally rewarding for them.

Read this book's section on your dominant group with particular care. You'll find examples and discussions of situations, attitudes, traps, and problems to which you may be particularly susceptible, as well as suggestions for dealing more effectively with the other groups. At the end of Parts Two, Three, and Four are (a) short quizzes to help you decide whether you may be too much of a Rebel, a Believer, or a Competitor, (b) ideas for what to do, plus (c) summaries of tips for managing and working with people in each group.

2

Joining the Tribe

Rites of Passage, Trials By Fire, and Ancient Secrets Your Boss Knows but You Don't

The hut is dark, but the night is alive with the sounds of drums beating, voices chanting, and bonfire crackling.

You wait and wonder what will come next.

Suddenly the door bursts open, and two warriors grab you and thrust you out into the great circle.

Your eyes ache from the brightness of the fire. The drums pound in your ears. All around you are people in strange and frightening masks, clad in ceremonial robes.

The warriors drag you in front of a demon, who holds a rattle made of human skulls in each hand.

You face each other. Abruptly the drumming and chanting stop.

"Tell me about yourself," the demon commands.

A lot of what goes on in a typical organization is ritual. Rituals are simply the way certain things are done by members of the tribe. The ways we greet one another, how we physically position ourselves in relation to one another, how we conduct meetings, and when and how we do the things we do—all these are rituals known and performed by members of the tribe.

Most rituals also have special meanings to the people who perform them. Some of these meanings are commonly recognized and understood. Job interviews aid in selecting new members of the tribe. Both the annual company picnic and the quarterly pep talk are intended to unify the members with the common purpose of the tribe. Other rituals are more subtle, and their meanings are more obscure. For example, some of the rites surrounding the budget may be known to and understood by only a few (such as how it's drawn up, who gets to see it, and what it's used for).

Whether obvious, widely practiced, and understood, or subtle, obscure, and rarely used, rituals are observed in almost every aspect of life at work:

The procedures for posting new jobs
How people get trained for their positions
How meetings are held
How supplies are requested
Where people go for lunch and how long they stay

The actions themselves may seem bewildering and, to the uninformed, even silly. The *meaning* of the actions is what is important, the shared tribal message. The way things are done at your company tells you who and what is most important and how you fit into the overall scheme. Members of the tribe who don't understand the tribal message are at risk of not fitting in, of not truly belonging to the tribe—or at least of not being eligible to enter the inner circle of Tribal Elders.

Not a bad day's work for a new lawyer. Susan put the finishing touch on her brief and looked at her watch. 5:30. Looked like she'd be able to get home at a reasonable hour. She put on her jacket and headed for the door, calling a cheerful goodbye to the receptionist on her way to the elevator.

The next morning, the news had spread throughout the thirty-fourth floor that Susan had left work before the senior partner.

* * *

This month, the management meeting was held at the plant, with the downtown staff coming up to do the ceremonial tour. Dana, a manager in the marketing department, was a little late in arriving. It didn't help that it took forever to get checked in at the plant gate. Next, she had to find a place to park in one of the green spaces that were always two miles away and then walk through rows of pickup trucks and vans with eagles painted on them. Finally she had to get her badge and hard hat. She always hated wearing that. It made a ring around her hair for the rest of the day.

As Dana came into the plant, she could see the managers' group up on the second level. To save a little time, she cut across an open area. All at once she heard three furious guys screaming at her, "Stay inside the red lines, lady!" Dana thought indignantly, Is this the way they talk to a manager around here?

* * *

Barry was ready for this: the chance to negotiate a multi-million-dollar contract. His attache case was full of charts and figures. What an honor to be a part of the A-team headed up by Jack James, known as "El Tigre" for the way he ate up the opposition. Barry expected the blood and guts to really flow today.

But what he found at the negotiating table were two middle-aged guys, talking about fishing and their kids. Except for a couple of casual references, they hadn't even mentioned the contract—and they'd been talking for half an hour. Barry wanted to know what gives.

What Rituals Reveal

If you are to understand and correctly perform your company's rituals, you should probably look beneath the surface to understand their purpose. Reasons for some of our rituals include

Showing and affirming tribal membership (e.g., company gatherings, meetings, orientations, and training). The ritual drum-beating and interview with the demon initiates the new member in a trial by fire.

Showing relative status in the dominance hierarchy (e.g., who goes first and who has the last word). In Susan's law firm, the daily ritual for leaving work spells out clearly who is the boss and how you must acknowledge his sovereignty each day.

Marking out territory or showing respect for the territory of others (e.g., actions signalling that you are in another person's territory). Down at the plant, Dana is not in Managers' Country any more. In the territory of factory workers, everyone wears the ceremonial garb and visibly obeys security and safety rules. If they don't, punishment comes swiftly in the form of a ritual chewing-out.

Performing certain actions with the subtlety and art due their importance (e.g., routine procedures or other recurring activities and events). If Barry had asked El Tigre why he didn't come to the point and ask for the money, Jack would probably have rolled his eyes and said, "Negotiating a multi-million-dollar contract is not like selling fish. We try to be a little more subtle and find out the lay of the land—who we're up against, what they're thinking about, and other absolutely critical things like that. It's just the way it's done." (Of course, Barry is enough of a Competitor not to ask. He learns by observation.)

If you're looking closely, a company's rituals can tell you a lot about the people you're dealing with: what they value, who they are, and how to get along with them. The rituals described in the preceding examples tell you which tribe you belong to, who you are, where you are, and what you're doing.

Another major purpose of rituals is to help us face the unknown. In our private lives, we may lock the doors and windows in a prescribed order, and recheck the locks before going to bed. In business, we observe decision-making rituals to help us ward off potential disastrous consequences of our decisions. These rituals help us cope with the need to predict the future—the outcome of our decisions—when the future cannot be known.

Decision-Making Rituals Protect Us from the Dark

If you think about it, it's frightening how many of our important decisions come down to sheer guesswork. Most of us, if pressed, will admit that guesswork, intuition, and hunches often play key roles in how we are rearing our children—or even in how we chose our spouses:

> "Bill is a nice guy even if he drinks a little too much. If we get married, his life will be less stressful, and he'll cut down."
> "Juanito should play sports—it builds character."
> "If I push her just the right amount, her grades will improve."

However, if someone suggests that our business decisions are hunches too, we balk at the idea:

> "How can you say that? Look at these degrees on my wall."
> "I'm a trained professional. I don't go just by instinct."
> "I consult the top experts!"
> "Look at this computer print-out!"
> "Check the mathematical model!"
> "We've used psychological testing!"
> "Check this marketing survey!"

However we might phrase it, what we mean to say is, "We take our business decisions *seriously* around here!"

Though some of the decisions we make at home might be clouded by emotions and doubt, business is business. Referring to business decisions as guesswork shakes us up. It directly assaults one of the great bulwarks of Competitor belief—that management decisions are always logical, rational, and objective. Yet all of the crucial decisions we have to make depend on being able to predict the future, which none of us can do. We have to guess, and we have to live with the results of the guesses we make. Nothing, not even management theory, is safe from that dark cavern of uncertainty that is our future. We use rituals to make the process less threatening.

Visualize the cave where warriors go to sacrifice a goat and read its entrails. Then they cast white or black stones to vote on whether to go to war. Now visualize the meeting room on the twenty-third floor, with its print-outs, charts, and reports—and the final vote being taken on whether to put out a new product.

Many business decisions are not logical. People band together in task groups and do the equivalent of casting runes and consulting the gods. It reassures us to get as much information as possible: We conduct surveys, evaluate and analyze past history, build mathematical models, or hire consultants. Nonetheless, when it comes right down to it, none of these strategies will give any of us the answer; rather, they stimulate us to come up with our own answers and give us the strength to act on the answers we come up with.

Often, as managers and professionals, we ignore emotional, psychological, and spiritual factors when we make decisions. We don't want to admit that the facts and figures really just give us the strength to grapple with doubt, because doubt does not officially exist—particularly in the work lives of Competitors. To admit doubt would make us vulnerable to direct assaults from other Competitors (who dominate the decision-making levels in any company). No sane decision-maker who wants to remain in a decision-making position would ever take that chance.

The Company's Perspective: Determining Who May Join the Tribe

Nowhere is the function of ritual more apparent than in the job interview. Because no one can predict with 100% accuracy a person's ability to do a job or to fit into the tribe, companies fill the darkness with rituals designed to make them feel confident about the decisions they make. When trying to predict skill on the job, some companies rely heavily on lists of qualifications, assuming that if new people have had certain experiences and training, they will be able to perform their new jobs well. Others rely on standardized tests to choose the good and screen out the unworthy. Some do extensive background checks; others put people into high-pressure situations to see how they handle them. All of these methods have their advantages and their shortcomings in predicting job skills.

Few, however (if any), can predict a person's ability to fit into the tribe. Thus, in the end, most companies make their decisions based on the job interview. We must see an applicant face to face to feel that we're getting the key information. Of all the methods in use, the interview is the most subjective, yet it is the one that can never be ignored. As in most other situations in the corporate world, however, we are forced to feign objectivity. Nonetheless, all the tests, qualifications, and references aside, the final accolade of tribal membership goes to the people we like the best—the people who can show us what we want to see.

Does this ability to fit in mean that these people will do the best work on the job? "Not necessarily," say all the objective studies. But that's not the key question the job interview is designed to answer or the real reason for many of the rituals. The real question is, "Do we want to work with this person?" After all is said and done, after layer upon layer of rituals, the boss must eventually guess that a particular candidate will be most able to fit in with the tribe and to do the job the tribe needs to have done.

Differing Views of Work Rituals

The specific rituals that a company (and a particular boss) use for determining who may join the tribe differ greatly. The reason things are done one way and not another always tells you something about the company and about the people who are involved in those rituals. However, exactly how you view the rituals depends on who you are. Rebels, Believers, and Competitors interpret the same rituals very differently. They all see and hear the same things, but what they make of them depends as much on their own beliefs as on what is actually going on.

We tend to revere our own rituals and those of our own group and say, "They aren't rituals. They're just the most logical way to do things." Of course, our values and beliefs determine what we consider logical. Other groups' rituals may seem just like a ridiculous waste of time—because they don't fit our values. So we pass up a chance to learn from them and instead get a good laugh at the other guy's expense.

Habitual ways of thinking and accustomed ways of interpreting are rituals, too. As Rebels, we may interpret daily corporate actions strictly in terms of our own struggle with authority. As Believers, we may look only for information about how to do things the _right_ way. As Competitors, we may see what happens purely in terms of winning and losing. Each of these habitual patterns of thinking limits our perspective and prevents us from understanding other people's actions.

The Job Interview: How Different People See It

The rituals associated with the job interview must serve more than one purpose. The expressed, obvious purpose is to select a person who can most effectively perform a particular job. A more important reason for the interview, however, is to help a company decide in advance who will and will not fit into the tribe.

Most companies also have other purposes for the job-interview rituals, such as the desire for the company to project a positive image of itself: "We're very choosy here. We pick only the finest candidates. It's tough to join our tribe." In addition, interviewers may have rituals to serve their own purposes, such as to make themselves look or feel more important. Understanding these multiple layers of meanings among the rituals requires great skill, and few candidates are prepared for the task.

There is much to be learned, but, as with all rituals, what we learn depends on what we look for. Let's look at the job interview and see how the three different personality types interpret it.

A Rebel's View of the Interview

We now go back to when our favorite Rebel joined Neander-Tek:

Luke arrived a couple of minutes late for his interview. His sweater and tie, while almost formal attire for him, were hardly the pinstripe uniform the other applicants had worn. The committee was just about ready to write him off when he sketched out a few ideas, off the top of his head, for inventory-control software that would solve a couple of nagging problems that had been costing the company thousands of dollars every month.

With a little more questioning, the committee discovered how well Luke knew his stuff. Repair computers? This guy could build them from scratch!

There *was* the question of how well he'd fit in, but the committee decided to take the risk and hire him.

Luke assumed he'd been hired to work on computers. Because nobody had mentioned attending meetings or doing paperwork, he assumed that they weren't in his job description.

A Believer's View of the Interview

Believers worry a lot about everything, and they worry even more about the interview ritual. They know they're supposed to make some sort of impression during the interview, but how? They know there are rules out there, and they try to find out what they are. They are often deceived by the interview's objective trappings into believing that the interview itself is an objective process.

Many Believers think a job interview is like a multiple-choice test, in which there actually are right answers somewhere, and whoever gets the highest score is hired. Often, in their concern with giving correct answers, they don't see that the interview is an essay test, and the grade is based on sounding convincing. Worse yet, they can be so concerned about what mark they're getting that they can miss seeing who is really doing the grading.

Lesley can't stop worrying. "What will I have to say to get the job?" She has read three books about what kind of suit to wear, what style of briefcase to carry, and what answers are best for which questions. The form of the interview is of paramount importance to her.

As the interview draws closer, Lesley's attitude swings wildly from moment to moment: One minute, she's anxious about every detail and what it will all mean. The next, she's belligerent: "They already know who they want, so what difference does it make?"

On the interview day, Lesley barely listens to the questions; she's too busy trying to figure out how she should act and what she should say to look and sound like the perfect applicant. When the interviewer smiles, Lesley smiles; when the interviewer looks serious, Lesley does, too.

She works hard at keeping her answers positive and diplomatic—and above all, she tries not to say anything that might rock the boat. Yet throughout the interview, there's also a part of herself that's watching her performance with disgust. She feels herself turning into a sleaze, a chameleon who tries to tell everybody what they want to hear.

But the interviewer is smiling at her, though, and she and Lesley are chatting amiably about career paths and Lesley's goals for the next five years. It seems to be going OK.

When the interview seems to have ended, Lesley is taken in to meet the division head. He seems kind of distant, and she has a hard time relating to him. She's glad the meeting lasts only about ten minutes.

At home that night, her husband asks her how the interview went. Lesley thinks about the smiling chatter from the Human Resources person who interviewed her, and the apparent disinterest of the division head, and shrugs. "It went OK, but I don't know."

Believers sometimes have a hard time telling where the power is. The interview was emotionally draining for Lesley, but at least she handled it better than her fellow Believer, Carl, who deals with uncertainty in a different way. As a Believer, Carl carefully researched and studied what you're supposed to do in a job interview. He found out that one of the things you should do is to find out about the company. What he didn't realize in his investigation is that this is supposed to be done by reading between the lines—not by making up a multiple-choice test to give to the interviewer.

When the interviewer asked whether he had any questions, Carl spoke right up. "Do you get to make your own decisions here, or are you told what to do?" The interviewer gave a sort of "Heh-heh, what-a-kidder" chuckle, but Carl waited for the answer. When none came, he asked the other questions on his list: "What are the real rules around here?" "Is this a very political company?" (The interviewer seemed to love that one, from the way she laughed out loud.)

Carl's last question, "How does this company stand on racism and sexism?" actually got a response. The interviewer said, as if reciting the *Pledge of Allegiance*, "We are an enlightened, forward-looking, equal-opportunity company with a strong affirmative action policy."

Carl deals with his uncertainty by trying to get the interviewer to spell everything out. The interviewer laughed at Carl's questions because she could *not* say, "Don't you know the rules of this situation? I'm a representative of this company. I can't admit to anything negative to a stranger (if there were anything negative to admit, which I'm not admitting.) All I can give you are stock political answers, not information. If you want information, you'll have to pay attention to my careful choice of words, my pauses between question and answer, and the things I don't say."

Subtlety is lost on him, the interviewer decided. If he were hired (fat chance!), he'd think I answered his questions with a pack of lies. I'm telling him what I can, but he's not listening. . . .

* * *

Both Lesley and Carl had to get through interviews at several companies before they were finally hired. Each interview was frustrating and perplexing. Often, they weren't called back after interviews they thought had gone well. It was ironic that Lesley landed her present job during the interview she thought she'd blown. Go figure.

The Competitor's Edge: Another View of the Interview

Competitors are very good at the interview ritual. They can sense what's going on from little details, nuances of words and procedures. They start by looking at the structure of the interview itself.

Bronson (the Competitor destined to become Carl's boss) knew it was time to take a career step. He had heard about an opening position at Universal Systems and, after doing a little homework on the company—the things they never tell you in an interview—he made a call.

Bronson was told he needed to pick up an application at the Human Resources Department. The screening day was Tuesday, the twelfth; he could have the 2:30 slot. All of this told Bronson that, if he wanted this job, he would have to go through the formalities. Did he really want to work for a company that wasn't looking for *him?* No percentage there.

Before the interview at Universal came up, Bronson got a call from a guy he knew at Neander-Tek. A good job, Bronson thought, a real step up. The guy on the phone said they knew about him and wanted to talk. The company was looking for somebody who could focus on the bottom line but still had good people skills.

Bronson knew the bottom line, all right. To him, "people skills" meant getting the best deal for himself with any people he met. In the interview, all he'd have to do was talk about participation, delegation of authority—all that management-textbook stuff—and it would go fine. Though he had no idea how to actually do these things—and little interest in learning—he knew all the right things to say to sound as though he had mastered them.

Bronson knew it looked good when the first person he met was the CEO, who poured him a cup of coffee and said, "Tell me about yourself." No problem. When the interview got down to the numbers (what other topic was there?), Bronson negotiated to get about twice the salary anyone else could expect to get for the position. Done deal.

Bronson would probably be better off making deals full time, instead of managing people, but if he had said so in the interview, he wouldn't have landed the job. Because he had made a good impression on the CEO, there was no need to check his references to see what previous bosses thought of him, or whether he really had the people skills that were called for. Bronson had something more important—enough understanding of The System to get what he wanted.

Competitors also realize that the higher you go, the more fascinating the interview rituals become and the more they reveal about the company.

In a company where Rich interviewed for district sales manager, he and other top applicants were flown to Regional Headquarters and met with the Vice President for Sales. In Rich's first meeting, the VP tossed him a pen and said, "Sell me this pen." When Rich looked at him quizzically, the VP said, "I can spot a good salesman immediately." But Rich knew that what the manager was really revealing was that he was The Boss, and his employees were going to have to defer to him, no matter how silly his request.

Rich saw that he had two choices. He could smile and play along, or he could refuse the VP's challenge. The fact that this would determine whether he was hired told him more than enough about what his job would be like.

He could see it all now. The whole region would be run on this guy's whims—getting calls at all hours if orders were down a point; listening to lectures on what it takes to be a great sales rep; being sent unqualified candidates whom Regional wanted him to hire. Rich knew the situation. One detail in the interview had told him clearly that he wasn't going to be allowed to run his own shop. Well, better to know it now than later.

Rich caught the next plane home.

* * *

Dana, a midlevel manager up for promotion, faced a trial by fire when she was invited for a friendly, "getting to know you" drinks-and-chat session with her boss and the CEO after work. Before the Scotch had even arrived, the CEO leaned forward, beamed paternally, and asked, "So tell me. What makes you think you're so damn much hotter stuff than all the other managers that we should promote you above them?"

Dana swallowed her tendency toward heated self-defense; instead she took a few moments to consider her response and purposely relaxed her posture. Smiling modestly, she said, "Oh, I think our entire management crew is great. I certainly wouldn't say that I'm better than any of them. I'm just fortunate that my own job gives me the chance for an overview. . . ." Then she proceeded to tell a few stories, each of which happened to illustrate what hot stuff she was.

". . . The Nielson project? Absolute luck on my part. Franklin here" (Dana smiled warmly at her boss) "was the guy who took all the risks by giving me a chance with it. It just happened that my work in production and my training in accounting led me to realize that we could save some serious money if we just went at it from a slightly different direction."

(Dana didn't mention that if she hadn't saved the bacon, another candidate for the same job would have blown the Nielson project big-time. She didn't need to mention it; she had successfully jogged the CEO's memory.)

". . . and I've worked closely with almost half the managers in the whole division. What a team!" (She then listed the names of the managers and all the money-making projects she'd been involved with—just in case the CEO had forgotten.) After mentioning Kate Anderson, a manager up for the same position, Dana said, "Now Kate has real depth of experience . . . in accounting . . . so it depends on what you're looking for. . . ."

At no point did Dana actually proclaim her own greatness, list her own qualifications, or bad-mouth other candidates, but in the course of conversation, she managed to compare herself favorably with all the other contenders.

At the end of the 150-minute cocktail hour cum interview (during which our junior executive had limited herself to a single Scotch), the CEO rose, put his hand on Dana's shoulder and announced, "You have my blessing."

At Dana's level, the job interview ritual can be loaded with traps. Dana successfully avoided potential snares by recognizing each of the CEO's gambits and using them to demonstrate—subtly—her own accomplishments. She understood the ritual clearly enough to take a "high road" approach, emphasizing cooperation among her colleagues rather than backstabbing her in-house competition.

If you're a Competitor, you will devote much of your work life to trying to prove something to someone. Nobody will ever tell you *what* you're supposed to prove, or to whom. If you can't figure it out, you're not management material. For Competitors, the job interview (like many other things they do) is deceptively simple. With Competitors, there's nearly always more than meets the eye.

As the preceding vignettes have shown, the way in which you view a ritual affects the way in which you handle it—and how effectively you handle it. If you don't understand the meanings and purposes underlying some of the boat-launching rituals, you may miss the boat. When you're a member of a tribe (or want to become one), you have to try to view the rituals from the perspectives of those around you, not just from your own viewpoint.

Some of the job-interview candidates described in this chapter were barred from joining the tribe because they couldn't see the rituals from the perspective of the tribal elders. They didn't understand the reasoning underlying some of the rituals, so they violated some of the rules.

"Cargo Cult" Thinking

Competitors seem to have the edge in figuring out most corporate rituals and turning them to their own advantage. However, even Competitors lack an ability to view rituals from the perspectives of some of their peers—and especially their subordinates. When Believers or Rebels are performing the rituals, the Competitors may misunderstand or ignore them. Also, when Competitors create new rituals, thinking that they know how Rebels or Believers will respond to them, they're often far off the mark. Not understanding the rituals and perspectives of other members of the tribe can have widespread consequences for all members.

Every company has its own set of rituals—the way things are actually done in a particular company—which is not necessarily the way people *say* they are done. Remember a few years ago, when the fashion was miniature versions of the corporate logo running amok on neckties or scarves that everyone was supposed to wear? Instead of being seen as symbols of company pride, those little trademarks became sure signs that their wearers were lower-ranking members of the tribe. Other than in carefully choreographed, "I'm just one of the members of this great team" situations, you never saw the company president sporting one of those little winged bowling balls on his $100 cravat or her $200 silk scarf, did you?

In the South Pacific during World War II, American forces had come and built airfields in remote areas, where the cultures had barely moved beyond the Stone Age. The natives would stand at the fences and watch the great American birds come flying down, bringing wondrous things: tools, jeeps, clothing, food—unimagined riches.

The natives figured this was a good thing, and they wanted to get in on it, so they started building their own airfields, complete with decoy planes made of sticks and leaves, and decorated with stars and stripes. They also developed dances that were similar to the signaling system the Americans used to wave in a plane for landing. Their idea was to lure the flying machines down from the sky so they could share in the miraculous cargo.

In some areas, "Cargo Cult" thinking is still practiced to this day—and not so far from home.

The Competitors in management at American Excellence & Quality came up with the slogan, "Excellence Is Our Middle Name." (The Rebels and Believers were not asked for input on this slogan.)

The Competitors assume that a good slogan will work like any other good advertising ploy. It will help the public and the workers at the plant to value product quality, which mainly depends on how motivated and dedicated the workers on the assembly line are. With a fine slogan like this to inspire them, surely the workers will take more pride in their work and do a better job!

(To the Competitor, the slogan is mainly an advertising device for the public, associating the company name with product excellence. The Believers are all for the slogan, and they see it as a genuine commitment to work harder and do better—the things Believers like most. They take the slogan literally and believe it means a change in company policy—more workers, better inspection systems, doing what it takes to achieve excellence. (The Rebels see the slogan as just another load of bull that's been dropped on them.)

The slogan is unveiled in an ad campaign for the public, and a huge banner goes up at each of the plants. The managers get lapel pins, and everybody else is given buttons that say, "Excellence Is Our Middle Name." Stories appear in the corporate newsletter extolling "the guys who go the extra mile for excellence."

A few days later, the first graffiti show up in the restrooms. (Bathroom walls are always appropriate sites for the Rebel version of alternative journalism.) "Excellence is our middle name, but quality comes last." The new slogan's message—be prouder and work harder—is as lost on the Rebels as a Tibetan prayer wheel: It definitely is not a part of their religion.

At the same time, the Believer middle-managers were presenting proposals to their Competitor bosses for the increased staff and better equipment needed to achieve *Excellence*. Their bosses' faces all wore the same unbelieving look that Competitors get when they have to explain the facts of life to corporate virgins: "Are you kidding? We just spent millions on the ad campaign for our new slogan. Where's the money gonna come from?"

The slogan story illustrates how each personality type responds to the rituals of others in ways the others don't understand, and each has its own rituals misunderstood, devalued, or subverted by the others.

Competitor managers are trying to invoke magic by creating something that looks good but has no internal substance. They say, "What do you mean that the slogan isn't true? Of course, it's true. Excellence *is* our middle name! Now we have a slogan—like all the Fortune 500 companies do!"

Unfortunately for these Competitors, they'll never convince the Rebels to share their points of view, and even the Believers eventually tire of the empty slogans that surround them. Virtually every company sees itself as being Number One in something and says that it accepts "nothing less than excellence." American businesses seem to be like the children in Lake Woebegon, Minnesota: *All* are above average.

The problem of Cargo Cult thinking is especially clear in the rampant use of corporate slogans. Everybody knows that at G.E., "Progress is our most important product," and that "IBM means service." Every company has a slogan about how excellent it is. These slogans usually sound good, but they don't necessarily express what the company believes in or does.

Corporate values come from the inside out. They cannot be changed by manipulating slogans, news releases, or employees' clothing. A business is headed for trouble if its corporate slogan hails excellence in all things, but its *real* motto should be, "*What It Looks Like Is More Important Than What It Is.*"

Hollow advertising ploys don't work well over the long haul. Even the most naïve of Believers grow weary of such gimmicks (and may secretly agree when Rebels call the gimmick-users "Neanderthals"). To develop a strong culture, a company has to start by understanding and accepting—accurately—what its culture is *now*. Pretending to be IBM won't automatically make you bigger or bluer.

No matter how much you want it to, a plane of sticks and leaves won't fly. It needs an engine. Corporate cultures are built on values and commitments, not created in slogan-drafting brainstorming sessions. The Competitors who are running companies need to recognize and understand the attitudes and values, myths and rituals, strengths and weaknesses of the Rebels, Believers, and fellow Competitors who make the products, provide the services, and keep the company in business. This is what the slogans should be about.

Rebels and Believers also have to learn to expand their perspectives. If they continue to misunderstand or simply ignore the perspectives of their coworkers, they will continue to drive each other crazy. Each must learn how to see the tribe from the perspective of the other.

Part Two describes more fully exactly how Rebels and their coworkers misunderstand one another and drive each other nuts—and how each can gain some understanding of the other's perspective.

PART TWO

The Rebels: Corporate Mavericks

3

Breaking All the Rules . . . Creatively

From the day he was born on a mountaintop in Tennessee until he fell at the Alamo, Davy Crockett was his own man. Out in the wilderness, there were no fences, no rules, and no bosses to tell you what to do. In the early 1800s, the American frontier was full of danger: wild animals, Indians, river pirates, or just the weather. Whatever trouble you encountered, Davy was the kind of guy you'd want on your side.

He made a brief and not completely successful sojourn into politics. He never did understand that people didn't take Congressmen who carry rifles totally seriously. Anyway, that was their problem. Let *them* try to filibuster a hungry bear.

America was founded by a rebellion. Most of our heroes are people who did their own thing, no matter what the authorities thought. You wouldn't catch Rebels such as Davy Crockett or Daniel Boone brown-nosing the CEO. They probably couldn't hold down a job in your company, either. But if the Indians attacked or your cabin was burning, they'd be the guys you'd want around.

To Believers and Competitors, Rebels are the "Neanderthals" who will never make it any further up the corporate evolutionary ladder because they lack the qualities that the two other "higher species" value most: motivation and the urge to succeed. The Rebel personality is maverick, irreverent, often maddening, but also creative, bright, and cool-headed. The challenge in working with Rebels lies in managing their independence and resistance to authority, while recognizing and making the best use of their virtues.

Rebels are good to have around. They're often terrific at handling emergencies or crises. If you look at the typical police or fire department, hospital emergency room, flight maintenance hangar, mental health center, or any other work setting that deals with crises, you'll find countless Rebels successfully handling the dangerous or high-stress aspects of their jobs. (They're probably behind in their paperwork, though.)

The whole billing program was down, and the "Suits and Ties" were wringing their hands about all the money they were going to lose. It must be a major breakdown in the mainframe, they moaned.

Then Luke, the computer troubleshooter from downstairs, came in, glanced at the screen, drawled, "Make my day," and typed in a couple of commands. The screen scrolled long strings of cryptic characters as he stared intently. When he saw the hieroglyphs he was looking for, he chortled and typed in a few new hieroglyphs. He then banged the [Enter] key, typed one more command, checked the screen again, grinned and nodded at the balding hand-wringer who had been surreptitiously staring over his shoulder, then got up and strolled out.

The managers thought that Luke had just gone out to get some tool he'd forgotten or that he'd gone upstairs for advice from the mainframe consultant. As the minutes ticked by and he still hadn't come back, the Suits and Ties began checking their watches and impatiently tapping their loafers—until a secretary noticed that the computer was fixed. The frenzied managers hadn't even thought to check.

The same qualities that make Rebels creative and good at crises—their independence, lack of subtlety, love of excite-

ment, and impulsiveness—can make them *seem* like bad
employees. They aren't—if you don't demand reverence,
and if you use clear, consistent rules and forget about the pep
talks.

Micki's boss shook his finger at her with mock sternness.
"Where's your monthly report, young lady? You promised it
would be here on my desk first thing in the morning, and I
don't see it anywhere. Is it lost in that dark cavern you call
your totebag?"

Micki slapped her forehead and started rummaging fran-
tically through her bright red attache. "I know it's here! I
stayed up real late last night to get it done for you, and I know
I stuck it in here, but . . . I could go home right now and get it!
I could be back in an hour for sure!"

The boss smiled indulgently. Who could stay mad at Micki
when she tried so hard to please everybody? Yelling at her
was like scolding a puppy. And the customers loved her. Her
stats were consistently higher than anyone else's. She was
definitely a people person, but when was this kid going to get
organized? The boss sighed loudly and said, "Don't go home,
Mick. Stay here and get going on your calls for the rest of the
day. But remember: tomorrow morning—without fail—that
report had better be sitting on my desk!" He went away, wondering (for the four-hundredth time) if the incompetence routine was just an act for getting out of the things she didn't
want to do.

Micki went to her desk, pushed aside the stacks of papers,
catalogues, and dirty coffee cups, and got down to her real
work—selling.

* * *

Troy turned off the alarm and squinted at the morning light
coming in through the bedroom window. It was going to be a
scorcher, but it was cool here. Too damn hot to sweat through
eight hours of planning meetings and economic projections in

the "House of Horrors," as he lovingly called the agency. Troy could easily do two days' worth of his real work—writing ad copy—in one morning. That was child's play to him—and he had awards and citations to prove it. The rest of the stuff they did at the agency was a joke.

Creativity Is Their Strength

The preceding examples clearly show that Rebels' strong suit is creativity; they have a knack for looking at situations in unusual ways. Among the biographies of the world's most creative people, you'll find few Believers or Competitors. Many of the great inventions have been based on some Rebel's fooling around with a new idea or fiddling with a new gadget—for 20 hours a day, 365 days in a row. (Unfortunately, some of these dedicated creators died penniless because of their appalling lack of business sense.)

Troy was the agency's creative genius, the clutch hitter who could whack the grand slam for the most demanding client. Wild-haired and argyle-sweatered, he would cruise in late to the presentation meeting, traveling light: no portfolio, no sketches, no notes. He relied only on the light bulb in his head that blazed on when his team most needed an idea.

He was always complaining about how stifling the agency's rules were, and he hated all the focus on planning and projection. People kept telling Troy he ought to start his own agency; then he could do things his own way. He'd probably have grateful clients lined up around the block. Troy would just grin that loopy grin, though, and say that he was happy where he was, "in chains in the House of Horrors."

The truth was that Troy knew how to write copy and design ad campaigns. He'd be scared to death to have to actually go out and try to find a client. Also, all that business stuff—the planning and projection—he didn't know anything about that, and he had no desire to learn about it, either. No thanks. For all his griping about how staid, conservative, and full of stuffed shirts the agency was, he had no plans to leave in *this* lifetime.

Troy didn't want to do the daily, caged-at-his-desk market research that his less flamboyant, more consistent colleagues regularly did. Start his own agency? No way. He didn't want to give up the funky sweaters for the pinstripe suit, or the tardy entrance for the bottom line. Troy didn't want to be in charge; he liked the Boy Wonder image too much to grow up.

Troy is an example of the Rebel attitude that says, unconsciously or directly, "I'm not going to do the parts of my job that I don't want to do." Most Rebels aren't lazy. Most of them will work their tails off, but their hard work will involve doing the parts of their jobs that they like or that come easily for them, not necessarily what is required or rewarded. Let's go back a few (dozen) years and look at an example:

When you were a kid, there were probably many times when you tried to do a job—mowing the lawn, for instance— and then got criticized for leaving out the hard parts (the raking and edging). Maybe your dad tried to tell you six- or seven-hundred times before you finally got it yourself.

Think of all the reasons you gave for why you didn't do the whole job. "The grass is too wet." "The edger doesn't work right." "The rake is bent." "I have homework." These excuses are what the Rebel culture is all about. You can't tell your boss, "I don't want to do this," and get away with it, any more than you could tell your dad. So you have to have reasons why you couldn't do what you're afraid of or don't want to do.

Then suddenly you realized that you couldn't get out of it, and you had to do the hard parts as well as the easy parts. The mowing wasn't fun, but the feeling of accomplishment was. The job wouldn't really be done until the grass was raked and the lawn edged. Until you figured it out, though, your dad might just as well have been talking to the garage wall.

The Rebel inside Each of Us

Your secret is revealed—you *still* sometimes make excuses and use other little tricks to get out of doing the tasks you hate! Even the most dedicated Believers among you probably can think of at least one or two things that you dread and put off as long as possible—indefinitely if you can get away with it. Maybe a small part of you still tries to get out of meeting with people you don't like or rechecking the numbers after you've finished the last draft.

Each of us, no matter what our job or level of management might be, has unresolved aspects of this Rebel attitude within us—a Rebel inside. It's the part that tells us to avoid the things at work that we don't want to do and then comes up with reasons that we don't really have to do them.

We all avoid what we don't enjoy, as do the people we manage. As we move up the ladder, it's easier to cover up for avoiding certain tasks. Even the most Competitor-minded managers among us may adopt a management style that gets us out of doing things we don't like to do—still Rebels at heart.

In managing, more than in any other kind of job, the demands are vague and the temptations are strongest to define the job in terms of what you like to do, rather than what is most important. Unfortunately, though, the unresolved issues come back.

The following are the things that the Rebel inside many managers and other professionals try to avoid: paperwork problems, policy/procedure problems, and people problems.

Paperwork Problems

Almost every job has paperwork: the tiresome task of keeping track of the work you do, and documenting to someone (a boss, a client, a committee) that the work you're doing is worth their paying you to do it. You may have expense reports to fill out, client records to keep up, progress/status reports to write, or any number of other forms and reports to fill in, fill out, and write up. Few of us really relish these tasks, and most of us try putting them off as long as possible, but sooner or later, you're going to have to write down what you've been doing and how you've been doing it.

Policy/Procedure Problems

Almost every company has rules, policies, procedural guidelines, and routines that absolutely, positively everyone must follow on all occasions—even when they seem ridiculous or even absurd. Naturally, when they're *your* rules, policies, and procedures, they make perfect sense, and anyone who can't understand their intrinsic merit must be some kind of Neanderthal. However, when they're someone else's, and they make no sense to you, the rules stir up the Rebel in each of us.

The confirmed Rebels just ignore any rules they dislike or find annoying—and often suffer harsh consequences as a result. Competitors find ways of getting around the regulations when they're pretty sure they can safely get away with doing so. Even Believers may inwardly rebel while compliantly following the procedures they don't agree with.

People Problems

As hard as it is to get along with policies and routines that you don't like, it's even harder to handle difficult people problems: figuring out whom you should talk to and what to say, what to listen to and how to listen, how to get others to do what you want them to do, and how to do what others want you to do.

Most people find it easiest to figure out people problems with people who are most like themselves: Competitors can relate to Competitors, Believers to Believers, and Rebels to Rebels. We tend to feel the most comfortable with the people who share our view of the world, so we tend to seek their company—particularly in the world at work. Most of our people problems arise when we have to deal with people who view things differently than we do. For example, picture yourself as a Competitor manager.

As a Competitor manager, you may really enjoy hanging out with other Competitors—such as the Big Bosses. However, to keep things running smoothly, you have to spend some time with the people below you.

Most managers feel that, if they have a good staff, then they won't have to keep interacting with them to keep them motivated. That isn't true. If you don't give Believers frequent feedback letting them know how they're doing, you'll end up with serious morale problems; like dandelions, you can chop off their heads but, unless you dig down to their roots, they'll pop up again. A manager needs to see widespread morale problems as *information about what needs to be fixed*, rather than as the ramblings of a few Rebel malcontents.

To avoid morale problems altogether, managers need to keep up with their day-to-day communication: answering questions, sharing information, following through on requests, and giving feedback on how well people are doing their jobs. This is particularly true for the Believers who do most of the crucial work.

This may also mean having to give the same information more than once: First you have to tell them you're going to tell them; then you tell them, and then you tell them you told them. If you haven't told them three times, the chances are that you haven't really gotten back to people with enough information. They're going to be asking why you never tell them anything.

If you're a Competitor, the Competitors above you will try to book up all your time with meetings, if you'll let them— and you'll be more than a little tempted to let them. You have to figure out which meetings are important and which you can skip, and how much time you can spend away from "home" and still keep your staff working effectively. Your boss *will not* help you with the decision.

Now picture yourself as a Believer manager.

As a Believer manager, you probably feel most comfortable among the Believers who surround your desk. To keep up your political ties to the executive suite, though, you have to spend some time with the people above you. The people below you will try to keep you busy with asking for advice, suggestions, and feedback—which you're all too happy to give. However, if you don't manage to tear yourself away from your home turf to go to the meetings and "power lunches" and other political gatherings, you may find your political position in jeopardy—no matter how much your subordinates adore you and work their Believer fingers to the bone for you.

As a non-Competitor, having to attend meetings is probably one of the routines you love to hate most. You rebel at the notion of having to attend yet another meeting, to listen to the same viewpoints over and over, to discuss endlessly something that could have been decided by one person in less than 10 minutes, or just to be forced to interrupt and leave the work you know you should be doing in order to sit around getting nothing done. Like it or not, though, most management gets done at meetings. If you regard meetings as time-wasters that get in the way of what you should be doing, you're probably not seeing an important part of your job.

If you want to know what's going on—which you *must* know if you're supposed to try to manage what's going on—you have to attend the countless meetings that fill your calendar. Participation in meetings is as important to a manager's career as campaign speeches are to a politician's career. A politician who thinks that campaign speeches get in the way of being an effective legislator or administrator won't have to deal with being a politician for long. A manager who considers meetings a time-waster may suffer the same fate.

Avoidance Is the Roadblock

Rebels *can* be shown the importance of "rake and edge" and why the business equivalent is important—if you understand that their real difficulty is fear. They're looking for some way to "make it" without having to do what they don't like or are afraid they can't do. Many Rebels don't understand exactly what it takes to get ahead at work, to feel a real part of things. Or maybe they do understand, but feel profound anxiety about doing what it takes. The result is that they never learn to face their fear.

Fear? If you work with or manage a Rebel, you may be thinking, "Wait a minute. He isn't fearful; he's the angriest, most cynical, battle-scarred old so-and-so I've ever met. . . . He's a lot of things, but he isn't fearful. Ornery, yes. Fearful, no."

Cynicism and tough talk are often a good cover for fear. If there's avoidance, there's fear somewhere. The anger is a cover-up to save face. Wouldn't you be angry if you thought you had no control over what you were required to do?

You can learn to manage Rebels effectively without having to become a psychotherapist. The strategies listed at the end of the Rebels section of this book offer specific suggestions for handling this difficult challenge.

Even Professionals Get the Rebel Blues

We all know people who marginally got through graduate school but were stopped by the bar exam or the licensing exam and now have to work in protected settings. Often they are masters of the theoretical aspects of their profession, but the practical things elude them. In university settings, they don't publish; they focus on teaching students, which is admirable but is not rewarded in our society. In private practice as physicians or attorneys, they go to seminars and learn notebooksful of theory and technique, but they don't go beating the bushes for clients.

Every job, every profession, includes tasks that you *have* to do to be successful, or even simply to keep your job. Going to meetings. Getting along with people (even the Neanderthals who drive you crazy). Keeping your paperwork up to date. Doing your homework. Following the company's or profession's general rules and standards. Many Rebels, however, think the rules shouldn't apply to them.

Paulette loves to do scholarly research. She has six projects going and publications that are regularly cited by almost everyone in her field. She is a scientist, not a sales rep—and she doesn't see why she should have to go out and hustle grants all the time. That's almost as bad as teaching a course to a brood of witless undergraduates.

* * *

Robin is in practice to do counseling, not paperwork. She's good at seeing clients and helping them deal with their problems. Maybe someone should help her with hers: chart notes six months behind, letters to referral sources unwritten, reports half-finished. One of these days she'll catch up. Insurance companies don't audit files, do they?

* * *

Jeff is an expert plaintiff attorney—at least on paper. Top of his class; a few well-written articles in journals. His briefs are impeccable and virtually airtight. He's the kind of guy you'd consult on all the fine points.

He wastes little time dealing with and explaining to people who know less about the law than he does. Unfortunately, those on the list include clients, prospective clients, and juries. Jeff may be smart, but he's not getting rich.

* * *

Ryan can really pick 'em. He's great at portfolio management, and other brokers are always coming to him for advice. But he doesn't do what's valued at his company—selling high-profit, in-house products. That means cold calls—and Ryan balks at those. He just will not pick up that phone and get turned down by a bunch of strangers. Give him his old reliable clients every time. If his sales quotas aren't as high as some of the glad-handers', he can live with that. Look at the steady and only occasionally spectacular gains in the port-

folios he's managing. But that doesn't seem to mean anything to his boss. The man won't stop bugging him about those cold calls.

Successful professionals learn a balancing act between the parts of their work that they relish and the parts that keep their jobs secure and their paychecks regular. This can mean teaching the Freshman Composition class, writing the research grant, taking the meat-and-potatoes cases to supplement your specialty, or getting out into the community to keep clients coming.

It also can mean keeping accurate records so that you can bill for your services, or paying closer attention to how you spend your time. You might even have to start attending the dull but mandatory department meetings instead of escaping to the lab, or to leave that exciting new project untouched until you've finished writing your overdue report on the last project.

In non-Competitor professional practitioners and managers, this Rebel attitude tends to creep into anything that has to do with selling yourself as a professional. If you're in private practice, you have the equivalent of cold calls and closing sales to new clients. If you work in an organization, you have to please your employer. Wherever you work, you have to keep up to date on paperwork, and you have to do the research to support your opinions and decisions—even if you can occasionally get away with doing less.

The Rebels in these examples all believe that they can get by without following the rules, and that they only have to do the parts of their jobs that they like to do. Each of these Rebels has let the internal rebellion get out of hand. Their rebelliousness is ending up hurting their professional or corporate careers.

Rebels can easily enrage their bosses by rebelling against authority and refusing to acknowledge what management values, or by simply not doing what they're supposed to do. This causes the boss to become more authoritarian, which makes the Rebel more rebellious and irreverent. The whole pattern just confirms what each initially thought of the other.

Another source of the Rebel's discomfort may be the corporate structure itself, with its rigid constraints and political games. People who are sensitive, intelligent and emotionally volatile, as many Rebels are, may find themselves better suited to the more relaxed atmosphere of a smaller company. They will still have to deal with politics and structure, no matter how small the shop, but they may no longer feel as isolated and alienated as they did in the huge, impersonal beehive.

Some industries and kinds of businesses are also more able to nurture the Rebel at work. For example, this personality type tends to be overrepresented in insurance sales, brokerages, financial planning, and real estate, as well as the crisis-oriented jobs where the work often is unstructured. Nonetheless, even in these jobs, Rebels still have to do some tasks they don't like doing, as well as the ones they like—at least if they want to get paid for the work they do.

4

Luck, the Big Break, and the Conspiracy Theory

A bunch of the guys were hoisting a few after work, and somebody mentioned the "Pet Rock." Everybody grinned in recognition; they all had one of those somewhere at home, probably tossed at the back of the kids' closet.

"Oh, man, if I could live my life over again, I'd want to be the lucky stiff who thought up that Pet Rock scam," Luke said. "Think about it. The guy comes up with one crazy idea and winds up with a million dollars for five minutes' work. That's what I need: just one lucky break—and then kiss this rat race goodbye!" He put his beer money on the table as he got up to leave and reminded himself to stop at the 7-Eleven for a couple of lottery tickets on the way home.

At the next table, a group of managers perked up when they overheard Luke mention the Pet Rock. "Greatest marketing triumph of this century," one of them murmured reverently as he held up a finger for another round.

Many Rebel myths have to do with luck in its many forms— good luck, bad luck, sheer luck. One of their common heroes is the guy who makes it big without working—the lucky so-and-so who wins the lottery or comes up with the Pet Rock.

The Pet Rock story is fascinating. When Rebels talk about it, they tend to focus on sheer luck—how somebody came up with one wild idea and got millions of dollars. (For Competitors, the moral to the Pet Rock story is, If you find the right niche, you can move anything!)

Stories like this give Rebels the explanation that they need to explain why some people succeed and some don't. The Pet Rock reinforces the Rebels' belief that effort is not what is rewarded. You can work like a dog all your life and never get anywhere. What it takes to succeed is that one lucky break.

Rebels aren't really trying to get something for nothing. They just believe that, with luck, you can do what you like doing and get paid a bundle for it. These people are always talking, literally or figuratively, about winning the lottery. "Making a killing in the stock market" is a myth they revere. There are always a few people, of course, who make the killing without having to do the things they don't like to do, but their odds for a score are nearly as random as the lottery.

Brad has an engineering degree, but he really sees himself as an "entrepreneur." He has sold all kinds of things, from soap to real estate. Occasionally he's made big money, but in the long run he's barely gotten by. If he looks back, he'll see that his wife Marsha's job has supplied most of the money that's come in—not including the money the couple got from Brad's parents to buy a house and a few other big purchases.

Brad is very charming and bright and can convince you of all kinds of ideas. He's willing to work hard on projects he wants to do. No one could call him lazy. Even in his periods of unemployment, he did meticulous housework and yardwork, and cooked gourmet meals, but his focus always has been on what he likes to do, rather than on what makes money.

When he was into investment planning, he spent hundreds of hours studying the stock and bond markets, designing brochures and business cards, and picking out just the wardrobe he needed for the right professional image. What he did not do was make enough cold calls.

Brad was willing to spend unlimited time talking to people about his new job and their investments, but he was never particularly good at closing a deal. The impression people had was that he was talking in the abstract, about something he was *going* to be doing, rather than something he was working on now. They thought of him as somebody who might be able to make them some money later, after he was established. Brad considered them immediate prospects, but he always had trouble asking for the money.

Marsha finally got him out of the investments game by insisting that he had to earn a certain number of dollars by the end of the year or quit investments and get a regular job. Of course, he didn't make the money—but it was always just around the corner.

Brad's problems didn't end when he got regular jobs. He found some work in sales but never made money on commissions. (No cold calls and no closings—no money.) He tried to sell insurance and automobiles, but he just wasn't ruthless enough. Finally, his engineering degree landed him a job as a safety inspector for a large electronics manufacturing firm.

Now Brad gets to attend meetings, read books of regulations, and go around doing very official things. He gets paid next to nothing, but he gets paid regularly. He still talks about the great scheme that's going to make millions of dollars, but in reality his career has never gone anywhere. He has never recognized how people become successful at their careers.

Believers Bristle at "Dumb Luck"

The Rebels' reliance on luck is a 180-degree swing from the Believers' view that people succeed through sheer hard work. To illustrate the difference in the two attitudes, we use Luke, our Rebel, and Lesley, our Believer archetype, in an exaggerated encounter at work.

Luke and Lesley sat on green vinyl chairs in the Personnel Department's waiting room. It was going to be a while, the receptionist had just told them with a plastic smile. The benefits coordinator was running late today. Luke groaned and slouched lower in his chair. Lesley reached for a copy of "Winning Ways," the monthly newsletter of Neander-Tek.

"Look at this!" Lesley said a few minutes later, pointing to the main story. "'NEANDER-TEK ALUM WINS NATIONAL HONOR: Years of Research Rewarded, Says 77-Year-Old Gold-Star Recipient.' Doesn't that just make it all worth it?" She passed the newsletter to Luke.

Luke scanned the story and snorted. "So the geezer spends his whole career locked in a lab, and what does he get in the end? No million-dollar bonus, no product license that he could cash in big-time. Just a pat on the back from some D.C. think-tank and his picture on the cover of the company rag. Not exactly my idea of a life well spent."

Lesley stared at him, shocked. "But the satisfaction! The knowing that your life's work has made a difference! Doesn't that mean anything to you?"

Luke looked at Lesley and wondered how anybody could be so dense. "Listen, kid, it's a well known fact that most of the great inventions in history were discovered by accident—not by a lifetime in a lab. Look at vulcanizing rubber—the guy spilled it on a hot stove and found that it got hard. Or penicillin—the 'genius' just had some moldy bread around and found it killed bacteria. And remember the guys who discovered the shape of DNA? They saw it in a dream!"

Lesley protested quickly, "Yes, but all of those people stumbled onto the solutions after years of working on the problem. Without all their research, they wouldn't even have known it WAS a solution."

Luke wasn't convinced. "Sure, but there were *other* people working on the same problem—and *they* didn't get a lucky break. We never even hear about them. Look, it's all luck. How do you think that idiot Marty Jenkins got his job as sales manager? He was the guy they were talking about when they made up the term *dumb luck*!

"Jenkins gives talks every morning at 6:30 that the whole

sales department has to get up for," Luke said. "'If you want to enough, you can move the world!' He has them close their eyes and visualize themselves closing million-dollar sales. What a crock. The guy's lucky they don't lock him up!"

Lesley bristled. "I *know* how Marty got that job! He is the most *motivated* person in this company. Do you know that every day he would get up and look himself in the mirror and say, 'Good morning, Mr. Sales Manager!'?"

Luke grinned. "You really believe that crap?"

Lesley glowered. "You don't?"

They gave each other the evil eye and retreated to chairs in the opposite corners of the waiting room. "Neanderthals like that will never understand *anything*," each concluded in disgust. *"They just drive me crazy."*

The real driving force for Believers is motivation. It's a religion with them. They believe that if you want to enough, you can do anything.

Luke is talking heresy to Lesley. If she would listen, he would point out to her that most things that happen to her are totally out of her control. Luke believes that if you start believing you're in control, you're headed for big-time disappointment.

Rebels have a hard time accepting that they have any control over their jobs. They tend to point to floods and earthquakes, then draw the conclusion that their boss's constant irritation with them is another fact of nature and has nothing to do with their own actions. Stuff happens. What can you do?

Of course, Believers don't always get what they want. Sometimes they, too, are tempted to believe that it's just bad luck. For Competitors, though, luck is a different story.

Several years ago, Bronson knew that Franklin, the division head, as well as a few other upper-level managers, played tennis at their club on Saturdays. That's why Bronson begged his second cousin to nominate him and willingly paid the exorbitant dues to join.

It's also why Bronson hung around the nets for three Saturdays in a row, until one afternoon Franklin wandered in.

"Bronson. You're a member here? What luck! I was looking for someone to beat!"

Competitors make their own luck.

The Conspiracy Theory

Rebels also have a theory to explain why nobody competent ever becomes chairman of the board. Why? Simple: It's a conspiracy. The message of the Conspiracy Theory is that, in the corporate world, the people who have power actively conspire to keep it away from people who aren't like them. (In most companies, this translates into "Competitors Against the Rebels and Believers.")

At its extreme, the Conspiracy theory develops into a belief that your company could have been designed by Robert Ludlum—nothing is as it seems, and everything is rigged.

One of the most common mythic tales related to the Conspiracy Theory is of "The Old-Boy Network."

Luke has heard rumors of Bronson's latest triumph.

So "Mr. Fast-track" got another promotion, did he? Well, what do you expect? He and Franklin belong to the same tennis club. In fact, it's the "in" thing for certain management types to "shoot over to the club" at lunchtime for a quick game. Those guys might as well hold all the management meetings in the club dining room.

Of course, you'll never see one of *us* over there, Luke thought sourly. "Why would anyone want to spend a fortune just to belong to a snobbish club and have to hang around with a bunch of Neanderthals who talk about—and think about—nothing but money and power?"

We're not saying that the "Old Boy" myth is completely untrue, but the network is not nearly as structured as people who aren't in it would imagine. The Old-Boy Network is not a group of silver-haired WASP males, having lunch at a downtown racquet club and plotting ways to keep women and minorities out of power.

The Old-Boy Network is really made up of Competitors, people who understand The System and have a similar world view, recognizing each other and doing favors for one another. True, the skills that a Competitor needs to learn are most similar to the training that white, Anglo-Saxon, Protestant males receive. It's also true that real restrictions exist on participation by women and minorities. However, most of the talk about the Old-Boy Network as a conspiracy comes from Rebels and Believers, trying to explain Competitor behavior without totally understanding it. Like all myths, the Conspiracy Theory is an attempt to explain the unknown.

The Old-Boy Network, conspiracies, luck of all kinds, and the Big Break—they all spring from the Rebels' central belief that what you do has little effect on what happens to you. To Rebels, luck explains what happens to them, and "conspiracy" explains what happens to other people. Rebels don't see themselves as "rebelling against The System" any more than teenagers do. (In fact, the people who *consciously* rebel at work tend to be morally outraged Believers.) Rebels (and Believers) don't understand The System, and Rebels think it's just their bad luck that they've never been invited to join an effective conspiracy.

Grievance Procedures

Complaining, a time-honored Rebel ritual, is an offshoot of the Rebels' belief in luck. (If you have bad luck, you complain about it.) As long as there have been undesirable tasks or managers who try to make people do what they can't or won't do themselves, Rebels have been complaining about them. Their complaints brand them as outsiders in the world of Believers and Competitors, whose mythology clearly states that complaints arise not out of problems with the job, but from defects in the motivation of the employee. Rebels think that the real question is, "How can I get people to leave me alone and let me do my job?" They don't realize that the real question is "How do you complain in a system where complaining is not allowed?"

For this purpose, Competitors have created the Grievance Procedure, a formal way of complaining that makes it look as if someone is listening. In most companies, if you have a dispute with your boss, you can take it to human resources personnel, who will tell you, in a very polite and understanding way, that your boss is right.

Grievance procedures exist because Rebels and Believers demand them. Competitors know that the cost of using them is higher than the worth of whatever might be gained. Believers want grievance procedures as assurance that everyone will be made to follow the rules. Most Believers, however, would never dream of filing a grievance because of their faith in the Myth of Motivation—until their outrage over a violated rule convinces them that a *truly motivated* person would speak out, especially for other victims.

Rebels just like to complain and will use the grievance procedure as another way of "standing up to the Neanderthals." Maybe they'll win; maybe they'll lose. Life is a game of luck. They don't see that much of their "bad luck" at work comes from being branded as a complainer. Rebels just think the Neanderthals are in a conspiracy against the people who really know what they're doing.

Paperwork. Luke's boss was a paperwork freak. Just because Luke kept forgetting his monthly reports, she never got off his case. She never gave Luke any praise, and she chewed him out regularly for little infractions, such as coming in five minutes late and making personal telephone calls. The boss didn't get on *other* people like that.

Luke had never forgiven her for making him stay after work that day until all the reports were in. He'd felt like a 12-year-old, hunched over his desk while the boss lectured him

about his work habits. He didn't have to take crap like that from anybody.

Luke decided to take his complaint to the Human Resources (HR) Department. The HR person listened, then said quietly, "Well it does sound as if your boss overdid it a little—but, Luke, I think you need to go back and do your paperwork." When he smiled sympathetically at him, Luke blew up.

"Thanks a lot for nothing! Well, no more Mister Nice Guy! I'm going to get that witch. It's grievance time! How do I file a complaint for verbal harassment?"

The HR person was able to talk him out of filing a formal grievance, but Luke left his office still fuming and convinced that the HR Department was just a part of the conspiracy. This is an unfortunate misperception of the HR person, who was just trying to protect Luke from himself. The HR person knows that the cost of winning a grievance is so much higher than anything that might be gained. Luke listened, but some Rebels are willing to get squashed flat proving that no one can push them around.

5

The Cult of Cool
and the Myth
of Purity

The eagle spied his prey and broke from his lazy circling. With talons extended, he dropped like a stone onto the hapless mouse, alone and unprotected in an empty field. Child's play.

Just before he hit, he was surprised to see the mouse stop running, rear back on his hind legs and raise his paw. It took the eyes of an eagle to make out that tiny middle finger, raised in a last, futile gesture of defiance.

How do you act in a world that you think is governed by uncaring fate? Be cool, man. This is how the religion of the Rebels, the Cult of Cool, was born.

The Cult of Cool is an attitude of detachment that psychologically protects you from things you think you can't do or don't understand. Try for that promotion? "No way. I like working for a living." Play corporate politics? "Give me a break. I've never been the good little boy who brings apples for the teacher."

Members of the Cult of Cool send others the message that they are too sophisticated to get involved in company life. Rebels are often the "teenagers" in a corporate family. They may be mature in other areas of their lives, but in their jobs they are still doing just what teenagers do—finding an identity for themselves that is separate from the authority figures. The Cult of Cool teaches them not to get too close, or their fragile, not-quite-solid identity will be swallowed up. The Cult of Cool is a way of acting, embodied in its heroes.

The heroes of the Cult of Cool are always the nonconformists:

Josh is the guy in sales who spends half his time on probation. Part of the problem is that he just doesn't adapt to the "corporate" image. The other reps dress in gray suits and subdued ties. Josh comes to work in cowboy boots and a bolo. He likes to hang out with the guys from the plant and have a few beers with them after work. He even drives a van with a (gasp!) mural painted on the side. Thank God for the company car he has to drive on sales calls. Behind his back, the other reps call Josh's style "blue-collar chic"; he just calls it being himself.

As to sales, sometimes he's way over quota, but once in a while he does nothing. You never know with Josh. Management says he's "not a team player."

But then the big emergency came up with the company's heaviest customer. There was a mix-up in paperwork, and the order got in late. When they found out about it, everybody else stood around, shaking in their wing-tips and moaning about how they were going to explain the failure to the customer.

Meanwhile, Josh drove down to the plant, rounded up the help of a couple of guys he'd shared a few brews with, and retooled the machines on the spot. They ended up getting the order out two hours *ahead* of schedule.

The next day, a grateful VP asked him how he had ever figured out how to solve the problem so quickly. Josh shook his head and said, "All I did was see that if somebody was willing to get his hands dirty, there *wasn't* any problem."

Josh saved the bacon precisely because, in the crisis, he didn't think like a member of the team. His creativity wasn't bound and gagged like the rest of the guys who, in his estima-

tion, were more concerned about keeping their suits clean than in saving a million-dollar account.

* * *

Let's just say Norm has his own methods. He's the unorthodox cop, the epitome of the Rebel. In the end, Norm embodies what *real* cops believe in—"getting the bad guys"—a lot better than his unimaginative, pencil-pushing lieutenant. Just turn on the TV. Norm's story in some form is on every night.

Rebels like to see themselves as the ones who actually do the hands-on work, while everybody else is shuffling papers and playing politics. Sometimes they're right, but not as often as they would like to believe. Somebody has to make the deals and keep the records, even if Rebels don't see those things as real work.

The Cult of Cool is the persistence of adolescent rebellion into adulthood. It has the vitality of anger and the creativity of looking at things in different ways, but it also has cynicism and disconnection. It is built on a strong sense of what you're *against* but offers little idea of what you're *for*. Among Rebels, authority definitely isn't cool. "Take this job and shove it" is the theme song.

Members of the Cult of Cool "worship" by getting together in groups and making jokes and snide remarks about whomever they're rebelling against. Cynical, put-down humor is very important; it's the tool that keeps Rebels detached. At times, the Rebel inside each of us uses Cult of Cool humor, just as we use other Rebel inventions, to help us get by in a world that sometimes seems unfair and out of our control.

Nonconformity, like everything else, has its rules and traditions. Whether it's the clothes they wear, how they talk, or what they think is funny, people who are rebelling usually display *at least one* (and usually quite a few) symbol of their independence somewhere or in some aspect of their lives. Non-Rebels can smirk about that, the way that Rebels smirk about the ties with the little dots, or we both can try to find out each other's symbols and what they mean.

The Cult of Cool Protects Us All

We all have some belief in the Cult of Cool. In fact, the Management Mystique is the Competitor version of the Cult of Cool. Both are trying to say, "I know all I need to know, and I'm in control." The difference between the Rebel and the Competitor versions are that the Rebel expresses it through cool detachment, whereas the Competitor shows it through arrogant conceit.

At its best, this reaction can keep us from turning into little, gray-flannel-suit, organizational clones. It can show us how to handle the role of Rebel with dignity when we need it. We are all Rebels sometimes; there are always clubs or cliques that we'll never get into. The Cult of Cool can also protect us from negative feelings by making us believe that the sources of these feelings are unimportant. Competitors and Believers, as well as Rebels, occasionally indulge in the vital emotional skills of detachment and rationalization.

For example, watch how Rich—a die-hard Competitor—shows his Rebel streak:

Rich came home from his trip to Regional with second thoughts about having refused the promotion. Sure, he couldn't stand the manipulative VP who would have been his new boss, but had he been a chump to turn down the higher salary and big career step?

His doubts eased as he and his wife talked about his decision that night. "You're right, honey," Rich said. "It would have been a terrible hassle. We would have had to sell the house, uproot the kids, find a new job for you—all in a strange new town where we don't know a soul."

He sat up straighter. "Yeah, but the main thing is I'd have to compromise myself too much, working for Chuck. The politics there are incredible. It wouldn't have been worth it."

What's more, even true-blue Believers such as Lesley occasionally feel the Rebel rising within them:

The day after she lost the promotion to assistant manager, Lesley had lunch with Betty, a secretary.

"Don't let it get to you, Les," Betty said as Lesley listlessly picked at her uneaten salad. "You know, it was all rigged from the beginning anyway. That brown-nose Andy had it locked. Besides, they don't pay you enough for the responsibility of being a manager.

"Besides, it didn't really have anything to do with you. They always knew it would be Andy—he *is* a member of the Racquet Club. So no matter who else had wanted it, it would have turned out the same. The posting was just a formality— everybody down here knew that. It's not like you failed or anything."

"Thanks, Betty," Lesley said, more relieved than she would have guessed. Her irritation at The System was helping her feel less depressed.

Messages such as these can help people deal with tough decisions and defeat but can also prevent them from figuring out what they're really afraid of or what they need to do to get the promotion next time around.

Cult of Cool, M*A*S*H Style

Some Rebels adopt a M*A*S*H unit approach to the Cult of Cool, exhibiting characteristic humor and independent behavior as they do their jobs well and tirelessly.

People in other departments of the magazine don't exactly feel comfortable with The Shooters, the staff photographers. There's no argument that their work is dynamite; they've won every major art and news-photo award three years running and have beaten out mags with twice the shooting staff. And

dedicated? Just mention a helicopter ride to the crater of a steaming volcano, and those hellions will be pushing each other to be first in line. They'll go anywhere, do anything for the best shot.

The Shooters have all had years of training. They've come up the hard way, from early years of wedding portraits and high school basketball close-ups, to reach the top of their field. Their work is never late; their van never breaks down on the way to a shoot. These people are veterans, real pros.

But the wild way they dress—all that torn denim and cowboy leather; the crazy way they laugh among themselves, telling stories about their riskiest assignments, then turn stone-faced when someone from another department walks in. They make other people feel shut out. It's as if The Shooters do it on purpose, as if they like being Rebels.

Cult of Cool Meets Myth of Purity

Many Rebels, Believers, and Competitors are convinced that *theirs* is the one group that really does the stuff that keeps the place going. We call it the "Myth of Purity," which can lead to self-inflicted moral isolation for any kind of personality.

The common definition of myth is a story that isn't true, or a quaint, unscientific explanation about how something started. In this book, we try to understand myth in the Joseph Campbell sense: the kind of story by which Rebels, Believers or Competitors pass along powerful information that the group considers important, true, and valuable. The stories are direct, convincing, and easily remembered. People hear them and tell them but seldom consider what they imply.

Purists believe that the attitudes and values of the other groups are so hopelessly self-defeating (Rebels), naïve and conformist (Believers), or corrupt (Competitors) that even *considering* them can cause psychological or moral damage. Followers of this myth are the Rebels who, on principle, will never wear a tie; the Believers who don't stoop to "playing politics"; and the Competitors who never ask for employees' opinions because they don't want to look indecisive.

The Myth of Purity keeps us persistently hanging onto our belief that we know it all instead of trying to see another point of view. This myth is especially important to Believers, who see themselves as the last outpost of morality in a wilderness of corrupt politics. They may not have power, but they're pure.

Gwen had been the head bookkeeper for Olduvai Inc. for 15 years when the company was bought out and consolidated into the Neander-Tek System. Then everything changed.

In the old days, Olduvai was smaller, more of a family operation, where procedures made sense. Gwen knew which information her boss needed and made sure he got it. Now her whole job seems to be making reports for the district office and for the exalted home office in Chicago. Most of the time, the information they want just doesn't make sense to Gwen.

Her former boss was a reasonable man, but he retired when the companies merged, and now she has to work for a 32-year-old MBA sent from Chicago "to straighten us out." Gwen could tell him a thing or two about how to run his office—such as using praise, for instance. Apparently, his mother never taught him that you can catch more flies with molasses than you can with vinegar. If you make the slightest little mistake, you're in his office with the door closed. But if you do something right, you never hear about it.

Her new boss's favorite saying is, "Just keep the old rear end covered. Whenever a problem comes up, convince 'em that it's some other department's fault." Well, Gwen believes in telling the truth. It's worked for her all her life, and she's not about to stop doing it now.

And look at the new people she has to work with. All they're good at is going to meetings. When it comes to knowing how to get the job done, most of them are out to lunch. Literally.

Gwen is miserable. She'd quit in a minute, but she could never make as much money somewhere else. She figures she'll just have to hang in there for another eight years until she can retire.

Who is to blame for Gwen's problem? That depends on what her problem is. If you think it is surviving in a company that has been taken over by incompetent sleazeballs, then we know whose fault you think it is.

Actually, Gwen is the biggest cause of her own misery. It's true that the management style of the new people is different from the old regime (and probably worse), but Gwen has set things up in her mind so that the old team was the Good Guys and the new people are the Bad Guys. Because Gwen is a "good guy," she feels she has to fight the "villains," instead of getting to know them or learning how to work under their system. That would be treason! Like many Rebel and Believer heroines, Gwen will lose in the end, but she will die pure.

She doesn't really have to lose at all. Maybe the bad guys aren't as bad as she thinks. Maybe Gwen's problem is not the struggle of Good versus Evil, but a simple case of culture shock. The easiest way to handle anything new that we can't understand is to label it *evil*.

What can be done? Gwen can choose to leave Olduvai Inc. and find a job that better suits her needs. If she decides to stay, however, not much will change until she stops playing that well-worn mental tape about how bad the new guys are and tries actively to get along with them. She could start by talking with her new boss—initiating a friendly conversation, trying to find out what he's really like, instead of mining him for little gems to add to her atrocity collection.

On the other hand, Gwen's young Competitor boss should ignore as much of her hostility as he can and accept the challenge of trying to win her over. How? By *listening* to her. Gwen has a lot to teach. The only people to whom 15 years of experience means nothing are people who haven't *had* 15 years of experience.

Political Skills or Brown-nosing?

For another example of the Myth of Purity, let's look at Stan and Erica, two employees in the same company.

Stan is the kind of guy who's friendly to the people above him. He jokes around with the boss and is usually quick with a compliment. He's always dropping in and chatting with the guys upstairs. When it's fishing season, he brings them a piece of smoked salmon. He occasionally volunteers to do extra work. Sometimes after 5, he'll go out and have a beer with the boss.

Describe Stan to a Rebel, and the response invariably will be a sneer and a muttered "That guy's a brown-noser." Erica, on the other hand, . . .

Erica is bright and competent, but she believes in doing a good job and going home. She doesn't play games. She is polite to her boss, but not overly so. She certainly doesn't go out of her way to talk to him or compliment him, but she doesn't avoid him, either. Erica doesn't think it's right that she should treat the boss any differently just because he's the boss. Erica is a woman of principle.
But consider how Erica treats her friends. She compliments them, jokes around with them. If her friends need her, she's willing to help if asked, and she doesn't say no to the occasional beer with her buddies.

Would you call this brown-nosing? "Hell, no," says the Rebel. "Those people are *friends*, not the boss. Erica's just being a nice person with her friends."

Terry is Stan and Erica's boss. He responds as most people do—on an emotional level. The way Terry sees the contrast

between Stan and Erica is quite simple. He thinks Stan likes him and Erica doesn't. Of course, this feeling shouldn't influence Terry in work-related decisions about the two employees, but Terry is human like the rest of us. Whatever Stan does just seems to show a little better quality than Erica's work. When Stan wants a favor from Terry, he's more likely to get it.

Erica knows this is true, but she says vehemently that she doesn't play that kind of game. It would mean compromising her principles. When you ask her what kind of principles she's talking about, she just looks at you as if you were some kind of pond scum.

Stan has taken Erica aside and tried to explain rudimentary political skills such as "How you treat people determines how they treat you." He never gets anywhere, though, because he's running headlong into Erica's Rebel religious belief that she is reacting in the only reasonable way to the things that are done to her. If somebody gives her grief, Erica gives it back. Not doing so would be compromising her principles. (Telling her what to do or commenting on her behavior is what she calls "giving me grief.")

Five years later, Terry has been transferred to headquarters. Stan is gone; he's a manager in another department. And Erica is still there, in the same position. Stan may or may not have been playing a game, but Erica was the one who lost. Why?

Erica made a poor career decision—but most Rebels and some Believers would say, "No, she didn't. Stan is a sleaze. He compromised his principles for wealth, power, and promotion." They have to say that. Within the Cult of Cool, any other response would be unthinkable.

Stuck in a Class by Yourself?
Do Your Rebel Attitudes Limit Your Freedom?

You don't have to move up in your company to be a good person. You don't even have to *want* to move up. Finding the job you love to do and having the freedom to do it your way is a rare and hard-won success. To reach this goal, your decision to rebel must be *conscious*, based on what you believe and what you want. Being labeled a Rebel should not be a choice that's made *for* you because you are unwilling to or don't think you can learn certain parts of your job.

Are You a Rebel?

The following statements may be indications of the kind of behavior that makes authority figures crack down. Take this quiz and decide whether your Rebel tendencies are helping you reach your goal or are holding you back at work. After the quiz, this chapter offers some specific suggestions for Rebels and for those who work with them (which includes just about everyone). Which of the following statements are true of you?

1. **I sometimes use humorous names implying incompetence for people who spend most of their time playing politics (empty suit, sell-out, brown-nose, Neanderthal).**
Different people have different skills. Just because people don't have *your* skills doesn't mean that they have *no* skills. Politics is a skill, too. It will be particularly helpful for you to read the Competitors section of this book. Someone as intelligent as you might decide that you need just one more skill to get to where you want to be.

2. **I usually use most of my sick leave and vacation time.**
It's your right to use your sick leave and vacation leave, and it's good that you don't come to work sick, or avoid relaxation. Believers pride themselves on accumulations of unused sick

leave and vacation time. Competitors seldom check to see how much they have. If you use all of yours every year, you'll be seen as having low motivation. This attitude gives you a *job*, not a *career*. Find out the unwritten rules about sick leave and vacation time in your company.

3. **In the past five years, I have held two or more jobs at about the same level.**

You may not be in a rut, but you're making no progress. Is it possible you left because you didn't know how to succeed? Were there personality problems? Did you blame the problem on the job, instead of seeing it as something you could have changed about your attitude or behavior? Hard-line Rebels sometimes have to experience the same problems at three or four jobs before they consider the possibility that it's them and not the job.

4. **In my life there are clear distinctions between work and play.**

True. We all need to know the difference between work and play. But if you see work as drudgery and miss its "game" aspect, though, you'll never learn to play the company game. You play to win on weekends, don't you? Why not try it from 9 to 5 on weekdays at the office?

5. **The people at the top don't follow the rules. I don't see why I should have to.**

Maybe you're right, but acting on this belief may get you fired. There are some rules everybody obeys. You need to know what they are. (*Hint:* Read the rest of this book to figure out which are the *real* rules in your office.)

6. **In the past year, I have chosen training only in technical aspects of my job.**

This is the way to stay focused and up to date, but *people* are important, too. Next time a training course on human relations is offered, sign up. Your sense of humor and creativity will make the group glad you joined—and you might learn a few things about yourself, too.

7. The bottom line is not my concern. Somebody else needs to see that there is enough money so that I can do my job correctly.

You have a clear focus on your job, but a "damn the expense" attitude may make your boss (who *has* to mind the bottom line) angry at you.

8. I call the conformists in my department Organization Men, Sheep, Cookie-Cutter Minds, or other humorous epithets.

You're a maverick, and sometimes your independence is a life-saver to the more conventional thinkers in your department. Faced with a crisis, you're often the person they turn to for inspiration. On the other hand, where would your company—the product quality or customer service that you value—be without conformity? Isn't it nice that there are a lot of conformists to please the boss and keep the boss off *your* back? Give 'em a break. Take a conformist to lunch.

9. My boss and I don't get along.

Your boss may well be an idiot, but doing your best to get along with him (or her) is part of your job. If you've had problems getting along with more than one boss (or if other people seem to get along fine), maybe the issue is authority rather than idiocy. Also, your boss is probably a Competitor and unable to see the world as you do. Read the section of this book that discusses Competitors, and find out how your boss thinks.

10. This place drives me crazy! I should go into business for myself.

Maybe you should, but if you do, you should be running toward new challenges instead of away from people telling you what to do. Even if you're your own boss, people still tell you what to do. (Ask the I.R.S.) If you want to start your own business, read the next two sections to find out how to combine your Rebel creativity and willingness to take risks with the Believer can-do attitude and the Competitor savvy that it takes to make any business succeed. Another (and less financially risky) possibility is transferring to a smaller company, where your special skills might be more valued and your style might be more compatible. Check it out.

Be sure to read the sections about the other personality types, too. If you tend to write off certain people at your office as Neanderthals, try answering the test questions following Chapter 1 again—this time as you think *they* would answer them. Then total their score, see which group they belong to, and try approaching them with some of the strategies you'll learn as you read the rest of this book.

If You Are a Rebel

If five or more of the preceding statements are true of you, you probably think or behave like a Rebel at work. You may be highly skilled and creative, and probably can see the same day-to-day situations differently and more productively than the people around you. You also may feel very frustrated because, no matter how hard you try to explain your ideas, people just don't listen to you. You may have to learn to speak their language to convince them to let you do what you're best at.

If you are a Rebel, you tend to think it's important to do things your own way. Why in the world would you want to change anything just because we say it's a good idea? Actually, there are some real benefits to being able to think like a Believer or a Competitor when the situation calls for it:

- You'll make more money. Promotions and raises generally go to those who operate within The System.
- Your job will be less stressful. If other people think you're a team player, you'll get into fewer arguments, and your boss will be less likely to criticize you.
- People will be more likely to listen to you. It always helps if you speak their language.
- People may finally appreciate your skills and creativity. If they don't feel as if they have to tell you constantly to

shape up, maybe they'll look at the value of what you're doing.

- You will be better able to buy your freedom. Outsiders are likely to be checked closely. Insiders have the freedom to make meaningful choices about their work.

One way to buy your freedom is by demonstrating to the people in authority that it will be in their best interests to let you do things your way. To do that, *you* have to know what *their* best interest is. Here are some ideas that may help you get what you want at work:

1. **Think bottom line.** In most companies, you can have wide latitude to do things your way if you can clearly demonstrate that your way is making or saving a lot of money. (Don't let your Cult of Cool thinking get in the way here and say, "That's for accountants. I know how to do my job the way it *should* be done, and if they don't want to pay for it, then they're just a bunch of bean-counting Neanderthals.") No matter what they are, you have to keep your own priorities straight. Recognizing your tendency to write off the "bean-counters" will help you keep it under *your* control.

2. **Show you can do what it takes.** The Rebel in you may make you act disdainful of things you don't understand, don't want to do, or perhaps even are afraid you can't do. Rebels sometimes tend to take shortcuts or to avoid a task by saying, "This isn't important," or "Somebody else needs to do this part." This leaves people thinking, rightly or wrongly, that you're criticizing something that you can't do yourself. Before you decide something is not for you, you need to demonstrate to other people that you know how to do it. Then you can make a case for not doing it.

Believers and Competitors think that a typical Rebel strategy is to say, "I can't do it" to get out of doing what they don't want to do. They'll be looking for evidence of this tendency. It's best not to give them any.

3. **Judge yourself on results.** If you want freedom and respect, you will have to think in terms of outcome. Your boss

does. Look at your job in terms of the final product for which you are responsible. Learn to do what it takes to make your final product of higher quality, greater usefulness, and lower price. Realize that you will be judged on the *outcome*, no matter how elegantly or painstakingly you do the rest of the job. If you're in sales, you'll be judged on the number of orders you bring in—period. If cold calls and closings are getting in your way, you'll need to do something about them. No amount of explaining or justification ever excused bad monthly totals.

4. **Pay attention to your own jokes.** What do you joke about most in the workplace? Whatever it is, pretend that's what you know the least about—and decide you'll learn more about it. If you're like most Rebels, you're bright and good at learning, but you tend to restrict yourself to what you consider your own areas. Make an effort to learn what other people do and what they think. If most of your jokes are about your boss's incompetence, spend some time paying attention to what he or she is really up against—the decisions, results, people, and problems in a typical week. Maybe the boss's work isn't worth learning, but you won't know until you've tried. There is absolutely nothing cool about ignorance.

5. **Focus on what you could do differently.** If you're not as successful as you'd like to be, you can't count on having other people change to help you. All you can do is change your own behavior. As we demonstrate throughout this book, changing your behavior can have enormous effects on how people treat you.

6. **Find somebody in authority you respect.** There's bound to be someone. (If there isn't, find someone who is successful in the area you care about.) Talk to this person about what it takes to be successful at your company. Ask him or her to tell you about how things operate, what you need to do to gain respect, how you can get people to listen to your ideas. We're suggesting getting a mentor—but having a mentor only works if you listen and try to do what your mentor suggests.

7. **Practice doing things you don't like to do.** No matter what your job, it will include some requirements that you don't like. Believers are very good at doing what they don't like to do. You might ask some of them how they manage it. You also need to develop strategies for yourself. We all make excuses and come up with good reasons why we shouldn't have to do whatever we don't like to do. Learn to recognize your excuses for what they are, and sometimes ignore them. If you know you have to do something to reach the outcome you want, then get yourself to do it. (We know this is a tough task. However, you wouldn't be reading this book if you weren't interested in making some changes.) This simple truth is the great wisdom of the Believers. If you've scored high on the Rebels' end of the scale, you could do well to learn from it.

Whenever there's a choice between the easy way and the hard way, choose the way that's most difficult for you. You can also learn from Competitors. Whenever there's a choice between your way and your boss's way, do it your boss's way.

8. **Look the part.** Maybe clothes aren't really important and have no bearing on the way you do your job. If you want to buy your freedom, though, you have to be able to look like part of the team. Pick your battles. If you're going to fight authority, why not let it be over something important—not about the way you dress?

9. **Let people tell you what to do.** Practice following instructions to the letter sometimes, just to see whether you can do it. If you're a real Rebel, your dislike of being told what to do may get in the way of new learning. Try to do it somebody else's way once in a while, just to see what happens.

10. **Practice boredom.** Be able to operate at peak efficiency even when you're bored. Sometimes the boring work is just as important, and you need to develop strategies to get through it. Some Rebels get into destructive conflicts with people in authority just because they see a blow-up as the only alternative to day-to-day boredom. Most people would say, it's better to be bored.

If You Manage Rebels

Rebels *can* be managed effectively—if you know something about the psychology of dealing with teenagers. (If you get angry, you're dead.) You have to accept that the Rebels' provocative style is important to them and that there's a reason for it.

Rebels tend to divide people into two categories—the people who know what they're doing, and the ones who play politics and avoid the real work. They place little value on the competence involved in organizing projects and managing people, and they may tend to rub you the wrong way by not acknowledging your value. Following are some suggestions for gaining Rebels' respect and cooperation by recognizing *their* value.

1. **Let them know which rules are important**. The important rules are the ones that relate to the bottom line and those that are critical to the Rebels' own performance. Clearly state that you expect them to follow these rules. You might need to let other rules slide. Rebels must learn to recognize the crucial rules, but if you demand that they do *everything* by the book, they may well resist your authority by neglecting something that's important.

2. **Don't make acknowledging your authority a job requirement.** Tolerate jokes about yourself. Try not to take yourself so seriously. If you get involved in a power struggle with a Rebel, you'll win, but you could lose the ability to be an effective manager. You might also lose a valuable employee.

3. **Show them you're not afraid to get your hands dirty.** Learn what they do. Rebels usually take great pride in their own work and have respect for people who are willing to do it with them. Getting into the trenches with them will increase your credibility if you treat their work seriously and pay them the respect they're due. *Don't* try to pretend that you're just one of the guys. Listen to them. Follow their directions, and pay attention to their suggestions. You could learn more than you expect to.

4. **Give them a chance to gripe.** If a Rebel in your department decides to talk to you about a problem, *listen*. This will make it less necessary for him or her to rebel against you in more destructive ways. Make it clear that employees have to follow the rules but also have the right to their own opinions about company policy.

5. **Put them where they can do what they do best.** Try to arrange it so that the Rebels can spend most of their time on the things they do best. Providing them with support staff will pay off quickly. (Dana discovers this when she deals with Luke—described later in this book.)

6. **Dare them to improve.** Rebels have a sense of adventure and excitement. They respond much better to dares, challenges, and bets than they do to demands.

7. **Be straight with them about who you are.** If you're an authority figure over Rebels, admit that you like power, authority, and money. Admit that you play politics. Rebels usually don't believe in altruism from authorities. Level with them about your own motivations and they may respond to your honesty.

8. **Protect them from above.** Don't become a mere conduit, passing on orders that come down from your boss. Rebels respect people who stand up to authority when they know they are right. If you want to win the Rebels' cooperation, you'll have to show that you can put yourself on the line for them.

9. **If you promote them, back them up with support.** Rebels often have very valuable skills, and some managers want to promote them so that other people can make use of their skills. Promoting a Rebel can be done effectively *if* you give the Rebel a Believer as support staff, to tend to the details. In this way, the Rebel can be free to do what he or she does best.

10. **Don't fall into the parent trap.** It's very easy to become parental with Rebels: to lecture them, to take what they do (or don't do) personally, and to feel "they should know better." Structure, rules they can count on, and having them face the natural consequences of their actions are the approaches that

work best (but even these strategies don't work *all* the time). These suggestions apply to Rebels and to the rebellious teen-ager who lives inside most employees—especially the dissatisfied ones.

If You Work for a Rebel

It happens sometimes (we didn't say *often!*). Rebels do get promoted to management. You might think that, with their sensitivity to authority, they would make great bosses. Actually, they are often among the worst. They tend to abdicate responsibility for the things they don't like. When pressured, they might adopt a leadership style that they call "military." (The military they have in mind seems most like the nineteenth-century French Foreign Legion.) People who dislike authority can become tyrants because that's what they think authority means. If you work for a Rebel, there is only one rule to remember: *Stay on the boss's good side.*

PART THREE

*Innocents
at Work:
The Believers*

6

Believers and the Myth of Motivation

Sir Thomas More, a man for all seasons, an idealist, author of
***Utopia,* friend and adviser to Henry VIII—that is, until he**
stood on his Catholic principles and refused to sign the 1534
Act of Supremacy, which would have helped Henry to engi-
neer his hostile takeover of the English Church from the pope
and, conveniently, to get a divorce from Catherine of Aragon.

Though he could have had power, wealth and influence at
the king's side, More lost his head rather than compromise
his principles. This is what being a Believer is all about.

We suppose you could say that More had the last laugh four
hundred years later, when he was made a saint.

On the surface, More may seem the quintessential Rebel.
However, his willingness literally to give his life for his principles gives him patron-saint status among the Believers. The
Believers' brown lunch bags hold more than just tuna sand-
wiches; they also carry a tradition of hard work and powerful
ideals.

Believers place their trust in the great principle of the business world, the Work Ethic: Work hard, do a good job, follow
the rules, and you'll be rewarded. Most of the time, Believers
don't talk about their moral code; they just live by it and, all
too often, get clobbered for doing so. To Competitors, Believers

are Neanderthals whose thinking is a million years behind the times. Rebels, too, see them as primitive thinkers, obsessed with rules (and with anything else written on paper, as if paperwork could, by some magic ritual, transform itself into something of value).

Many Believers are self-motivators who find a genuine sense of accomplishment in the hard work they do, just as following the rules gives them a sense of ethics and personal value. These internal rewards are real and important, and the corporate world would collapse without them.

Few Believers in today's business world are willing to wait 400 years to be appreciated. They'd like to see something *now* that recognizes and rewards their value to the company. A raise would be nice. Or a promotion. Heaven knows, they've earned it.

Lesley believes in doing a day's work for a day's pay. She knows what needs to be done, and she does it. She often works late to finish a job the right way, when instead she could probably get away with rushing through it. Whatever she does, she does as well as she can. She couldn't live with herself if she did any less.

When Lesley noticed an error that messed up a whole month's worth of reports, she stayed at the office until 2 A.M., correcting every report. (It was her error, so she felt she had to do it.) She didn't put in for compensatory ("comp") time, either.

Lesley knows she's doing her job the right way, and that gives her a lot of satisfaction. Her hard work doesn't seem to have much effect on her performance reviews, though. She gets good ones, but so do people who don't work quite as hard as she does (and some people who really goof off.)

Lesley is running head on into the biggest problem with the Work Ethic. Most Believers expect that their hard work will be rewarded on earth as well as in heaven. They don't realize that business doesn't operate that way. The real rewards go to those who know what to work hard *at.* The people who get the raises and promotions are the people who understand The System—the unwritten rules about how things are done. Most of these people work hard, too, but they also do something else, something Believers don't approve of. That "something" nearly always means playing politics, which, to many Believers, ranks right up there with signing the 1534 Act of Supremacy as distasteful, if not downright immoral.

This is the last straw. Carl has been working his buns off for the promotion to office manager, and instead it goes to Kasey, that lazy, good-for-nothing, brown-nosing, back-stabbing witch! It seems as if nobody values hard work any more—just a big smile and big. . . . Well, Carl can be fair. They want a politician; that's what Kasey is—that's *all* she is. . . .

A more objective observer would disagree with Carl. Kasey may be a "politician," but she is neither lazy nor good for nothing—nor any of Carl's other bitter put-downs. Kasey works hard and smart. She'd rather greet people with a smile than a martyred sigh (and she knows the right people to smile at.)

Maybe in his heart, Carl knows this, too. Carl knows what it takes to get ahead. He just can't bring himself to act like Kasey. Carl is bound and determined to get promoted, based strictly on the quality of his work. He'll work himself until he drops. Maybe the boss will notice—someday.

Carl may work himself to death, but his anger may burn him out long before then. What he *won't* get is that promotion to office manager—not unless he accepts that politics is part of his job.

Other Believers pick up on the challenge and begin to learn what they don't know. They hang onto the Believer ethic of hard work and personal integrity that has taken them this far, but they will also borrow a page from the Competitors' notebook. They will come to realize that politics is *hard work* and a kind of work that they know nothing about. When they enter this jungle of secret rules and mysterious rituals, things will never be the same again.

Even if the promotion doesn't come and the bonus doesn't show up in their paychecks this week, true Believers will keep giving 110 percent. They have something more powerful than dollars and cents to keep them going.

The Myth of Motivation

The pillar of Believer wisdom is the Myth of Motivation: If you want it enough, if you believe in it enough, if you can muster that internal drive, it will happen. To accomplish anything in the business world, you have to know this. If you think you can and you're willing to work hard, you can. If you're motivated enough and work hard enough, nothing is impossible.

Unfortunately, the Myth of Motivation also hurts Believers if they believe in it too strongly without knowing *what they have to work hard at.*

If you take myths literally, they are always untrue—larger-than-life distortions of reality. However, if you regard them as metaphors, they tell you what to believe about life. The story of St. George slaying the dragon, for example, is not meant to tell us that, at some time during the Middle Ages, a particular saint killed a particular dragon. Rather, the story is meant to tell us that Good triumphs over Evil, even when the evil is fearsome and mighty. Rebels, Believers, and Competitors each have their own myths that point to what is true for each group.

The Myth of Motivation answers the central question, How do you get yourself to do a task that you don't want to do? The answer is, You *make* yourself do it (often because you're afraid of what will happen if you don't.) By doing the difficult, you grow to love how it makes you feel about yourself. You know that you deserve to get ahead. You get a morality high just thinking about the success you deserve. In doing so, you feel even more motivated to work harder.

For Believers, there are no higher virtues than motivation

and hard work. These are the keys to success, Believer-style. Rebels, on the other hand, tend to avoid doing what they don't want to do. Their religious beliefs include no Myth of Motivation. (They're too cool to have one, anyway.) Rebels know that The System and the old-boys network determine who will and who won't succeed.

Neither view of motivation is completely right, but this difference in doctrine causes some Rebels and Believers to feel for each other the same warmth, trust, and affection that Protestants have for Catholics in Northern Ireland.

(Competitors believe in the Myth of Motivation, too, but they see it as a part of the greater Cult of Winning. Their motivation is to beat the other Competitors. To Competitors, the skill involved in winning—especially knowing the rules of the game—goes without saying. A winner works hard at whatever scores points. The Believers' more vague understanding of the game sometimes leads them to put the ball through the other guy's hoop.)

Rebels are convinced that luck and conspiracy explain why some people win and others lose. Believers believe that all power lies within themselves. Competitors, on the other hand, believe that The System determines who wins or loses, and that because they know The System and know how to work it, *they* will be the winners! More than anything else, the Myth of Motivation is the source of the energy and vitality of American business, most of which is made up of Believers. The Myth of Motivation gets them to do—and to take pride in doing—the hundred million tasks that have to be done every day. As much as paychecks and praise from the boss, belief in this myth keeps Believers going.

The myth also drives Believers crazy because it leaves out one important detail that Competitors know but don't tell: *You also have to understand The System.* Motivation alone is not enough to ensure success. When Believers confront this fact, their first tendency is to doubt themselves. They try to come up with a little more motivation and to work a little harder. (Their bosses will sometimes encourage this solution.) When this doesn't work, Believers may blame the boss for not playing by the rules. Finally, they begin to doubt the myth itself. When they do, the result is burnout.

"How do you do it?" friends of super-salesman Tom ask him in amazement. "How do you face being told 'No' again and again, but keep on asking?"

Tom just gives them that wall-to-wall smile and says cheerfully, "Well, first, you have to have motivation. You have to believe in whatever you're doing, with your whole heart and soul. You have to tell yourself that it isn't personal, and that 500 'No's' to one 'Yes' is a great ratio! There's no room for naysayers in this world. People with positive attitudes win, and people who aren't positive deserve what they get!"

The gurus of the Myth of Motivation are the people in sales, like Tom, who every day face the cold calls and the personal rejection, yet somehow come out smiling—and then do it all again, a hundred times. For Carl, the smile is starting to wear thin, and a martyred sigh is all he can muster. In fact, for most of us, this would be a superhuman effort, but there are people who thrive in this setting. Without them, industry would fall flat.

What the Myth of Motivation Leaves Out

It's a good thing that Believers have heaven, because earth surely seems to belong to Competitors. Companies need to have tasks done every day, but because most of those tasks carry few rewards, business must rely on the hearts of Believers to get them done. The Myth of Motivation can drive Believers crazy because of what it leaves out. It doesn't mention skill and selectivity—the ability to figure out *which* tasks get noticed and rewarded. The myth leads Believers to rely too much on heart.

Many Believers go on working hard, being positive, and expecting that the external rewards will come. If the rewards don't come, the Believers feel cheated and burned out. Eventually, they complain, then feel guilty for doing so. They seldom ask themselves what is really going on here—and their Competitor bosses don't tell them. (Competitors teach themselves how to recognize which tasks are rewarded, and pretty soon, spotting those tasks is as natural as breathing.)

Why aren't many Believer tasks rewarded? The answer lies within the Cult of Winning, the central belief of the Competitors. The Competitors' world is divided into winners and losers. No matter how much of anything there is, there isn't enough to go around. The winners get the biggest share. Yet a company made up only of "winners" wouldn't have anybody to do the day-to-day work.

How Marty Jenkins Got to Be Sales Manager

At his famous motivational seminars, which everyone at Neander-Tek is required to attend, Marty Jenkins (a successful Competitor) tells people how he became sales manager.

"I wanted it so bad I could taste it. Every day I looked at myself in the mirror, straightened my tie and said, 'You *will* be sales manager! You can *do it!* You can do *anything* you set out to do! You're a *winner!* All you have to do is *sell!* If you stay Number One, the job is yours! Now *go get 'em!*'"

Marty read the road-to-success books and played the inspirational tapes on the way to the office every day. He knew that one day—soon—he would walk in the door and see a big red banner that read, "CONGRATULATIONS, MARTY! OUR NEW SALES MANAGER!" If it didn't happen today, Marty didn't get discouraged. He would do whatever it took, would overcome all the odds, to make his dream come true. He knew he wasn't the first to be walking down that road. . . .

In the dim mists of time, 1949, Dale Sutter, the founder of Neander-Tek, had risked everything on *his* dream, "with only a transistor in a garage and a can-do spirit as big as the state of Indiana," Marty reminds his audience. "Dale and his sales manager, Samuel M. (the "M" is for Motivation) Kirby got the company off the ground. They wouldn't even admit that the

word 'No' was in the dictionary. They took their vision and turned it into the institution that we are all a part of." Marty is proud—no, _honored_—to carry on his legacy as sales manager of The Greatest Company in the World!

Marty knows he is only presenting part of the story (overstated for dramatic purposes, of course), to point out the importance of motivation in getting tasks done. He knows but doesn't state that the tasks have to be the right ones. He doesn't realize that people will understand his story to mean that everyone who is highly motivated will receive tangible rewards, such as promotions and raises, but this is just what many Believers expect.

Competitors such as Marty Jenkins are not consciously deceiving the Believers. They're just practicing Cargo Cult thinking and encouraging Believers to do the same. The jobs need to be done. There aren't enough rewards to go around. So, if you believe and pretend hard enough, the rewards _are_ there—and planes of sticks and leaves can fly. The Myth of Motivation is completely true inside your heart: If you believe, it _will_ come true. However, if you take it literally to mean that tangible rewards are sure to come in the real world, the myth is false.

Believers miss this fundamental distinction, and it drives them crazy. To Competitors, the distinction is so obvious, it drives _them_ crazy that Believers can't see it. If you want real rewards, just do what's rewarded. If Believers still don't get it, Competitors are not eager to correct the misunderstanding. To become a Competitor, that's what you're supposed to figure out for yourself (and the work _does_ need to get done. . . .)

Quality versus Quantity? Why Not Both?

The Myth of Motivation has other powerful properties. It can resolve the Quality versus Quantity dilemma.

Don, Lesley's husband, works as a sales rep for a telecommunications company. He's meeting with Eddie, his boss, who is studying a printout on his desk.

"Your sales totals this month are a little lower than we'd like to see, Don," Eddie says.

"But you know how busy I've been," Don says. "Bryce Industries has been installing the new equipment I sold them, and I've been spending just about a day a week helping them get set up. You know: 'Service Is Job One.'"

Eddie sighed. "Of course it is, Don, but if we don't sell, we don't have anything to service. Maybe you should let the techs handle the questions."

Don interrupted eagerly, "The techs can tell people how to operate the equipment, sure, but I show them how to *think* about it. Right now, most people don't know enough about our system to even ask the techs an intelligent question. If I spend the time with them now—they're already my biggest customer—in a few years, when they expand and need a new system, they'll want ours."

Eddie nodded impatiently. "Sure, Don, I know that. But that's the future. This is now. Look, if it were up to me, you could spend all the time you want getting Bryce set up. But I get these little notes from the VP's office. . . ."

Don frowned. "So you're saying I shouldn't be over there, setting them up?"

Eddie shook his head. "No, no, no. Service *is* Job One. Just spend maybe a little less time."

Don leaned forward. "Eddie, you were a sales rep. You know how much time it takes to do a job like this right. Are you saying I should give them less than the best? That doesn't make sense."

Eddie picked up the printout again. "No, Don. I'm just saying you need to get your totals up."

Don's voice rose. "Well, something has to give! I'm working sixty hours a week this month. You know that. How do I keep my totals up and give my accounts the kind of service they need? How would *you* do it?"

Eddie said heartily, "It takes real *motivation* to do a job like this!"

And so it goes. Eddie knows that quality and quantity are both important. He can't tell Don to sacrifice one for the other, so he relies on the mythic Power of Motivation. He knows that when he was a sales rep, he was able to keep the two balanced. Where there's a will there's a way, Eddie always says. If Don can't figure it out, he's just not trying hard enough. That's it, Eddie decides. That has to be it.

Don feels he is going crazy because he's getting two different messages that seem contradictory to him. He isn't sure which side of the issue Eddie is on. He suspects that Eddie favors quantity, but Eddie has also implied that his attitude is actually closer to Don's. Eddie's mixed message increases Don's confusion and makes it very clear that this is Don's problem, not Eddie's.

Though it would certainly benefit Don *to be able to see* the world through Eddie's eyes, it is not absolutely necessary that he *does* so. Don could be content simply to recognize Eddie's real message—that is, to get ahead, dump quality and focus on quantity—and then decide for himself how much he wants to get ahead, in relation to his other values. Maybe for Don, keeping his customers happy gives him enough satisfaction that he's content not to "progress" as quickly as Eddie thinks he should.

The Myth of Motivation can make problems magically disappear. This is also known as the "trickle-down" effect. Thus, responsibility for management's most difficult decisions can trickle down to the next lower level. From Eddie's point of view, Don is too naïve to pick up the answer to the Quality versus Quantity dilemma for himself; he has to ask the boss to settle it. Eddie also infers that Don disapproves of the company's position. All this drives Eddie crazy. Doesn't Don know that, to get anywhere, you have to get with the program? That's what Eddie thinks motivation is all about.

Every manager must take some stand on Quality versus Quantity. The most difficult part of management can be striking a balance between these goals. Like Eddie, many managers don't know which side of the issue to come down on, and they use the Myth of Motivation to avoid resolving the problem. "I'm motivated enough to do *both*," they tell themselves, "so everybody else should be able to do it too." The problem disappears because it has trickled down to the next level.

Corporate Catch-22

Motivation is the word that applies to all those intangibles that are rewarded but not explicitly stated. If you have it, nobody has to tell you what to do. If you don't, no amount of telling will work. The Myth of Motivation is the Catch-22 of the corporate world. We hear it everywhere. Whether you call it "motivation" or "will," "drive," "personal power," "passion," "vision," or even "true grit," most people in the business world would agree that there is an intangible quality that explains why some succeed and others fail. (Rebels, of course, think it's all luck.) If you believe strongly enough, your dreams will come true. Is it true? Absolutely! Is it the whole truth? Well, no. It takes motivation *and* skill to become a winner. Marty Jenkins and Eddie would certainly tell you that.

Unfortunately for Believers, motivation alone does not promise success; it takes something else to reap the rewards of this world, and Marty and Eddie probably would *not* tell you about that missing something else: To win, you have to know how to play the game. This is the missing information that makes the Myth of Motivation so misleading and that drives innocent Believers crazy.

7

The Need to Measure (and Other Confusing Customs)

Lesley, team manager of Neander-Tek's softball team, frowned at her star shortstop. "Luke, we missed you at practice yesterday. Where were you?"

Luke's voice was heavy with sarcasm. "I had to stay after school because I didn't turn in my homework."

"What do you mean?" Lesley asked.

"I mean that I was three months behind in my monthly reports, and Her Highness wouldn't let me leave until I filled 'em out," Luke said.

Lesley said quickly, "But Luke, those monthly reports are so simple if you just do them every day. If you leave them to pile up, they take hours."

"Yeah." He shrugged. "But I get busy and I forget."

Lesley smiled. "Oh, come on, Luke. You're the guy who can debug three programs at the same time—and you can't come up with a system to remind you to fill in three little boxes every day? I mean, if you *wanted to,* you could."

Luke glared at her, and his voice rose. "Look, those reports are just a bunch of made-up numbers for the accounting department. It's not like they show anything I really do."

Lesley didn't understand his attitude. "But all you have to do is fill 'em in," she argued. "You've got to do the paperwork to be *allowed* to do the things you really do! There have to be some records so your time can be charged out to the right cost centers.

"It's really easy," she went on earnestly. "I keep all the information I need for my reports right in my day-planner. I mean, it's not a big deal."

Luke grinned at her and drawled over his shoulder as he walked away, "Guess I'd better hustle out and get me a day-planner. . . . Yeah, right. . . . See you at practice, Les."

Lesley went back to her desk, shaking her head. That guy really drove her crazy. She didn't understand him at all. She knew he'd keep on doing things his way—and even though he was a crack computer expert, he'd always be a step away from probation.

The guy has talent and brains; he could move up, Lesley thought. For what he's giving up for them, it seems like not doing those monthly reports must mean a lot to him.

From monthly reports to the sacred Goals and Objectives and the solemn Performance Review; from the posting of memos to the filing of grievance procedures—Rebels will fight it, but Believers embrace the business world's need to measure and record itself. There it is in black and white—proof of all the hard work they're doing. Now maybe somebody will listen.

Performance Review: The Ceremonial Goals and Objectives

Believers want to do a good job. "Just tell me what to do, and I'll do it well" is their battle cry. To lead the Believers into battle, every company has a goals system, which usually includes a written document titled something along the lines of "Goals and Objectives." However, just exactly what that document means, how it's used, and how it relates to what happens the rest of the year is not clear. These fuzzy interpretations are what drive Believers crazy.

As Lesley and her boss, Jack James, went over her Goals and Objectives statement, it occurred to Lesley that the whole process was a lot like a time capsule. The Goals and Objectives were a relic that told how she and her boss had been feeling about her job *a year ago,* not a working document that defined Lesley's current responsibilities.

Lesley scanned the page. Look at this stuff: Revise job description; learn new software package; attend career development workshop. You bet, she thought with a silent laugh. Her job had been restructured so much that it was nothing like the plan they'd drawn last March. You can't drain the swamp when you're up to your neck in alligators.

Jack looked up and said, "Lesley, you were supposed to be up to speed on that new software package by now. The department equipment inventory is starting in two weeks, and you have to know how to use it by then."

As she picked her jaw up off the floor, Lesley thought, Wait a minute—I didn't get to go to the software training. HE told me to do other things.

Lesley is feeling *very* crazy here. It looks to her as if the procedure for assignment of tasks, written and verbal, is binding on *her,* but not necessarily on her boss. It's not that she thinks Jack is trying to make her do more work on a technicality; it's actually worse than that. At this moment, Lesley thinks she has been working her heart out for a boss who forgets what he tells her to do!

Lesley has missed the point in deciding what is important. When Jack and she first determined her Goals and Objectives, she viewed the written document of their agreement as a comprehensive, unchangeable, unbreakable contract—like maybe a job description. She hoped her hard work—all of it—could be measured, recorded, and rewarded. After a few weeks of being given assignments that bore no relation to their recorded agreement, she said to herself, "Oh. Now I get it. This was just one of those pep talks from management that's supposed to motivate me but has nothing to do with what I really do. I think I'm figuring out The System."

When Jack suddenly started saying that some of the goals are important and some aren't, Lesley thought, "He's driving me crazy. How in the world am I supposed to know which goals I'm supposed to meet—no matter what—and which goals I'm supposed to forget about the minute I leave the room?" On the other hand, it drives Jack crazy that it's so hard for Lesley to see which are which. Anyway, if she were a real Competitor, she would know that monitoring contract compliance and calling for renegotiation of your goals statement are always your own responsibility. Competitors would never trust anybody *else* to look out for them.

Goals and objectives systems were designed to clarify the working relationship. Some companies put great effort into setting clear priorities for employees and making the Management by Objective (MBO) system actually reflect what is expected.

In other companies, though, the MBO system is more of an attempt to bow to the Believers' desire to have their hard work spelled out and evaluated. They go through the motions of setting goals and doing evaluations, but rewards and punishments are based on something else—the opinions of Competitors.

Performance Review: Flattery May Get You Nowhere

Checking the accomplishment of goals and objectives is just a part of performance review, the most solemn of business rituals, which Believers especially take to heart. Central to the "Cult of the Brown Bag" is the belief that the good will be rewarded and the evil punished. If there were justice, *they*, the Believers, would be rewarded with high marks for all their hard work—just like at school. At school, grades really *meant* something.

Bronson knows enough "people skills" to realize he has to be tactful in his performance reviews. Otherwise, his staff will drive him up the wall with such questions as, "Where?" "When?" and "Can you be more specific?" To avoid their nit-picking, he presents everything in varying degrees of positive-ness for performance reviews, so he writes Carl is "Above Average" (read that "reasonably adequate") at doing his job. If he thinks Carl, the Believer who wants everything spelled out, is bad at something, he says that Carl is "Fair." ("Below Average," of course, means probation.)

Bronson uses the ratings to send Carl a subtle message, but subtlety is not Carl's forte. (Bronson is already anticipating the accompanying ritual argument, when Carl will make his case for changing the "Above Average" to "Excellent." Sure, why not? Bronson figures. All he's getting is a cost-of-living raise anyway.)

As always, Carl demands that *every* rating be changed to "Excellent," or at least "Superior." He wants it all on paper, but he doesn't realize that what's in black and white is much less important than what's in his boss's head. Carl argues vehemently, and finally Bronson wearily agrees that, yes, Carl is at least "Superior" across the board. Carl ends up with good ratings on paper but a boss who is wondering whether he can work with Carl at all.

Carl will find that these rites cause a great deal of trouble. Later, if he expects a promotion and big raises because he has such great performance reviews, he will feel extremely per-secuted.

If you don't know what the boss thinks of your performance, the performance review is definitely not the place to find out! Both Carl and Lesley are hard workers, and they want their work to be appreciated. Carl demands the letter of the law, but Lesley is beginning to see that maybe there is no objective way to tell whether she's doing a good job. She doesn't know yet how to get the acknowledgment she needs, but she'll keep looking.

When Bronson came up for his own performance review, he privately dismissed the process as play-acting for losers. He already knows The System—how to get the work he wants and how to publicize what he's done. (To him, the company is made up of a lot of losers whom you can mostly ignore and a few winners whom you have to watch every minute.)

For Bronson, the only important part of the performance review is the *numbers*—the quotas that can be measured, the due dates, and the like. Bronson knows that his numbers are what's being checked—not his winning personality or the flattering comments on his performance review.

The purpose of performance review and MBO systems is to make a very subjective relationship look objective. These systems are supposed to be a clear contract, binding in both directions, that gives people an idea of what they have to do to be successful in their jobs. This is a good idea, in theory. In practice, the task is so complex that few managers have the time or even the ability to do it the way it's "supposed" to be done. So they just do an adequate job (read that "go through the motions") and develop their own, often unspoken, ways of evaluating people.

Believers don't recognize what is going on. They know there's something wrong, but they're not quite sure what it is. It drives them crazy. Won't *anyone tell* them what they have to do to succeed? No.

For Competitors, the most important part of the job is figuring out The System—the unwritten rules by which the game is really played. (Rebels think the whole performance review process is a trick to cover up the fact that the rewards go to the brown-nosers, and whatever you do, the bosses will want more.)

The Posting of Rules

Bronson has assigned Carl to develop a manual of procedures for their department. (The Big Boss had sent around a memo reminding all managers that the Head Office was requiring every department to produce a manual.) Bronson knows that nobody will want to read the damn thing, but it has to be done, and Carl, a stickler for rules and details, is the perfect choice.

The project has taken months because Carl wants rules for everything. His writing style is jargon-filled and confusing. He has omitted some basic information (such as how to fill out mandatory forms) because he thinks everybody should already know how to do that. On the other hand, there are massive chapters that chronicle his own "simplification" of cross-referencing procedures, recording of requisitions, and other paper-processing dear to his own heart. The thing is, the system works. Doing it his way is definitely more efficient, but the way it's written, nobody would ever want to try it his way.

Imagine Carl's pride the day the manual is finally handed out. Each one weighs almost 20 pounds and is encased in an Executive Silver looseleaf vinyl binder. All the managers get one. Now picture Carl's frustration when, several weeks later, nobody is using the procedures as outlined in his manual.

This kind of manual is something that Competitors have but do not read. The rules are in there somewhere. Competitors figure that if their requisitions are too far off the mark, somebody will inform them. Carl takes the Believer's view that everyone will benefit by following the same rules. Because they are written down and official, he assumes everyone will follow them. They *have* to. They're the *rules*.

Bronson, even if he doesn't care whether people follow the procedures, is pleased that Carl came up with the manual

**because now the department has met Home Office regula-
tions. Carl's stock has gone up in Bronson's eyes.**

In some companies (especially those in which the bosses
are Believers), precision in these matters can help people get
into the winner's circle. Precise forecasts, reports turned in on
time and written in the correct format, completion of a required project—all of these can make a boss's life easier and
boost the reputation of the person who played by the rules. In
most workplaces, however, most of the rules are flexible, but
some are carved in stone. Competitors *always* know which is
which.

What most companies need—and what would minimize the
blood spilled in the battle between Believers and Competitors—is a set of realistic rules that are explicit and binding.
Believers would be quite willing to write them, but they seldom see the entire System well enough to come up with work-
able rules. Competitors have the overview, but they would say
that what they do is far too complex to be specified. They
might come up with *something* to please the Believers—but
any Competitor knows that the *real* rules are far too . . . subtle.

The only way to make meaningful change in a corporate
culture is to be very specific about what that culture actually is
and how it works. The problem is that the people who could
write the explicit rules don't think it's in their best interest to
do so. To them, it ain't broke, so why fix it?

The posting of the unwritten rules would be a revolutionary
act, and most companies aren't ready for revolution. Thus, you
have to learn The System on your own.

Memos

Many Competitors' rituals are based on the fact that managers
usually don't do work that leaves many visible products, other
than the bottom line. Competitors know that, especially in
large corporations, it's always important to keep your name in

public view. The sending of memos is one ritual that accomplishes this goal.

Jim is a vice president in the central office, one of the company's cost centers. His office doesn't earn money directly (that's what being a cost center means), so he has to justify his existence by keeping a hawk's eye on the places that do produce. If production or sales are down a half-point—if anything at all goes wrong—there has to be a memo with Jim's name on it, asking, "What's going on here?" He can't look as if he's asleep at the switch, can he?

Memos from Jim get action (he *is* a VP), so when he writes, people read and do something, even if they think Jim's a pain.

* * *

Carl (king of the procedures manual) keeps firing off nasty memos to managers all over the building, informing them that their people have failed to follow standardized procedures in filling out forms and are guilty of other infractions clearly spelled out in his manual. Bronson tries to explain that "you just fill in the blanks for them if you can and don't antagonize them over the little stuff."

"Little stuff!" Carl says huffily. "Standardization of procedures is one of the top corporate objectives this year. These people *need* a few reminders!"

Bronson just shakes his head.

When memos come from people of high power to people of lower power, they are taken seriously and acted on. It doesn't work the other way around. Rebels and Believers (and even some inexperienced Competitors) don't understand the ritual: It's not the memo itself that has the power or even the worth of the ideas in the memo; it's *the person who sends it.*

Bronson is not really supporting the idea behind the manual, Carl thought bitterly. The more Carl stewed, the more betrayed he felt. Well, maybe Corporate Headquarters would realize what was going on and take some action (maybe even have more respect for all his hard work than his own boss did). He sent out a new round of memos to the Home Office, asking their opinion about his manual and whether they thought compliance was important.

Carl's memo didn't come right out and say that Bronson was encouraging people to ignore the manual, but he hinted at it by saying that perhaps it was lower on the priority list down here than at the Home Office.

Two days later, Carl got two little notes from upper management people, saying, "Of course, the policies and procedures manual is wonderful. Compliance with procedures is important." That was all the encouragement Carl needed. He marched in to Bronson's office and announced, "Here's this memo from Home Office, saying we have to do something about compliance." Bronson looked at him as if his calendar were missing a couple of Thursdays. . . . To Bronson, the memo said nothing at all.

Tattling is the lowest level of corporate politics.

If you need to have upper management intervene to settle every problem, you're never going to rise much higher than you are now. Some corporate headquarters make it a policy to return *any* communication they receive from branch-office employees—including "confidential" tattletale memos, FYI stuff, or requests for transfer—directly back to the complaining employee's boss. (The rationale for this is usually the Competitor idea of "teamwork"—doing what you're told without complaint.)

The memos Carl got didn't direct anybody to do anything. If they had really been serious, upper management would have sent a memo or made a call to Bronson. They wouldn't have sent orders to a subordinate to relay to his superior.

Carl would have gotten much more mileage from sending positive memos about the manual, praising the people who were complying and emphasizing how much money standardization would save. He could have done a great PR job for himself as the manual's author and given his career a boost.

Carl won't do that, though. Like many Believers, he feels that there would be something a little bit wrong with using the manual to advance his own interests. Carl feels that he wrote the manual and lobbied for compliance because the rules are _right_ and the procedures should be followed. He's in it for the principle, not for personal glory. It is his principles also that cause him to want to punish the noncompliant. Carl doesn't realize that he needs to do a real sales job to get the manual accepted, or no one will even read it, much less comply.

Carl succumbs to the great tragedy of the Believer. Even though he's bright, talented, and right, his ideas are not used and he feels unappreciated, even discriminated against. He believes it is management's job to tell people to use the manual. He doesn't recognize that promoting it is partly his own responsibility and opportunity. Like so many Believers, he thinks the actions it takes to succeed are simply not in his job description.

8

My Boss Is Driving
Me Crazy

What to Do about Problems with Misguided Authority Figures

The Believer's creed says that merit is rewarded and hard work will pay off, but every day, Carl sees evidence to the contrary in his department. Nobody checks; goof-offs get promoted; the rules aren't followed. It happens again and again. Plain and simple, people are being lied to. Somebody ought to do something.

Carl would heatedly deny it, but he is a corporate innocent. He believes all the major Believer myths that tell of rewards for hard work, merit, and following the rules. He just doesn't understand the pressures and contingencies that are part of Competitors' lives—and Carl's bosses haven't tried very hard to understand the things that are important to him.

The result, for Carl and many like him, is that Believers and Competitors face off across a Great Divide. The two groups work side by side within the same company, each misunderstood by and in conflict with the other.

Believers don't usually complain. They rely on their motivation to pull them through. Some bosses don't play by the rules, though, and eventually a person of principle, such as Carl, must speak up. When Believers complain, they sound very much like Rebels—although the Believers would be insulted by the comparison.

Some Competitor bosses assume that they're smarter than their employees, and they pretend or otherwise try to trick Believers into doing what they want them to do. The message comes through—loud and clear—that the boss doesn't value what the Believers value—or, in some cases, doesn't even value *them*. Carl, a valiant Believer, has worked for several manipulative and insensitive managers.

B.J., Carl's first boss, made it a practice to hire only very inexperienced people, then impress them by his total knowledge of the field. To learn or do anything, Carl and the other green recruits were completely dependent on him.

B.J. liked to picture his department as a wheel, with himself at the hub. All communication went through him. Nobody else knew exactly how much money was available for a project budget, or what the guys on the top floor were planning, or anything else that affected his turf. His people had to come to him for the real scoop, and that was exactly the way B.J. wanted it.

When Carl and the gang progressed beyond entry level, B.J. tended to pick fights with them because of their "bad attitude" or the fact that they wanted more pay or some say in what happened in their job. Some, like Carl, were shipped out. For B.J., the departed employees were "out of sight, out of mind." Carl, however, had to deal with the painful consequences of the abrupt change in his job assignment.

Carl met a common response to the chronic underfunding of a department that upper management considers a low priority. There's a lot of work to be done and not enough money. So the best strategy is to hire as many entry-level people as possible, appeal to their motivation and sense of justice, and hope for the best. Promise them anything, but if they want money or power, get rid of them. When they gain more experience, the company either keeps them at the same low salary until they quit or moves them to a department that's valuable enough to be worth paying for their experience.

The problem is that most Believers expect to stay wherever they are and gradually move up through the ranks, according to their merit. In B.J.'s department, there were no careers but his own. Everybody else was supposed to move along. Carl and the rest of the staff were considered raw recruits, and their work was considered unimportant.

Instead of wrestling with these issues, B.J. developed a system that was confusing and deceptive—but his reasons for doing so were not quite what Carl thought. B.J. didn't tell people anything because he didn't know; nobody told *him*, either. He was focusing on getting the most done with the resources he had. His boss kept telling him that, if he were motivated enough, he could make his department provide quality services within its meager budget.

Carl Goes on a Guilt Trip

Lorraine, the boss to whom Carl was transferred, was very unclear about standards. Whatever Carl did, Lorraine always pointed out that there was a little bit more that Carl could have done. Lorraine also tried to keep the psychological books out of balance in her favor by giving Carl something—a minuscule raise, a nominal promotion—and then describing the transaction not as something Carl had already earned, but as a privilege that he had yet to earn through loyalty and obedience.

One day, Lorraine called Carl into her office and said, "I backed you for this promotion, so don't let me down."

What Lorraine did *not* say was, "Carl, your performance was good enough to earn you this promotion under your own steam." Bosses like this always phrase it, "I gave you this." The idea was for Carl to do what his boss wanted because the boss had made Carl feel that he owed her. If Carl didn't do what Lorraine wanted, Carl felt guilty. The problem here is that guilt always breeds resentment. Carl may not have been able to stop it, but he knew what was going on, and he hated it.

Asked to defend her policy, Lorraine would probably not recognize herself as manipulative. Like B.J., she would probably talk about getting the most done with limited resources. She would be surprised and disbelieving of the impact of her "little comments" on Carl. She would probably say defensively, "Well, if Carl was going to take everything *that* personally, maybe he should have left. He obviously didn't understand the way business is done."

Lorraine would never admit to what she did, even if she recognized it (which is doubtful). Carl would have gotten much more mileage from asking her to clarify any vague statements at the time she made them. Then Carl could have responded, "Does this mean that my work up until now hasn't been what you want?" or "What do you mean? How might I let you down?"

After Carl had accepted the job on Lorraine's terms, though, it was too late to change the ground rules.

Carl Gets Intimidated

Two years later, Carl was looking for work. Lorraine had fired him for "nonperformance." Carl gratefully accepted an offer from Neander-Tek. He quickly discovered, however, that his new boss, Marv, intimidated his employees by blowing up unexpectedly and irrationally. He also tended to trigger anxiety attacks by saying such things as, "Well, I heard in the management meeting today that the crunch is coming and there might be lay-offs."

Marv's strategy was to keep people off-balance, worrying about their own job security and whether he would blow his stack today, so that they didn't pay as much attention to the real issues.

The manipulative management styles that drive Carl and many Believers crazy often rely on implied threats and promises. Marv counted on the fact that Carl wanted to please him, and he used this to try to control Carl. He tended to ask a lot of questions until Carl said something that Marv didn't like. Then he found a way to remind Carl of his error, usually disguised as help: "You know, Carl, you wouldn't be in the mess you're in with this project if you'd only. . . ." The debt mounted.

Marv left Carl wanting never to talk to Marv again, but, of course, there was no avoiding it. If the next encounter was filled with friendliness and compliments (intimidators tend to switch behaviors, which keeps people further off-balance), Carl found himself thinking, "Maybe from now on he'll be reasonable." Carl knew that it was only a matter of time, though, before Marv's disapproval would come through again.

Actually, Carl could have handled an intimidating boss fairly easily if he had kept his wits. Marv counted on Carl to stop thinking and merely *react* whenever Marv put on the pressure. Then Marv always won. Instead, Carl could have followed a few suggestions for breaking the cycle of intimidation and disapproval.

Most important, Carl would need to accept that "getting back at the boss" will never work. Most people have fantasies about making the perfect, scathing putdown, or finally having the guts to tell the bully off, or—better yet—getting the CEO herself to do it.

Sometimes, warring Believers go for the "Big Lawsuit" for harassment or discrimination. Most of the time, they're disillusioned because they don't understand the legal system any better than they understand The System at their office. Carl's idea of what constitutes grounds for a lawsuit is based on a commonsense idea of justice (which he might have to abandon after he visits an attorney and discovers that suits are won and lost based on laws that, mainly, are written by Competitors and don't correspond to his innate sense of fairness.) The "Big Lawsuit" seldom works, but Carl could dream, couldn't he? (Believers, with their reliance on rules, see a lawsuit as a strategic solution. Rebels, however, would not choose this route.

Rebels distrust authority figures—in court as well as in the boss's office.)

The more Carl argued, fought, or got pumped up with thoughts of revenge, the calmer Marv became, and the more he would explain, wide-eyed, that "I didn't mean anything. You're the one who's overreacting." The angrier Carl was, the more control Marv had over him.

Carl is acting like a Rebel, but his reason for rebelling sets him firmly in the Believers' camp: He is fighting for a principle. He is seeking justice. Carl needed to be more calm and vague in his responses to Marv. There's no law that says Carl had to answer every question that was asked. He could have offered generalities or a variation on "Let me get back to you on that." Before he gave information or an opinion, he should have thought about how Marv might twist it. Think Joe Friday: "Just the facts, ma'am."

Some people in Marv's department let criticism roll off their backs. Carl could have sought them out and found out how they did it. (He would have needed to avoid his impulse to label someone a "brown-noser" if he or she can get along with difficult and intimidating people. Getting along with difficult people is a valuable skill, not a sign of weakness. This is what has kept Carl from being more effective and less frustrated at work.)

Instead of avoiding contact with Marv and griping about him behind his back, Carl needed to be able to deal with Marv directly. Carl should have focused on what he wanted to have happen—not on trying to tell Marv what he had or hadn't done to Carl. He could have said, "I'd like clear priorities on this project," instead of "You never tell me what you want."

Carl Goes to War

At first, Bronson, the boss Carl inherited when Marv retired, won Carl's loyalty with vague promises and suggestions that he was bound to go far. Then he started confiding his negative feelings to Carl about other employees—followed by rumors

and negative comments about Carl that Bronson said he "thought you should be aware of."

Soon Bronson pulled Carl aside and whispered conspiratorially, "There are sharks out there, and you'd better stick with me or you'll get eaten alive!" It took Carl awhile to realize who the shark really was.

Competitors such as Bronson think that the end is what's important, not the means. Nothing in his code suggests that there is any value in considering the implications of your own behavior. Philosophy is not for warriors; it is for Neanderthals such as Carl, who, in Bronson's view, are too naïve to realize they're being used.

As to the means, Competitors have the Management Mystique, which says, "Go ahead, you know what you're doing. You have to. You're a manager." Many Competitors decide that to get people to do what they want them to do, trickery, intimidation, and seduction are the only methods. (Competitors, of course, don't call those methods by those names.)

Bronson would say, "Hey, you want information? It's not my fault if you can't handle it." This is another of those statements heard so often on the front lines in the battle between Believers and Competitors that is neither true nor false.

Manipulative management is guaranteed to create resistance and resentment. People won't forgive these kinds of tricks. Believers expect to work hard. They also expect to do things that they don't want to do. That's part of working. They don't, however, like being made to feel guilty and dependent or frightened and off-balance.

What does Carl do when he has to face all of this disillusionment? He is smart and energetic, and he could learn to channel his talents into learning how to become part of The System, instead of standing above it. He could also learn to recognize the real rules, as well as the ones written down.

Carl doesn't realize that he has a choice, though, and that he could learn something from the Competitors. Instead, he will cope with his anger and disillusion in ways that will leave him feeling more frustrated, angry, and helpless than ever. This way of fighting back is based on the Believer's mythology about how the business world should be. Unfortunately, there are very few "killer Believers." Ralph Nader is one of the few examples of people who work The System well enough to enforce Believer values on Competitors. The rest of the Believers just keep hoping they can do it.

Carl Has Had It

Believers usually don't complain, unless the situation becomes so destructive that others may be hurt. In their frustration, some Believers turn to their company's grievance procedure and expect it to operate like a federal court on their behalf. For the company, the most important thing is preserving the legitimate lines of authority. No matter how much evidence you have, it's hard to win when the Competitors are the judges. If you do win, you may lose more than you were fighting for.

Carl and several other employees in his department got together and complained about Bronson's "obvious incompetence": He never met with staff. He didn't enforce the rules about attendance. He hadn't done a six-month review in four years. Their solution was to ask for a consultant to come in and "clarify job responsibilities and authority in the department."

Unless things are falling apart, upper management doesn't call in Clint Eastwood to investigate.

The first time, instead of the consultant, the people in Bronson's department got a two-day seminar in "Getting Along with People the E-Z Way," in which Carl discovered his own personality as an "Ideal-Enforcer," and Bronson's personality as a "Fact-Processor." They should talk about their differ-

ences and do a few role-plays together. Of course, nobody took *that* seriously.

Carl persisted. He came up with the "clarification of job responsibility and authority" idea. The consultant came in and did just what he'd hoped. Bronson was told that he had to revise job descriptions, meet with staff, enforce the rules and do reviews. Unfortunately, though, the sweet taste of victory turned to sour defeat when, six months later, everything was exactly the same as it had been before. Except for one little detail. Now Bronson owed Carl one, and Bronson had honed his Competitor's craft for paying these debts in full.

Even though it may be self-defeating for Carl to keep complaining, it is also self-defeating for Bronson to keep ignoring his complaints. Besides being annoyed by the employees who complain, upper management also gets annoyed with the managers whose employees complain frequently.

It's very rare that anybody listens to complaining. If a wrong is done to an employee, there really is no way to set it right without going to a tremendous amount of difficulty and expense. There is almost no way to force management to treat people fairly. The truth of the Ritual of Grievances is that, with the possible exception of Superior Court, there is no grievance procedure that anyone in power takes seriously. The real way to get things done is to understand The System and to operate within it.

Carl often feels angry, but he's not sure at whom. He keeps wondering, "Is it the job or is it me?" If he decides "It's me," he will learn from his experiences. If he blames all his problems on the job, he might deny his anger and work even harder, eliminating any possible joy until he eventually gets depressed and burns out.

By now, it's crystal-clear to Carl that nobody at the top understands that Bronson is evil incarnate. There's no point in talking to management about him any more. Instead, Carl talks to other people about how bad he is. Talking to Bronson would be pointless. Bronson would punish Carl, or, at least, be insensitive (which is a pretty good bet if Bronson's a Competitor and Carl's a Believer). So Carl communicates to his peers, in "support" groups, or via one of the great Believer inventions, the office grapevine.

On the grapevines in most offices, most of what you hear has to do with breaking the rules, the lies that bosses have told, people's moral deficiencies, and other injustices. The tagline to most of these news bulletins is the Believer's battle cry, "... and nobody's doing anything about it!" The same issues that Rebels use as a justification for slowing down their work just shake up the world of the Believers.

(A further complication is that Competitors use the grapevine to their own advantage. Competitors can manipulate Believers by planting certain kinds of rumors on the grapevine or using it to tell what's going on in Believer's minds. In fact, people like Carl often unwittingly play right into this strategy.)

Carl believes that people should know what's going on, so he has become the keeper of one part of the grapevine. He knows all the negative things that Bronson says or thinks about other people. He's well informed because he digs out that information. He gets people to talk with him about how bad Bronson is and then tells Bronson, "People are saying. . . ." When he gets Bronson's response, he quickly sends it back along the grapevine.

It feels like power and respect to Carl. Even though Bronson needs Carl to disseminate some of this information at a safe distance, Carl and the people he talks to all consider him reprehensible. He thinks he's letting people know how bad Bronson is, but he's really just doing Bronson's dirty work for him.

Sometimes, burned-out Believers like Carl, especially those who have battled The System unsuccessfully, will turn traitor and become watchdogs, tale-bearers to management. They mistakenly conclude that The System is evil (it may be callous, but it's not really evil) and decide that, to win, they must become as corrupt and underhanded as they perceive those around them to be. There are managers who will reward them for this decision.

In some businesses, people can make a profitable career from being the hatchet man and doing the boss's dirty work. They're not afraid to be mean; they don't care what other people think of them. Only the boss's opinion counts. These employees are particularly valuable to conflict-avoiding bosses and to bosses who have gained their positions within a political system in which it's not a good idea to have enemies.

Carl had had it. He'd tried to slay the villain, but the villain was still alive—and now everybody else thought he was a spy. It didn't pay to try to change the world. He was thinking small now—small but safe. He had spent weeks setting up a fail-safe system of rules and procedures to protect himself and his department: Code yellow for routine requests, blue for rush jobs, and orange for Bronson's orders.

Plus, all requests must be made in triplicate and every research fact sheet verified by three different staff members (just in case anybody questioned Carl's accuracy later—give them no ammunition!). Let enemies try to invade! Carl hunkered down in his little fortress in the data department.

Some people cope with the Believer Blues by staking out their own territory and defending it from all comers—becoming the guardian of the fax machine, for example. Like Carl, people who feel they can't control the bigger issues in their jobs become petty martinets and set up all kinds of rules and regulations for access to the services they are in charge of. Fax machines, data departments, human resources departments, and the like are often the home of this kind of strategy.

The ultimate revenge of the Believer is setting up bureaucracies where the rules are more important than the product. That's Believer heaven (or so it seems until they have to work there)—the kind of structure that Believers set up to protect themselves and others against Competitors. (This is also as good a one-sentence description of government as we can think of.)

If you're a Competitor in management, why should you change the way you act to accommodate people who don't understand The System? The answer: money. You can't afford not to change. Understanding the way Believers and Rebels think is the way to get the best work from employees for the least money. Conflict costs. Loyalty pays.

The Competitors' Challenge

Most managers typically react with disdain to the Believer strategies we have described—and they feel justified in their disdain, because what the Believers are doing looks petty. Competitors don't recognize the pain and sense of helplessness that lie underneath. Instead, they tend to lump the Believers with the Rebels and to see them as lazy or as fighting legitimate authority. There is no greater insult to Believers than to call them lazy. Because the Believers already feel under attack and without much control, the result can be an entire department or company armed for in-house combat.

Any self-indulgent Neanderthal can control people who think they aren't in control of their jobs and don't know what's going on. The real test is helping them to change these fundamental beliefs and to develop their own abilities and skills so that they will be a value to the company. The Competitor's challenge is recognizing the Believers' value *as they are*, instead of expecting them to turn into Competitor clones. The real test of leadership lies in helping Believers develop their own abilities and skills so they will be of top value to the company.

9

The Myth of the
Man-Eating Job

Burnout is made up of psychological traps that you can fall
into if you don't see them coming. The more you know about
this disorder, the easier it is to avoid. Before reading this chapter, take this quiz to find out how much you already know
about burnout. The answers to the quiz are given at the end of
this chapter.

Burnout Quiz

1. Exhaustion and burnout are so similar that they can be
   thought of as the same thing. True or false?
2. In occupations involving high stress and high uncertainty, burnout is
   a. inevitable.
   b. almost inevitable.
   c. highly likely.
   d. not possible to determine without more information.
3. The people most likely to burn out are those who don't
   talk about their frustrations. True or false?
4. Burnout is contagious. True or false?
5. People who see themselves as "givers" are less likely to
   burn out than people who see themselves as "takers."
   True or false?

6. One of the best things you can do to prevent burnout is to get away from work as often as possible. True or false?
7. Your task is to arrange four coins into two straight rows containing three coins in each.
   a. This task can be done.
   b. This task cannot be done.

Now that you've explored some of your own ideas about burnout, see whether you identify with the people in these situations. You—and they—may be candidates for burnout.

Another reorganization, just when things were getting back to normal—if you could call it normal. Another few people laid off, a few managers' job descriptions altered—as if it will change anything. Mitch had *had* a decent job with some responsibility, some chance to be creative, and a chance to move up. He had had the illusion that he was getting somewhere, until the company was "restructured." "Gutted" is more like it.

Now what does he have? Piles of paper, headaches, and demands from the head office to do more with less. Plus endless meetings about the nifty new software that's sure to make things easier. The ship is sinking, and they're putting new curtains on the portholes. It's so pointless.

Lately, his energy has been at an all-time low. Mitch snaps at his coworkers, and he's smoking again. Who wouldn't, with stress like this? He's given 15 years to this company, and what does he get back? Nothing. Just one broken promise after another. Mitch spends a lot of time staring at his desk. He just can't seem to get motivated any more.

* * *

Alice is a good social worker. She really puts herself out for the people on her caseload. But the need is so great—you can't imagine the human suffering she sees every day. If there were ten of her, she still couldn't get it all done. Her boss, however, doesn't care *what* she does in the field, just so that

the reports are all there to show *his* boss. All he wants is for her to make more contacts, see more people, do a sloppier job.

More contacts, fewer results, so they can play their political games, pretending to care about clients. Well, Alice cares. She cares so much that her colitis keeps acting up. The doctor says it's stress-related, and she knows where the stress is coming from. There's so much work to do, and she's been out a day or two every week for months. The doctor says she has to do something about her stress, but obviously he hasn't taken a look at her job.

* * *

Jesse sighs to himself, "The bottom line. That's all they care about here. The corporate slogan is 'Excellence in Customer Service'—but their idea of excellence is to slap a bandage on a problem and shove 'em out the door. If, by chance, the customers complain to your boss, it's your rear end that's on the line."

Lately, there have been more complaints. Jesse just doesn't have the patience with the petty issues that he once had. Most of those fools are just coming in because they can't read instructions anyway. If Jesse has to smile just one more time today, his face is going to crack.

Believers aren't afraid of hard work, of doing their share and a little bit more. These are the people who get the job done. They also win world wars, champion the downtrodden, and do the word processing. They're so reliable that everyone seems to take them for granted. Their rewards just aren't commensurate with their value. In many companies, though, that's business as usual. Mitch, Alice, and Jesse's problems are even more serious.

What's wrong with the people in these examples? They're good employees who have given a lot to their jobs, but now their motivation is lagging. They're feeling irritable and experiencing stress-related symptoms. What would you call a disorder like that? They call it "burnout."

Burnout is not really a single disorder; it has different faces with different people. In most cases, it is self-diagnosed and self-treated. Treatment usually involves doing more of what caused the problem in the first place.

When people feel that they're not in control of their jobs, they often start looking around for someone to blame. Usually, this feeling comes on when they've reached some sort of dead end: They've been passed over for promotion, had their sales totals go down, or perhaps faced a major project or responsibility that intimidated them.

Certainly, there are people who do burn out from sheer overwork, but their symptoms are usually different from the people who diagnose their own condition. The burnout that was first written about 15 or so years ago is a disorder of successful people who rarely realize that they have it. They have achieved and achieved, to the point at which they have pushed themselves beyond their physical or psychological capacity to respond.

As first described, the disorder was similar to what is called "karoshi" in Japan—dying from overwork. Today, when the word burnout is used, the meaning is very different. The reason, we think, lies in the name, burnout, which perfectly embodies what Believers think their job does to them. It uses up their substance and gives back no rewards; nothing is left but a charred husk.

The first sign is usually increased irritability. Something is stirring inside. Most people don't know exactly what it is, but it bothers them. They don't know what to do to make it better. They think, "If I'm feeling this way, somebody must be doing something wrong." They want to point a finger somewhere. Sometimes, they look first at themselves and say, "Oh, the answer is simple. I'm a failure." Later, however, the target becomes the job itself. Or the boss.

"No wonder I'm never caught up. This damn job just sucks people in like quicksand. It's terrible. Nobody could get a handle on this job. No wonder I feel so stressed out all the time. I've never felt so burned out in my life. I have to get away from this job! Maybe if management were a little more competent, things would be different."

It's easy to get caught up in this attitude and its attendant belief in the Man-Eating Job—the idea that, *through no fault of your own,* you just can't succeed. The horrible job destroys people because of its inhuman demands; it eats them up and drives them to the edge. People in this stage might find themselves spending more and more of their time trying to explain to people why the job is impossible to do and why it's driving them crazy.

(We're not saying that there aren't jobs that eat people alive, or bosses who exploit people, or any of the other horrors Believers have nightmares about. We *are* saying that a person's response to such bad situations can make them worse.)

The Romantic Disorder

Enter the Myth of Burnout. People who accept this myth believe that burnout is an inevitable consequence of the stresses of the job and that it's only a matter of time before they go up in flames. Burnout is the only disorder named by the people who have it. The term *burnout* suggests an image of someone being consumed rapidly by fire. Its victims see themselves as romantic heroes—dreaming the impossible dream, fighting the unbeatable foe: Don Quixote martyred in a world of pragmatic Lee Iacocca clones.

Actually, the syndrome is not like burning out at all. It's more like rusting, a form of slow oxidation that corrodes and makes things brittle and fragile. (How many people would want to associate themselves with a disorder called "occupational rust"?)

Burnout is really a kind of depression that its sufferers believe is caused by the job. In fact, it's caused by feelings of helplessness and an inability to accept that they are in control of their own lives and jobs. The Believers think they have made a deal with their jobs—"If I work hard, then I will be rewarded." Now the job is reneging on the deal, and they don't know what to do about it.

Their typical response is to rely on the Myth of Purity (the conviction that theirs is the only true, right way) to save them. They work harder than ever—when this was probably what got them into trouble in the first place. They don't take the time to take care of themselves, do things they enjoy, or get emotional support. Of course, their mood gets worse. They feel that their job isn't giving them enough, so their response is to give more and more to the job. It may not help the pain, but at least their wounds are honorable—not like those of *some* people they know!

We have said that Believers use burnout as a metaphor, to express to themselves and to the world what's wrong with their jobs. Burnout, however, is a disorder of the person, not of the job. What they're really saying is that there are some fundamental things about their jobs that they don't understand, don't think are fair, and are not in their control.

Burned-out Believers don't recognize their lack of success as a sign that they don't really understand what's going on and should be trying a new approach. Instead, they simply work harder and obey more rules, then are shocked again that they have no control. In other words, they're using Believer strategies to accomplish Competitor goals. They don't see the central truth that all Competitors have recognized: That it's not how hard you work, but what you work hard at that makes the difference. (Later in this chapter, we discuss measures that will help with some of the symptoms, but the only real cure for burnout is recognizing that the people in charge *do* think differently. You certainly don't have to want to be a Competitor, but it's to your advantage to understand how they think.)

Burnout is characterized by apathy, strong negative or ambivalent feeling about the job, declining productivity, increased illness, a decline in the quality of personal relationships, and perhaps even substance abuse (alcohol or other drugs). Self-diagnosed burnout is a cover-up for not realizing that people do have some control over their jobs (and their lives). Instead of seeing themselves as noble knights, tilting at windmills, a healthier role model would be the Don's less romantic, more practical sidekick Sancho Panza. A little Rebel cool can also help to ease that burning sensation.

Job-induced stress exists, of course, but the most damaging thing is a person's *reaction* to the situation, rather than the situation or environment itself. Few jobs are universally stressful. Some people learn to cope with the situation, no matter how bad it becomes. Stress is really like exercise. If you begin with a little and practice dealing with that, then tomorrow you may be able to deal with a bit more, and a bit more the day after that. That's how we grow in our ability to manage stress. When people begin to think, "I shouldn't have to cope with this," they stop growing.

Would You Bow to Burnout?

Let's look at some examples of people who have bowed to the Myth of Burnout.

Karen sighed and turned resignedly back to the folders that covered her desk. It would take her all afternoon to pull together the material her boss wanted for the mock-up—that is, if it were done right, which was the way Karen would do it. . . .

Her boss had said casually, "Just run off a couple of photocopies of the pages—let the copy machine 'shrink' them to fit the dummies—so we can get an idea of what the real thing will look like."

Karen didn't think "shrunken" photocopies would be good enough, though. Instead she decided to call up all the computer files on which the reports were stored, recode each report to print out in smaller type, so they'd fit the demo pages, and print out and paste up the results on dummy sheets. That way, it would look professional. Shrunken photocopies, indeed— not from *her* desk.

She'd have to kill half her day and skip lunch to get it done, but what other choice did she have? Somebody had to set some standards for this office. . . .

Six hours later (including two hours of unpaid overtime), Karen rubbed her aching head and breathed an exhausted sigh. Finished—and the mock-up was perfect. Not that her boss would appreciate her efforts. When it came right down to it, nobody appreciated her around here. Karen could hardly stand it any more. "I work my butt off, and they don't even know it. If I didn't need this job, I'd just go get in a canoe and paddle out to some deserted island and stay there forever." She was so tired that she'd be lucky to make it all the way to her car in the parking garage.

When people feel victimized by burnout, as Karen does, they often start doing more and more irrelevant work until they wear themselves out and thereby gain some justification for why they feel so bad. Other burnout candidates might focus on some small issue or cause that everybody else thinks is irrelevant and blow it out of proportion. The effect is the same.

Find an Escape

The people who experience the worst burnout symptoms usually are the ones who feel the most trapped. On the one hand, they're screaming that the job is impossible and they can't handle the stress. On the other hand, they aren't looking for other work. They typically say, "Well, I just couldn't find another job that pays as much," or "I'm vested in the retirement system," or "I have family obligations, you know."

Unless perhaps you're a union journeyman with a certain number of years of seniority, there *are* other jobs. Yet people in distress have the characteristic idea that, though they think their job is impossible, they can't or won't leave it. They fear the unknown more than the pain they're in. Like an abused spouse, they keep hoping against hope that the job will change and be fair to them, that they'll be recognized and rewarded for all their work and devotion.

There also are people who do quit the job—then take the unresolved problem on with them to the next job. For those who tend to repeat the burnout pattern from one job to the next, leaving won't make much difference. (This is not to say that there aren't awful jobs that people ought to quit, or that burnout victims are treated fairly on the jobs they're in. They're not usually. They're exploited, not told the truth, conned, and used, all of which adds injury to insult. The sad truth is that they may discover that things are the same all over.)

A Few Different Responses to Burnout

"I'm getting old and gray and in the way."

Nancy turned quickly away from the mirror, but she didn't need the looking-glass to be reminded of the gray streaks and crow's feet, the flab around her waistband, and the dowdiness of her skirt and jacket. In two hours, she would be standing in front of an audience of 250 professionals, delivering a presentation on instructional techniques. How could any of those people take her seriously when she looked like this—old, fat, and dowdy?

Some people who are feeling bad about their jobs will transfer those negative feelings to their own body image. The turning inward of hostility toward the job is a common pattern in burnout. For many people, because of The System's emphasis on image and its restrictive standards of beauty, their body is the perfect target.

They decide that the problem will go away just as soon as they tone up certain muscle groups, drop a few pounds, or buy a tonic for thinning hair. They don't consider that their self-image would improve if they worked on flabby job skills with as much energy as they might give their daily workout. Nancy, for example, might take a course in public speaking, or spend an hour a day rehearsing her presentation until she felt comfortable and confident enough to look in the mirror and wink.

Illness as metaphor (with apologies to Susan Sontag)

Ed knew he should call in sick, but he hated to be away from the office, especially right now, when there was so much going on. The pain in his gut was almost killing him. If he even turned a certain way, his insides felt as if a giant fist were twisting everything down there into wire ropes. It was the worst pain he'd ever had, and it made him so tired that he could hardly hold his head up. None of the doctors he'd seen could give him anything to make the pain go away. Stress, they told him. Stress. Yeah, right. He didn't have time for stress. There was work to do. He dragged himself into his office for another eight—or ten—or twelve. The work was there; somebody had to do it.

Some Rebels use illness as a way of getting out of work they want to avoid. Believers use it as a way of getting out of realizing that they have tough choices to make about their job. Rebels stay home at the least hint of a sniffle. Believers come in and work till they drop—then maybe someone will realize and do something about the problem.

Believers firmly believe that nobody can do the work the right way except themselves. The illness, and their often-conspicuous ignoring of it, is their way of telling the world what's wrong with their job. "My job is killing me. See?" This whole process is usually unconscious. These persons see what the job is doing to them, not what they're doing to themselves. Everybody else sees that, though.

"No respect."

Things were not going well for Kerry. The bid she'd worked so hard to get her boss before his vacation was still in his mailbox. He hadn't even looked at it! Kerry had been up until 3 A.M. each night all week.

Her boss's reaction *(non*action) was typical, Kerry thought bitterly. What else could she expect from a Neanderthal like that? She had mentioned her boss's oversight to the division head (he frequently says, "My door is always open"), and all he had said was, "It's Jim's decision. I guess he figured it could wait." Maybe she should go hit the sales at the mall. So what if her checkbook was overdrawn? That's why they invented plastic! Maybe if she bought herself some decent clothes, people would treat her with more respect around here. Everybody knows, when the going gets tough, the tough go shopping.

People who feel like victims of burnout (or anything else) may retreat into substance abuse—not only caffeine, alcohol, and other drugs, but also plastic abuse. Some people will start buying things, as if the things they buy will solve the problem for them and add whatever they think is missing in their lives. This type of abuse feeds on the struggle between image and reality that so many businesspeople face today. There has been so much emphasis on *image* within corporate cultures—what you wear, how you talk, the car you drive, the toys you own, the "outer you." It's understandable, then, that many people's first reaction to an internal problem is to go out and try to buy a solution.

The truth is that, when people are wrestling with basic attitudes toward their jobs, nothing will work except confronting the issue and making some decisions.

"The job or me?"

That was what it was coming down to, Bob thought: The job or his wife. She griped when he had to work late; she nagged when he went in on Saturdays and had to miss the kids' ball games. She sulked when he was too wrung out for sex at night.

Did she think he was staying away from home on purpose? Did she think he enjoyed working around the clock, with no time to be part of the family, no time for himself, no time for anything except the damn job? Didn't she realize the pressure she was putting on him? Maybe, Bob thought, it would just be easier if he packed his things and got a little room someplace, where nobody would be there to blame him for something he couldn't change.

Some people will blame their spouses for their own unresolved feelings about their jobs. Many a marriage has broken up over the feeling that the wife or husband is saying, "It's either me or your career." The reality is that the problem may not be in the marriage at all; instead, it stems from the inability to change the attitude toward the job. The mind does not always work in a direct line. Often, if people are trying to deal with a problem they can't cope with, they transfer it to another area—where it usually becomes just as hard to deal with—but at least now there's something to point at.

Review the Burnout Quiz

Now that you've had the chance to find out a little more about burnout, review what you know about it.

1. **Exhaustion and burnout are so similar that they can be thought of as the same thing. True or false?**
Answer: FALSE. Exhaustion is physical. Burnout is a psychological reaction to stress, similar to depression. Rest can cure exhaustion, but rest usually makes burnout worse. Actually, people with burnout don't rest. They spoil their weekends and vacations by resenting the fact that they have to go back to work.

2. **In occupations involving high stress and high uncertainty, burnout is**
    a. **inevitable.**
    b. **almost inevitable.**
    c. **highly likely.**
    d. **not possible to determine without more information.**

Answer: d. Burnout is not a disorder of the job; it is a disorder of the individual. Some people can work for years in highly stressful jobs without burning out. This is usually because they have developed effective strategies for dealing with stress, not because they have sold out.

3. **The people most likely to burn out are those who don't talk about their frustrations. True or false?**
Answer: FALSE. In most cases, the more you talk about how bad you feel, the worse you feel. This is not to say that people should never talk about their frustrations (perish the thought— How could psychologists make a living?)

Talking about frustration can be helpful given two conditions: (1) you talk to people who can help by changing the situation or by offering emotional support. Talking to people who merely agree that things are awful can be damaging. (2) Don't repeat yourself too much. Repetition usually is not a way of communicating. It is a way of convincing yourself that the situation is terrible.

4. **Burnout is contagious. True or false?**
Answer: TRUE. Only the Black Plague spreads faster. Infection is spread by getting together to complain about the people and situations that are causing all your problems.

5. **People who see themselves as "givers" are less likely to burn out than people who see themselves as "takers." True or false?**
Answer: FALSE. First, there are no such things as "givers" and "takers." Everyone has to give *and* take to get by. People who see themselves as "givers" sometimes have to burn out or break down before they will allow themselves to accept support from others. Classifying people as "givers" and "takers" is just another way of saying "good" and "evil." Dividing the world up into good and evil can be a destructive addiction to Believers with burnout. They have to ignore anything that's different from themselves, because it wears a hat of the wrong color.

6. **One of the best things you can do to prevent burnout is get away from work as often as possible. True or false?**

Answer: FALSE. There is a practice of taking sudden, unplanned sick days when the pressure builds up. Some people call this "taking a mental-health day." The practice is actually terrible for mental health. If you stay away from work when you have left a lot of unfinished tasks or situations, your body may be at home, but your mind will still be at work. Days off and vacations that are planned can be beneficial if you can stop thinking about work.

7. **Your task is to arrange four coins into two straight rows containing three coins in each.**
   a. This task can be done.
   b. This task cannot be done.

Answer: a. The task can be done. Actually, there are at least three solutions to this problem. Read the question carefully. Don't be distracted by rules for the solution that are not stated in the problem. Here are some solutions:

- Line up the four coins. One row is the first, second, and third coins; the other row is the fourth, third, and second coins.
- Stack the coins. (This solution is really the same as Solution 1.)
- Arrange three coins in a triangle and stack the remaining coin on any other one.
- Hold four coins in your hand. Take out three and make a row. Put them back. Take three coins and make a second row.

See? One of the best ways to avoid burnout is to stay flexible. The hallmark of the disorder is getting hung up on rules that aren't really there.

If you had trouble with this problem, or if you find yourself saying, "That's cheating!" when you see our solutions, then you've come head to head with the kind of thinking that tends to mistake your own personal preferences for the laws of the universe.

Avoiding Burnout in Two Not-So-Easy Steps

No matter what the cause of your burnout, you have to look at the behavior that's involved and do something about that before you do anything else. The behavior, of course, is working yourself to death. Alcoholics Anonymous has a saying that's appropriate here. "When you find yourself in a hole, the first thing you need to do is stop digging." Beware of any thoughts that suggest that there is no possible way for you to slow or stop.

How do you avoid burnout?

First, take care of yourself. Realize that whatever the job conditions, your mental health is your responsibility. Learn a relaxation technique, and use it every day at work. Set up rewards for yourself. Pay attention to your diet and exercise. Choose a partner, and give him or her the right to ask you the hard questions, such as, "So what are you going to do about it?"

Second, take control of your job. Set priorities, then check how you're spending your time against your priorities. Know what the real rules are. Avoid the tendency to place blame. Expect change. Think of your job as a problem to be solved—not as a moral issue. Like any psychological symptom, burnout can serve a positive function by warning you that there is something you aren't paying attention to. Burnout is always a sign that there are things you need to know about how your job really works—that there is a bigger challenge for you if you are only willing to take it up. Forget the windmills. Among the Competitors, there are real dragons.

Too Much of a Good Thing?
Are Your Believer Attitudes Holding You Back?

Which of the following are true of you? They may be signs that you are too much of a Believer for your own good.

1. **I sometimes use humorous names (sleaze, shark, shyster) for people who work The System, to imply that they're immoral or untrustworthy.**

It might help you to think of politics as a job-related skill, not a lapse of morality. When two or more people gather, politics is inevitable. You need to learn to understand the game better, even if you decide not to play.

2. **I cite my unused sick leave and vacation time as evidence of how hard I work.**

You probably think this is an indication of hard work and high motivation. It may also indicate candidacy for martyrdom. Beware of burnout. (You might want to read the preceding chapter on Burnout again—carefully.)

3. **For the past five years, I have held the same job.**

If you like what you do and feel happy and valued in your job, then there is no problem. However, if you feel as if something is holding you back from getting the job you really want, you may not know how to get a promotion. You may be steadfast and solid, but you need to read the Competitors section—and take a few notes.

4. **When I play, I give it my best, but I don't mind losing if someone is better than I am.**

You pick your battles and avoid reflex competitiveness. This is not necessarily bad—unless you want to be a manager. In fact, even if you do want to be a manager, this is fine, but you should probably avoid admitting this to your boss and other Competitors. You may be considered "not management material" if you don't push yourself to win.

5. **It bothers me when rules are not clear or not clearly enforced.**

The Rule of Law is a great ideal, but not one that's enforced in most companies. You may be in for a lot of frustration unless you learn to figure out rules for yourself. Look for a mentor who can teach you the *unwritten* rules of your company. Your mentor should not be your boss. Try to find someone you trust who has Competitor tendencies (there *are* trustworthy Competitors) and a willingness to show you the ropes.

6. In the past year, I have had training in human relations and anything else I can get my hands on.

Good for you! This is the way to learn. Avoid the tendency to rely too much on "experts," though—even us. Many companies don't see this eagerness to learn as a positive trait. You will need to develop your own instincts and decision-making ability. Suggestions lie ahead in the next two parts of the book.

7. I can think of a number of things more important than a good bottom line.

Though there may be numerous things more important than the bottom line, you have to have a good bottom line before you're allowed to talk about them. The bottom line is not the be-all and end-all, but in most companies it does determine what is feasible.

8. I have no respect for people who are lazy.

Hard work is important, but value judgments are seldom helpful. You may mistake people's fear of failure for laziness, or you may consider them morally deficient because their values differ from yours. If their behavior isn't making your job more difficult, leave them to their own values. If their behavior *is* getting in your way, tell them exactly *how* you're affected by their behavior—*without* value judgments.

9. I try to get along with everybody.

You may be a "people person," but you may also be too concerned about being "nice." ("You can't make an omelet without breaking eggs.") Read the stories about Bronson in the next section, and try to imagine yourself—just once—talking or acting as he does.

10. My boss drives me crazy, but I don't want to leave this company.

You already know how to work hard, and your motivation is still high. Now it's time to lose your corporate innocence and find out how your boss thinks. You *know* you could do it if you found out how to!

If You're a Believer

If five or more of the preceding statements are true of you, you probably think or behave like a Believer at work. You're certainly not afraid of working hard. You're probably good at paying attention to details, and you're not afraid of doing difficult tasks. You probably do your job well and thoroughly, but you may feel some frustration because nobody really sees what you do, and nobody appreciates all you do.

Your hard work is probably not rewarded as it should be because (a) your boss is probably a Competitor who doesn't pay much attention to day-to-day details, or (b) you may not have a clear idea of what your company rewards. Maybe you focus a bit too much on the rules that are down on paper instead of the ones that the company actually operates by. Here are some things you can do that may help you feel more in control of yourself and your job.

1. **Find out your company's high priorities—the real ones, not the ones they tell you at pep talks.** As with Rebels, you can buy a lot of freedom and respect by tending to the things that your company considers important. You can be pretty sure it's the bottom line. Other priorities might be generating good publicity or bringing in new customers. Whatever it is, that's Job One, and you will get the most rewards for doing it even if it's not the most difficult or challenging part of your job.

2. **Take responsibility for getting your own information.** Most Believers feel frustrated because nobody tells them what they need to know. However, learning by observation is a valued skill in the world of the Competitors, and they expect everyone to know how to do it. You need to develop good sources of information for yourself. Having a mentor is an ideal way to solve this problem (as Lesley discovers in the next section)—but nothing beats learning by watching the people in power. Be careful, though. If you're like most Believers,

what may be most apparent is the rules that Competitors *break*. You really need to look for the rules they *follow*.

3. **Take care of yourself.** You have to know how to negotiate for what you want, whether it's a promotion, appreciation, or simply the resources you need to do your job. Believers are often frustrated because their bosses don't recognize what they need or see that they get it. Don't wait for the Competitors to solve this problem. Competitors expect you to take care of yourself—so do it. You need to be able to make a case for whatever you need or want. The more closely you can tie your case to making or saving money for the company, the more likely you'll be to get it. ("Because it's the right thing to do" is seldom a useful argument with Competitors.)

4. **Stay close to your own ethics.** If you're a Believer, you may be called upon to fight ethical battles and to stand up for what you believe is right within your company. As you know already, this is perhaps more of a curse than a blessing, but you are needed. You are probably much better suited for this than your Competitor boss. The clearer you are about your own values system, the better able you will be to choose the issues worth defending. Nobody listens to people who bring up ethical issues every day, but at some point in your career, you may have to go to the wall for something you believe in. It's going to be tough, but you'll be able to handle it if you're very sure about the principle you're defending.

5. **Speak for yourself.** Many Believers have a hard time asking for things for themselves, so they adopt a position of "protecting others." This can cause problems. If you want to get anywhere with Competitors, you have to be able to admit that you're acting in your own interest. Otherwise, they won't respect you. Certainly, you can help other people to fight their battles. Beware, though—don't take on their cause if they are unwilling to take it on themselves. If you do, the results will almost always be frustrating and destructive, even though you will be operating for the best of reasons.

If You Manage Believers

The biggest complaint Believers have about their bosses is that the bosses don't listen and that they either don't tell them anything or give them inaccurate information. Here are some ideas for better communication between you and the Believers you manage.

1. **Give them honest feedback even if you're afraid they can't take it.** Give them as much information as you can. Assume that all that they know is what you tell them. Do whatever you can to make information more available to them. Answer their questions. Set up ways of providing information, including regular meetings and perhaps even newsletters.

2. **Make your priorities clear and specific.** Be sure you know how your department's priorities square with the goals of the company. If making you look good is the highest priority in your department, say so. Believers will recognize your deceit and will feel insulted if you tell them that quality is Job One, when the real first priority is covering your rear end.

To make your priorities clear, you need to resolve the Quality versus Quantity dilemma yourself. Even if your boss has delegated the issue to you, don't delegate it to your staff and hope they are motivated enough to handle it. Your primary responsibility as a manager is to draw the line clearly between quality and quantity and to set limits. You have to let people know the real standards by which they are being evaluated.

3. **Make the requirements for getting promoted clear.** In most companies, it takes considerably more than hard work to get ahead. Let your staff know how you did it, but don't pretend that just working hard and getting good scores on their ratings will automatically put them in line for promotions. Recognize that if people don't see moving up as a possibility, they may try to move out.

4. **Say what you mean, and mean what you say.** If you must do things for show, let your staff be part of the production rather than the audience.

5. **Remember that evaluation is important.** It should relate directly to your employees' goals, your goals, and the company's goals. You should work hard to explain to Believers exactly how they fit into the larger scheme. During their job evaluation, let *them* educate *you* about what they do and how their tasks can be evaluated. A good question to ask is, "How can I tell you're doing a good job?" Listen to what they say, then ask questions that relate to your goals and the company's goals. Try to think of evaluation as an ongoing experiment or a series of approximations, instead of a final product, carved in stone. (If pleasing you or making you look good is a major part of people's jobs, rate them on that. Even the staunchest Believer will agree that success is at least partially determined by how well you please the boss.)

This approach to evaluations also will work for Rebels and Competitors. If you're going to do an evaluation, it might as well mean something. (Don't forget—evaluation goes both ways.)

If You Work for a Believer

If your boss is a Believer, according to our criteria, it's possible that the powers-that-be consider your department a backwater where the work is easy or boring. Believers are rarely bosses, and they're even more rarely bosses in departments considered important to the executives. The usual rule of thumb is that if your department does not have a bottom line, it's more likely to be considered a backwater. Sometimes, however, the only indication is that yours is one of the only departments that has a Believer as a boss. If you're happy where you are, then there's no problem. However, if your goals involve moving up, you'll probably have to transfer out of that department. Whichever is your situation, here are suggestions for working for a Believer.

1. **Follow the rules.** Know what you're supposed to do, and see that it's done. Your boss will be checking. Count on it.

2. **Recognize your boss's limitations, especially if the company is volatile or you want to move up.** Your Believer boss may not be able to protect you or promote you. You may need to develop mentors outside of your department. Have other sources of information about what's going on in the company and how others view your department. Find other ways to send out positive information about *you.*

3. **Demonstrate motivation and willingness to go the extra mile.** If your boss is a Believer, you will be rewarded for being a team player or looked down on for advancing your own interest ahead of other people's. If your boss is a Competitor, though, the rules may be completely reversed about this. Be sure you know who's who.

PART FOUR

Warriors at Work: The Competitors

10

The Cult of Winning and the Management Mystique

The Secrets of Competitors' Power

Alexander the Great came to the Shrine of Gorda, where he found an enchanted and very complicated knot that was rumored to give the power to conquer the world to the man who had the skill to untie it.

The crowd hushed as Alexander approached the Gordian knot. They knew he was good—but was he good enough?

Scarcely glancing at the knot, Alexander drew his sword and hacked it to pieces.

Now was this guy a Competitor, or what?

The story of Alexander is a classic example of the Competitor's view of winning. Alexander is a winner, going for stakes higher than anyone else has dared. The sheer nobility of his quest puts him above the rules designed for mere mortals. Let the Believers try to untie the knot. People didn't call Alexander "the Great" for screwing around with regulations. He had a job to get done.

Nobody else loves a winner as much as a Competitor does—especially winners who, like Alexander, ignore conventions in their quest for the Big Prize. Believers value the work it takes to win (they would have disqualified Alexander for breaking the rules), but Competitors value the winning itself. They see their world as a conflict, with the strongest emerging as the most successful and success as its own justification. For Competitors, it's the winning, not how you play the game, that counts. Competitors see themselves as sophisticated and knowledgeable. However, to the Believers and Rebels who work with them, Competitors are the Neanderthals who turn the office into a primitive jungle.

The Cult of Winning tells the Competitor that there is nobility in imposing your will on the universe, in setting a goal and accomplishing it, in being the best and beating other people. Mythic stories focus on what it takes to be the best: the ability to balance the opposing forces represented by the myths of the Rebels, the Believers, and the Competitors. To pursue excellence and catch it, you need the Believers' motivation, the Competitors' knowledge of The System, and the Rebels' imagination. *Nothing* great was ever accomplished without the drive to win.

Bronson's Battle Strategy

Bronson was on a negotiating team to work out a contract to buy excess inventory from American Excellence & Quality. Because the making of deals is what gets people into the history books at Neander-Tek, Bronson wanted to do this right. To him, this meant extracting better terms than Jack James did in *his* last deal. This was the victory Bronson wanted so much he could taste it. First, however, he had to fight and win two other battles:

- **Establish dominance on the negotiating team so that everyone would know it was Bronson's Team. (At Neander-**

Tek, it was understood that, even though deals are made
by a team, a leader will emerge. Winning breeds winning.)
• Soundly beat the AEQ team by getting the inventory at a
rock-bottom price.

A few days before the negotiation, Bronson had worked
himself into a competitive frenzy. He knew that, to win the
Big One, you had to believe in yourself, _and_ you had to know
how to win. You had to have a strategy.

Bronson's favorite strategy was doing careful research on
his enemy's weak points, then hammering those points with
everything he had. Bronson saw this approach as military
tactics. It was the way Stormin' Norman Schwarzkopf had
beaten Hussein, and it was the pattern for virtually every
interaction in Bronson's life. It was how he played tennis,
made deals, and argued with his ex-wife. It was how he
won—and winning was what Bronson was all about.

He started with the negotiating team. His only real rival for
leadership was Max Jacobs. The other three team members
were definitely spear-carriers. Bronson knew that Max had
been involved two years ago in making a deal that lost a few
bucks—the Culligan project. Max wasn't the head of that
team, but Bronson felt sure he could get the lingering stain of
that defeat to stick to Max.

Bronson's tactic was to get the other team members to see
Max as a loser, thereby neutralizing him as competition for
leadership. He carefully studied what had gone wrong with
Culligan and referred to Max as "the mastermind of the Culligan deal" to a couple of other team members.

At the first team meeting, when Max made an initial comment, Bronson said, "Now hold on a minute, Max. You'd
think you'd have learned something from the Culligan fiasco,
but what I'm hearing is the same kind of fuzzy thinking that
caused us to lose big on that one." He then recited an en-
cyclopedic run-down of the Culligan deal and its outcome.

Max was stuck. If he said he wasn't in charge of Culligan,
he would reveal he was too weak to take control of the previous team and was not leadership material. If he pointed out

that what he was saying here wasn't the same as Culligan, he would still imply that he should have said something during the Culligan negotiations that could have avoided that defeat. Checkmate. Max was enough of a Competitor to realize that he'd been outmaneuvered.

Bronson had maneuvered the second most able person on the team to a position in which he had to keep his mouth shut and take orders. It never occurred to Bronson that Max might have offered some valuable insights that could have helped the team against AEQ. To Bronson, once a loser, always a loser.

Bronson is a fundamentalist in the Cult of Winning. He sees everything as a win-lose situation. Every battle is individual, and cooperation is little better than defeat. He bears the risks and dangers gladly; when the smoke clears and the body count is tallied, all the glory is his. Bronson doesn't see that you can win battles and lose wars.

Now Bronson had control of the negotiating team. He knew from his research that American Excellence was badly strapped for cash. Their earnings were down, and they had debt to service—soon. They were over the proverbial barrel.

He announced his plan at the negotiating team meeting. "We've gotta send these birds a message from Day One. They need to know who they're dealing with.

"We have to know the exact date that they have to service their debt. Max, you'll have to make a few calls to find out. Get me all the facts and figures so I can call on you to cite them, chapter and verse, if they get cute on me.

"I'll start out by saying we have to work fast to get this deal made by whatever the debt-service date is. I'll just let it hang in the air a minute, so they'll know that we know." Bronson smiled, but his eyes were hard.

"That ought to cut 30K off their asking price right there. We need to remind them that beggars can't be choosers.

"Making a deal is like war," he told his troops. "You have to let the enemy know you have the upper hand from the beginning. Let 'em know they're going to lose. Demoralize 'em. Hit 'em with everything you've got right from the start."

Bronson made the deal, which worked out just as he had predicted. He won. It really didn't matter to him that he had left a wake of humiliated people who wanted to get even. Let them try to get back at him. He was ready. Ah, the thrill of victory. It was what his life was all about.

Bronson wins by pushing himself. He knows you have to push to be a winner. Anything that stands between him and his goal is the enemy. Personal limitations, tough tasks, rival coworkers, tennis opponents, other drivers on the road—he treats them all with the same aggressive nerve. He gets mad, then he gets them. He doesn't see his temper as a problem. Far from it. To him, it's more like his secret weapon; it gives him the extra motivation he needs to win. Incompetence from any of the "Neanderthals" around him drives him crazy. When he explodes at his subordinates, he's not being emotional; he's exercising his divine (or at least hard-won) right.

Heroes of the Cult of Winning

Competitors listen with rapt attention to the top military, sports, and business figures when they try to explain, in their autobiographies or after-the-game comments, that elusive edge that gives them a higher batting average than everyone else. Even the most inarticulate of winners has something to teach Competitors that ordinary people cannot match. Winning itself somehow bestows grace _and_ wisdom.

Bronson likes to consider himself in the company of the great winners of America that he reads about in the glossy business magazines:

"He turned the company around, from big loser to industry leader in six months."

"Billionaire at 29"

"Nobel Prize for Scientific Discoveries"
"He single-handedly changed the face of bond financing."
"Builds Latest Hotel Grander Than Taj Mahal"

However, the unchecked drive to win can also destroy. All too often, if you follow the news, you'll read about the collapse of the financial empire and even the indictment of the king. The message Bronson reads in that is simple: If you slip up, you're dead. He accepts these terms gladly. You can't be a winner without taking risks.

There is an even darker message in the Cult of Winning: that winning somehow makes Competitors superior. Like Alexander (at least in their own minds), they're exempt from the rules that other people have to follow. This part of the myth confirms the Rebels' distrust of authority and drives Believers crazy. If Competitors would play by the rules, Believers would follow them anywhere. Some Competitors too readily ignore what their subordinates think. They may talk of teamwork, but to them, the role of the team is to aid in the captain's quest for greatness. Too-rigid adherence to the Cult of Winning can turn leadership to exploitation.

Bronson won the AEQ deal, but he ended up with a team that hates his guts—especially Max Jacobs.

Well, not everybody wants to string him up. Howard Endicott, the junior member of the team, looks up to him with awe and with the hope that Bronson will become his mentor.

Winning through Teamwork

Winning does not have to be as cutthroat as Bronson makes it. Let's look in on Jack James, working with his negotiating team.

"I think the first thing we all have to understand is that we're making a deal—not fighting a battle. Every deal can lead to another deal," Jack says. "No victory is ultimate.

There's always a bigger win in the future, and you never know whose help you'll need to pull it off." (This is the essence of El Tigre's strategy.)

Bronson is not on Jack's team, and it drives him crazy that Jack is so successful. To Bronson, Jack's approach sounds like weakness. Bronson told his wife, "People should be wiping up the floor with him. One day, I will. Just wait."

Jack James is a member of the Cult of Winning, too. Victory is every bit as important to him as it is to Bronson, but his strategy is more long term. Jack knows he needs allies if he's going to win the really big ones. This means that he may have to turn away from a few battles that he could easily win. He knows that, if he has to beat everybody at everything, all they'll want to do is get back at him.

Jack's drive to win is just as strong as Bronson's. The hardest lesson he's ever learned is to hold back, but now that he knows it, he sees its value.

Back at the meeting, Jack grins and says, "Enough of my prattle. Let's hear from you guys. How do you size up the situation? Let's go around the table and see how we scope this out."

Jack has a clear plan here. He knows that if he takes over and directs people to do what they are dying to do, he will be perceived as the leader. (There's his reputation to think of, too.) He wins leadership as quickly as Bronson, but without shedding a drop of blood.

Jack knows that the Competitors at the table will all be leading with their best shots, vying for the second position. He will have the benefit of their best ideas from the outset. You can bet that everyone's ideas will be considered, and everyone will have a role in making the deal. Jack knows that Alexander, in addition to cutting the Gordian knot, was one of history's most able administrators. That's how you win the really big victories.

Competitors' Blind Spot:
Bronson's Reverence for
the Management Mystique

The Cult of Winning can blind Competitors to the point of view, or even the value, of people who haven't reached the upper level or who haven't embraced the creed that Winning Is Everything. To members of the cult, if you're not a winner, you're a loser.

The Competitor's power comes from motivation and a knowledge of The System. Ignorance is no excuse; it's a crime. In the ranks of big winners, there is no room for people who don't know the score. Competitor cool requires that all doubts, fears or uncertainty be completely denied. Rebels have their Cult of Cool; the Competitor version is called the "Management Mystique."

Bronson's list of accomplishments at Neander-Tek is impressive. Whatever needs doing gets done. No excuses. Upper management regards him as a real comer. He reminds some of Dale Sutter, the founder, in his heyday. Maybe it's the leather suspenders . . .

Of course, there are a few who, while agreeing that Bronson is brilliant, have some doubts about his ability to really lead. And one or two hate his guts. That's the way he affects people.

Bronson is our caricatured personification of the Cult of Winning and the Management Mystique, the ritual requirement that managers never guess; they *know*. Always. The effect of the mystique on Bronson, as on many hard-driven Competitors, is that he sees little that's right about his opponents and little that's wrong about himself—at least, that he'll admit. Internally, however, Bronson is always criticizing himself and making new demands. To him, if you're not Number One, you're nothing.

He brushes off criticism from anyone else, especially from "Neanderthals" who don't have the least idea about who he is or what he's doing.

The consultant presented Bronson with a long list of complaints from his staff about his leadership. At the top was their fear of his shotgun temper (with a page of examples of past blow-ups), followed closely by irritation at his disregard for their opinions.
"How can they say that?" he shouted. "My temper isn't all that bad! I blow up, then it's over. I don't hold grudges. They're always bringing up my past. It's over for me. Why can't they let it rest? Aw, hell. What do they know, anyway?"

Bronson's anger covers his feeling of hurt. He mistook his subordinates' fear of him for admiration.

Bronson has been a Competitor since about age eleven. He was a smart kid, smart enough to know that just being smart would never get him anywhere. In childhood, he had figured out that the world loves a winner, and he's been winning ever since. He wins because losing is unthinkable.
To Bronson, the big winners were all in business. He carefully picked his courses in college—just enough tough ones to show he had brains and enough easy ones to keep his GPA up high enough to get into the best MBA program. Basic training for a corporate warrior.
He likes to say he learned three things in graduate school: Bottom line, bottom line, and bottom line. He also learned another trick there, which he still uses from time to time: inventing studies and reports on the spot, to gain the upper hand in an argument.
". . . remember the Johnson article in the Harvard Business Review? . . ." he'll say.
". . . that new study, just released by the Defense Department . . ."
"As Peter Drucker has said many times. . . ."

The references sound so plausible that other Competitors seldom question him about their accuracy. Most of the time, his references are correct; Bronson does know a lot, and he does his homework. Sometimes, though, if he needs a corroborating quotation to gain an edge, he'll invent one. People seldom call his bluff; they don't want to reveal their ignorance of something so elementary that everyone should know about it.

This is the kind of trick that only works on Competitors. (Believers would usually admit they don't know and might ask questions in their sincere desire to know more.) Bronson knows the psychology of highly competitive people: Never admit to doubts, fears, being wrong, or any other weakness that might erode your position. His real trick is using Competitors' own characteristics against them.

Bronson understands the unwritten rules for managers at Neander-Tek (and most other companies.) Managers have a lot of responsibility and a lot of privileges. They are expected to know what they're doing. (Other people are allowed to guess.) Everything managers do is supposed to be based on knowledge and forethought—and, it seems, on superhuman powers. Doubt, fear, uncertainty, ignorance and other human frailty? Within the Management Mystique, they aren't allowed to exist.

Management Mystique is not just a creation of Competitors. Believers require that their leaders be more qualified than they are, and they can be downright cruel to authorities who try to suggest that they are only human. (Remember Jimmy Carter? Competitors remember him and have learned from his mistakes.)

The Management Mystique arises from a number of sources, but it comes down to a powerful demand that managers *know*, not guess. If you haven't lived with this kind of pressure, it's hard to understand its burden.

The Management Mystique implies that everything that managers do is planned and calculated to achieve an effect. Let's say, for example, that a manager doesn't like to sit at a desk but prefers to walk around her department a lot. The Management Mystique can turn her simple stroll into her "management style." In the same way, many managers perpetuate the mystique by implying "I meant to do that," whether their successful actions were deliberate or just a lucky shot. Luck is for Rebels. Competitors *know*. Believers are impressed and think, "I couldn't do that."

Competitors who are caught up in the seductive power of the Management Mystique know that other Competitors are watching their every move—and that, as the commercial warned, you should *never* let 'em see you sweat.

Dana could feel her shoulder muscles tense as soon as she walked into the conference room. Charts, stats, survey results—everything was ready and filed in her briefcase. She had done her homework—so why was she so hyper?

Dolan. She was worried about old Dolan the Shark, whose daily dietary requirement was one manager on rye, barbecued to a crisp. He loved to slouch in his chair during presentations, eyes closed, head nodding. Many unsuspecting victims thought he was a harmless old duffer, but Dana knew that when he went into his naptime act, he was just resting before the kill. What the hell would she do if Dolan asked her a question she couldn't answer? Would she be able to talk fast enough and sound confident enough to bull her way through, or would everybody know he'd nailed her? Would everybody see that she'd failed?

There is an implicit demand that Competitors in management never say, "I don't know." Inspiration may come from not knowing, and learning often is the result of making mistakes, but the Competitor's burden is to need to know it all already. At the far fringe of the Management Mystique, you're not *allowed* to not know it, and you're not allowed to make mistakes. In this, Rebels and Competitors agree: Mistakes are the stuff of losers.

The most important thing about learning how to behave in Competitor-driven situations is that *you must never admit to winging it*, even when you are. Sometimes, like Dolan, you might want to appear to be out of it, so the competition will underestimate you. It's OK to keep *them* guessing, but *you* have to know.

In most companies, the projected image is that management is based on facts, hard work, solid judgment, and, most of all, *numbers*. The Management Mystique demands that all agree that management is a rational process, even if it isn't. Managers are human beings who, like the rest of us, are guessing most of the time. However, they know that if all you have are doubts, questions, and human failings—with no numbers to back them up—you have no authority. You either have to make something up or admit to being a loser. (Nobody said being a Competitor is easy.)

The other possibility is to assume, as Bronson does, that what you don't know is unimportant. In Bronson's case, this means that people who don't think as he does are ciphers; they drive him crazy. Don't they understand that there's a better way to be? They should be like him. If they aren't, that's their problem.

Ask anybody who knows Bronson. Ask his employees. Ask his family. They will tell you that Bronson doesn't give a damn about who they are or what they think. (Actually, he does, but that is the deep, dark secret he can never admit to anyone—or even to himself.)

Bronson's Divorce

It had never been an easy glide up the corporate escalator for Bronson. His climb to the top had taken an all-out commitment: killer hours, too many nights away from home, family dinners missed, the thousand reasons why he couldn't be there when his wife or son needed him. Finally, they just stopped needing him.

He couldn't figure it out. He thought he was doing it all for them. Every step up the ladder meant a bigger house, better clothes, classier cars. His wife had loved to throw it up to him that he was never home to enjoy any of it—but who did she think paid for the new BMW and the tennis club dues? The tooth fairy?

* * *

Bronson's wife, Meredith, has a different story:

"Even with his temper, he wasn't so bad," she said slowly, remembering. "I know he loved us—and he had a great sense of humor. Nobody could make our son laugh the way he could. We had good times together, the three of us—when we got to see him.

"To me, the house, the cars, the tennis club, and all the other toys didn't mean a thing. What I wanted was *him*—to spend time with us, to talk to us, to find out what we thought. I don't think he ever saw us as separate people; we were just extensions of him. If *he* wanted something for us, then *we* should want it too. That's what drove me crazy."

* * *

Bronson had really wanted to make the marriage work, but he didn't know how. When it ended, he was alone again. Sometimes he felt as if he'd been alone every day of his life.

Jack James had tried to help. "Want to talk about it?" he'd asked soon after Meredith had left him.

Bronson had shrugged. "What's there to say? It's the oldest story in the book. She thought I spent too much time at work and not enough with her and the kid. She didn't understand what it takes to succeed in a business like this—and she didn't realize I was doing it for *them*. They were my family. I wanted them to have the best. It's just not . . ." he caught himself midsentence and shrugged again. "Oldest story in the book."

Jack recognized that Bronson had just shut the door on any real chance to talk. "Yeah," he said. "If there's anything I can do, let me know."

"Sure, Jack. Thanks."

Like the Rebels' Cult of Cool, the Management Mystique can be a prescription for emotional distance from other people. Bronson would tell you that you have to make sacrifices to win at the corporate game. It's always lonely at the top.

The Cult of Winning and the Management Mystique are the sources of Competitors' power. These mythical systems give Competitors the strength to do the things that are demanded of them to manage, to lead, to win. Without these beliefs, there would be no corporate excellence to proclaim on company slogans.

However, if Competitors take the Cult of Winning and the Management Mystique too literally or see them as the only truth, these myths also become the sources of Competitors' weaknesses. If they cannot understand and accept that others can be different from themselves, they become less effective as leaders and more lonely as people.

The Cult of Winning glorifies strength, power, and masculinity. Corporate cultures that are set up totally by Competitors often resemble the cutthroat jungle of *Liar's Poker* or *Bonfire of the Vanities*.

Yet, without Competitors, there would be no excellence, because nobody would be striving for it. The Cult of Winning reveres not only the material triumphs, but also the triumphs of the spirit. Many Competitors respect great art, great music, and great writing as much as they venerate great management. Without Competitors and their aggression, there would be no greatness.

Baby Boomers and Competitor Cool

Because of the Vietnam War, many Baby Boomers joined the Cult of Cool in the '60s, when believing in their country was dangerous to the health of their generation. These Competitors-to-be decided that authority and rules were meant for other people, not for them. They rebelled and got away with it. They learned that, like it or not, *they* were in control—and there were ways around the rules. Perhaps they learned it too soon.

Some of these Baby Boomers grew up and became Rebels; others returned to the Believer values of their parents' generation; but a surprising number found that their Cool defense against a heartless system had turned into a basic cynicism: All that's important is winning, money, and power. Look out for Numero Uno. Everybody else is a loser. Economic development forgives all. By the early '80s, they had gone beyond "The Establishment" they had fought.

Now, in the '90s, many of these former emotional dropouts have gained all the riches, won all the battles, and are looking for something to believe in. The Cult of Winning may no longer be enough. A life of commitment to yourself alone may not be rewarding enough, no matter how much you win.

11

Founders, Warriors, and Entrepreneurs

Corporate Heroes and Mythical Tales

Neander-Tek was founded by Dale Sutter, who started out with the legendary transistor in a garage. It was his garage, but it wasn't his transistor. (He did buy the patent, however.)

Dale was an entrepreneur; inventing things and managing people were not his fortes. His genius was recognizing a good idea and being able to get together the capital to make it work. From the beginning, he believed in diversification. "Don't put all your eggs in one basket" was his financial philosophy. The phrase could be carved in stone on the lintel of N-T's corporate headquarters today.

Dale was great at picking the businesses to get into. His ability to choose them was legendary—no one knew (and he wouldn't tell) how he made his decisions. Everything he touched just seemed to turn to gold. When asked, "How do you do it?" Dale would say only, "Some got it, some don't." Then he'd smile, straighten his leather suspenders, and reach into his desk drawer for a victory cigar.

He didn't just pick the right properties; he was also a master at putting together the deal. The stories of how he acquired some of N-T's major divisions sound like military campaigns: carefully planned and well funded, but, in the end, relying on Dale's skill at the negotiating table. At Neander-Tek, making the deals is still recognized as the highest art, followed closely by sales.

Dale believed that having a good product was never enough. "You need to let people know what you've got." From the start, he relied on a crack sales force to move his products.

His original sales manager was Samuel M. ("Motivation with a capital M") Kirby, whose requirements were simple. "You're Number One in your territory, or you're gone. If you're not Number One, you're not motivated enough to work for us."

Later, Dale jumped onto the marketing bandwagon, too, when he saw the insatiable postwar demand becoming more specialized. In his later years he became a fanatic about data, numbers, and recordkeeping. Sloppiness in any area was not to be tolerated at "The Greatest Company in the World." N-T was one of the first companies in the country to become computerized and still relies heavily on its computer operation. From Day One, N-T's people had to have the numbers to back up their decisions.

Dale believed in sports as a way of training people in what's really important. He was an ace tennis player and delighted in beating men half his age. It was rumored that he chose his executives as much for their backhand as their business skills. He believed in being a well-rounded person, which meant being a first-string athlete and a first-string dealmaker. "If you're not going to win, why play?" Dale liked to say.

He was killed in an auto accident in 1973, but his ghost— trim, suspendered, and graying at the temples—still strides down the halls of Neander-Tek and lives in the attitude that winning—making big deals and big sales—is more important than any one product. (That doesn't mean that the products are *un*important, you understand. . . .)

In many companies, the founder is the major corporate hero. Mythic stories of his or her exploits illustrate what a successful person should be. Often, the founder's personal characteristics, beliefs, prejudices and even fears become the basis for the way the company does business. (Sigmund Freud had a phobia about looking people in the face, so from his day until now, psychoanalysts sit behind the couch, out of the patient's line of sight. Psychoanalysis can drive you crazy, too.)

The founder is often held up as an example. If she (or he) could do it, you can, too. If not, maybe you have some sort of attitude problem. What is seldom considered is that founders may have had great talents in areas that others may not be able to match. Also, founders stood to gain tremendous rewards for their hard work. Many of their heroic deeds were motivated by desperation—they were the only way to get the company going. Besides, they *owned* the company. If they had failed in their early gambles and feats of arms, there wouldn't be anybody to recount their heroics. They'd all be working for someone else.

Of course, legends grow in the retelling and are subtly shaped by the belief systems of whoever is doing the telling. It is no accident that the founder usually symbolizes the Myth of Motivation and the Cult of Winning. The stories sometimes put unreasonable performance pressure on today's employees. It can drive them crazy.

A producer in a West Coast record company remembers his first job in the industry. "The company was about 14 years old when I joined, and the stories about how the current CEO signed up some star artists (with no advance on their contracts, mind you—and my clients think *I'm* cheap!) served as the model for subsequent generations of producers.

"These myths were very influential," the producer said. "If you wanted a contract bad enough, you could motivate any artist to sign with you—at terms distinctly worse than the competition—and they'd be glad they did."

Part of that myth was that "Our Company" was not for

everyone, the producer said. Only a special breed could operate there. "We didn't like those other companies that simply bought talent. We literally thought that we were the greatest company in the world."

Sometimes, management will point to the founders of other companies as examples of heroic qualities and values.

The Entrepreneur: Competitors' Hero

The great hero of the Competitors is a particular kind of winner and creator. If there's anything that makes American business spirit great, it's the entrepreneurial spirit. Entrepreneurs are the go-getters who have the motivation, the guts, and the skills to make something—a company—out of nothing but their will to succeed.

Who are these mythological creatures?

They are the winners who understand The System so well that they can see market niches that no one else has seen. These wizards master technology so brilliantly that they come up with a product that revolutionizes the industry; the founders accomplish the heroic feat of starting a business that actually makes a profit. Entrepreneurs represent what Competitors value most about themselves: the magical ability to turn ideas into money!

Believers revere the entrepreneurs for their hard work and high motivation; Rebels admire their creativity and maverick qualities. Competitors, however, admire only their money and their power; without these, all else is academic.

At Neander-Tek, they like to talk about Joe Sinclair, the founder of Banana Industries, new star on the software horizon. Jack James tells about how Joe started his company from nothing, using some really ingenious ideas about financing— and how his marketing is so precise that he (almost) always clobbers the competition. The fact that Joe's firm pulls down 40 mil a year is of interest as well.

Lesley likes to point out that even though Joe Sinclair *could* just sit around and . . . manage . . . he doesn't. It's well known that he still writes software. He also lets his employees have a say in everything.

Luke likes to talk about how creative Joe's software is. The guy's a flat-out genius. Also, Joe has never worn a tie to work in his life, and he's been known to flip a Frisbee around the table at his board of directors' meetings.

Manufactured Myths

Remember how Marty Jenkins got to be sales manager? He was so motivated that nothing could stop him. He believed he could do it and, despite mountainous obstacles, he *did it.* Marty tells the story at his seminars to illustrate the power of motivation. In effect, he is using himself as a corporate hero to embody the myth that's so dear to his heart. Maybe he embellishes a little, but he really does believe his motivation is the secret of his success.

This story is a distortion of reality, but it's not a lie. Corporate myths are stories used by people in companies to impart company values, just as other cultural myths impart other cultural values. With all the recent writing on corporate culture, managers recognize the power of myths to control behavior. The temptation is strong to manufacture them in the way that the practitioners of the Cargo Cult built artificial planes.

Myths can't be made up like advertising copy, no matter how much management would like to manufacture them as a way of manipulating the corporate culture. The culture produces the myths, not the other way around. The myths that stick arise in the form of the stories that members of a group choose to tell. Stories that don't fit what's there get rejected as propaganda. When you use yourself as the hero of your own mythical tales, you run the risk that others don't interpret your life story in the same way you do.

Something Else the Myth of Motivation Leaves Out

Never mind that Marty Jenkins knows the product better than the guy who invented it. Never mind that Marty has the ability to listen to and even remember the names of well over 300 customers. And never mind that he can figure out, and even anticipate, what people want, both in the corporate hierarchy and among his customers, and he can give it to them, too.

Marty will tell you it's his *motivation* that's at the root of it all and is the only thing that really makes him different from any other Joe in the company.

What Marty won't tell anyone is that when he becomes sales manager, he will expect all the sales reps to be able to do what he can do. He won't recognize that he tops most people by 20 I.Q. points. When they can't store as many facts in their head as he can, he will think their problem is lack of motivation, instead of a lack of ability. It drives him crazy that they can't do what he can do.

Marty won't consider setting more reasonable standards for his sales force. (Lowering standards is pretty tough for a guy for whom 110 percent is average.) Instead, Marty will give his famous lectures and pass out motivational books and tapes. If they don't work, Marty will get irritated, maybe shift some people's sales territories around and put a few people on notice, to send everybody a message.

Hey, if he can do it, anybody else can, too—*if* they have the motivation.

The Myth of Motivation gives Marty strength and meaning, but it can also blind him to important issues. The blindness, as happens with many Competitors, shows up in his dealings with other people. What makes Marty strong as an individual makes him weak as a leader. Think about how it would feel to be working as hard as you can and have your boss subtly imply that you were lazy. Needless to say, it drives his employees crazy.

Myths as Metaphors

The myths we work by—our beliefs about work—are passed along through stories, wisecracks, jokes, and even rumors, in office hallways and across lunch tables. Just as early myths told stories about events that weren't scientifically understood, Believers make up mythical explanations for the things in their universe that they don't understand—the behavior of their Competitor bosses, mostly.

Carl is always trying to explain Bronson's behavior to anyone who'll listen. He favors an interpretive approach, vaguely influenced by New Age psychology and, more heavily, by a large dose of Believer morality (which New Age psychology is, anyway).

Carl is positive that Bronson must be an "adult child," and you know how they are. They lie even when the truth wouldn't hurt them. That's what they learn in the kind of environment they grew up in. Carl just knows that Bronson's father must have been a heavy drinker. That's why he's so threatened by powerful and competent men. Any time a man does something significant (such as write a policy manual), Bronson just has to cut the guy down to size. Bronson doesn't realize that he's just perpetuating the cycle of abuse.

Believers such as Carl are often attracted to New Age "recovery" approaches to psychology because they translate the confusing aspects of life into something they can readily understand—victimization.

New Age psychology, like other Believer religions, tends to view people's lives and behaviors in a moralistic way. What is good (the Inner Child, honesty, self-understanding) and what is evil (parents, codependency, dysfunctionality, not understanding yourself) are so clear that there is little ambiguity—unlike, say, real life. Undesirable behavior was caused by someone else—the Alcoholic, the Abuser, the Parent—and presents the Believer as a victim. The effect of past experiences clouds Believers' vision of the present; they can't see the role of their own behavior in a negative situation. They *can*, however, regain their emotional health by following a set of rules (12 is the typical number.)

Carl takes comfort in his belief that he knows more about Bronson than Bronson knows about himself, though it doesn't help Carl to deal with Bronson any better or to predict Bronson's behavior any more accurately. (This is mainly because Carl doesn't understand how Bronson conceives of himself.) Nonetheless, Carl's Bronson myths do help Carl to feel superior to him. To Believers such as Carl, people who understand their own shortcomings (and those of others), and who are honest and pure are far better than those shallow souls who don't think about such things.

Bronson heard Carl's interpretation of him through the grapevine. He didn't like it. That soft-headed psychological stuff drives him crazy. He says it's a lot simpler than that. "I'm just trying to get the job done. Period. Save your self-help for someone who needs it."

The Rebel interpretation of Bronson is simpler and more to the point. To them, Bronson is the mythical big-headed boss who's not as smart as he thinks he is. Rebels say things like, "The guy's a Neanderthal. Too bad his brains are no match for his ego, or he might actually *know* something or be able to *do* something around here—besides trying to make our jobs a living hell."

Believers, too, would think these comments were funny, because of the implicit message that conceit is wrong. To Bronson, however, modesty is not a virtue, and conceit is not a fault. He knows you have to structure situations so that people will find out how great you are. (He calls it "promoting yourself.") He might be mildly offended at the Rebels' slurs on his intelligence, but their comments about his ego would be lost on him. So, he thinks, I've got a big ego. So what? Besides, who listens to subordinates—particularly subordinates who aren't Competitors?

Bronson has his own slurs for non-Competitors and tells a joke that reflects his view of the inadequacies of Rebels and Believers:

> A farmer had a new hired hand who could plow, cut wood, and slop hogs three times as fast as any of his other workers. After four days in the fields, the new guy consistently worked harder and better than anyone else.
>
> On the fifth day, the farmer decided to let him take it a little easier. He took the hired hand to the barn, where his job was to sort potatoes. There was a board with holes in it and baskets underneath. Big potatoes go in the big hole, medium in the medium, small in the small.
>
> Just before lunchtime, the hired hand stormed up to the farmer and shouted, "I quit! I can't take this any more!"
>
> The farmer was perplexed. "You've been working so hard all week. I thought I'd give you an easy job so you could relax today."
>
> "Easy!" the hired hand fumed. "What do you mean 'easy'? All day long, making decisions!"

Bronson tells this joke to Competitor buddies whenever Believers and Rebels act up. (To Bronson "acting up" means griping or complaining about how he does a job that would be too difficult for *them*.) Viewed in the context of the Cult of Winning, the comment he makes by telling the joke is, "Losers run away when they're given a task that's really hard."

In fact, Bronson will use "They just can't sort potatoes" as an in-joke to his peers to describe people who can't handle the pressure of the way things are at work. He says it about Carl all the time.

The stories told by other Competitors are less biting and seem more closely tied to the Myth of Motivation.

Marty Jenkins also has a favorite joke that, to him, has mythical significance.

> A young grocery clerk is approached by a woman who wants to buy half a head of lettuce. He says he has to have his manager's approval, then goes to the manager and says, "This stupid old lady wants half a head of lettuce." He hears a cough behind him, turns and sees that the woman has followed him—so he quickly says, "And this nice lady would like to buy the other half!"
>
> The manager is impressed. He offers to back the young clerk as a candidate for manager of the store in Detroit.
>
> The young clerk says, "Detroit! All they have there are ladies of ill repute and hockey players."
>
> The manager says coldly, "I'll have you know that my wife is from Detroit."
>
> To which the young man replies, "Oh, what team does she play for?"

When Marty tells the joke (and he has told it in at least three sales meetings in the past six months), he uses it to point out how, with enough motivation, you can think on your feet and turn potential defeats into victories.

The victory here is over the young man's own sense of good judgment. Marty doesn't see that, in using this story as an illustration, he is pointing out the darker side of the Myth of Motivation, as well. If you're motivated enough, you don't need critical thinking or even basic good sense. If you have guts, who needs a head?

Much of what you hear along the corridors of the typical corporation are myths—stories, offhand remarks and jokes that point us in the direction of a particular belief system.

If we take these stories and jokes literally, we miss their message, at least consciously. We don't realize that we are sharing myths any more than does the shaman who points to the mountain that was formed when the God of Thunder tossed his rival out of the sky. Each of us is just stating the facts as we see them—and everybody else could see them, too, if they were just motivated enough.

12

Warriors' Codes of Combat

Bronson, Jack James, and Dana were on their way to the quarterly Input and Informational Meeting. As they stepped into the executive elevator, Bronson said, "These meetings drive me crazy. As soon as Big Al [Neander-Tek's CEO] gets up there, the hands start waving in the breeze. It's always the same people, saying that somebody in management didn't play by the rules." Bronson's voice took on a mimicking whine, "So what are you going to do, Al, to punish them?"

Bronson snorted. "I don't know how Al can keep a straight face. Those people are so picky about every little detail—always wanting to know what's the policy on this and what are the rules about that. They're so obsessed with The Rules. It drives me crazy."

Dana smiled. "They aren't the only ones obsessed with rules."

Bronson frowned. "Are you trying to tell me something?"

"No," Dana said. "Just that we all operate by rules. Some of 'em are on paper, and some are just in our heads. Look at us. Three gray suits, riding in an elevator." Jack James smiled as Dana continued. "Do we have a dress code? No. We don't need one. We know how to dress, how to act, what to say—and how to keep score. I was talking with Lesley—you know her?"

The elevator stopped, as Bronson said, "Yeah, the softball queen."

"Come on, Bronson, she's not a bad kid," Dana said as the three started down the corridor to the auditorium. "A little naïve, but that's what we were talking about. She wants to be a manager, but she hasn't figured out how to act like one."

Bronson smirked. "She could start by taking off that stupid baseball cap."

"That's what I mean," Dana said, then lowered her voice as the three reached the auditorium. "We all know not to wear a baseball cap—but where do we learn that?"

Bronson rolled his eyes. "Just look around you, Dana. How many high-level management types do you see in team colors?"

Dana purred, "It's true that we don't wear baseball caps, but we *do* carry tennis bags, don't we, Bronson?"

Jack James burst out laughing, and Bronson snarled, "That's different."

"Is it?" Jack asked as they took their seats. "Dana's got a point. But there's more to it than what you wear and what sports you play. It's how we gauge the moves we make all the time. How we score points. If we didn't have rules, we wouldn't know how to keep score."

Dana looked around the room. "Just watch when managers get together. There are always rules. We always keep score."

The CEO entered as Bronson whispered to Dana, "You know, this is getting too theoretical for me. Have you been to one of those management-training seminars lately?" She shot him a glare before turning her attention to the front of the room. Bronson grinned. That gets her back for the tennis-bag comment.

Big Al draped his suit coat over the back of his chair and started rolling up his shirt sleeves. Bronson groaned inwardly, "These meetings drive me crazy. . . ."

Competitors' rituals are like those of the warrior classes in every society. Competition is the name of the game, not only at work but on weekends as well. Remember when running, cross-country skiing, surfing, *Trivial Pursuit*, and the like were activities anyone could participate in for fitness or fun? Then the Competitors realized that performance in all these areas could be *ranked*, and there could be a "Best in the World." Overnight, in all these areas, there developed a class of "real" runners, skiers, and Pursuers of Trivia. For corporate warriors, business is a game, but games are serious. You play to win or not at all.

The Business Meeting

Competitors excel at doing meetings. No matter what you were told in the last Meeting-Effectiveness seminar, the *real* purpose of most meetings is to show connection, bonding, and status—and to demonstrate that you know how to follow the forms and behaviors appropriate to your rank. Conveying information and making decisions are usually low priorities.

The players gather for the Input and Information Meeting, in which the CEO (in shirt-sleeves) asks 250 assembled headquarters employees of Neander-Tek for "input." This is really a meeting about who's boss. When Bob, a new manager in Accounting, raises his hand and asks a question about a production snafu, the CEO nods regally.

"That's an interesting problem. We're working on that," he offers. "It seems that there was a misunderstanding about the number of units called for. There were two figures on the printout. The production run was adjusted to the lower number, to avoid a costly overrun. As it turned out, the number of units required was higher, so we had to add another run. The time it took to gear up for that delayed several shipments, which resulted in the cancellation of a few orders. It's a regrettable incident, and we're doing what we can to see that it doesn't happen again. Next question."

Bob sits down, confused. Yes, he knows that was the problem—and that it had cost big. What he *didn't* know was how

such a mess had happened. Why hadn't anybody caught it, and what was being done to tighten up the controls? Bob thought that discussing this issue might be helpful to everyone. He has some ideas about plant management that he could bring up and. . . . Next question. Input and Information? It's becoming obvious to him that things at Neander-Tek are not as he had expected. It's beginning to drive him crazy.

If somebody asks an embarrassing question (maybe Carl will demand to know why management isn't using his manual), his name will be noted, and the CEO will tell him to talk to his own manager about that. (Bronson *won't* need to be told to rebuke *him.)*

Bob looks around him, bewildered. Why are most of the other managers so uncharacteristically silent? This is supposed to be an *input* meeting, isn't it? (Being a Competitor, he does what Competitors always do when they are confused. Check to see what other Competitors are doing, and do that.)

Bronson, Jack James, Dana—nobody is saying a word. They know that the correct Competitor behavior at "Input" Meetings is to sit and nod. Bob adjusts. Learning by observation is a Competitor's most indispensable talent.

Competitors also know that at certain kinds of meetings, certain behaviors are never allowed.

The real estate sales staff flipped through their books of new listings while Adele, their manager, concluded, ". . . and I see no reason why this can't be a banner season, not only for the agency as a whole, but for each of you, personally. The market is *hot, hot, hot,* and . . . yes, Vinnie?"

Shaking his head, Vinnie held up his listings book and measured its thickness between his thumb and forefinger. "I don't know," he said gloomily. "Looks like pretty slim pickings for this time of year. Now if it were *last* year we were talking about, I would agree with you, Adele, about a hot market. But I sure wouldn't go making any down payments on a new yacht, based on this year's commissions."

As worried frowns began to sprout on the younger agents' faces, Adele stared through Vinnie as if he had suddenly vaporized. "As I was saying," Adele continued in a heartier tone, "there is absolutely *no reason* why this can't be a record-breaking season for *each* and *every one* of us. There is *nothing* this staff can't do, no house this agency can't sell! Why? Because we are *professionals!* We believe in our product, we believe in our clients, and we believe in *ourselves!* Right?"

"Right!" The frowns disappeared and the cheer echoed throughout the agency. What was left of Vinnie got up from his seat and went to pour himself a cup of coffee.

At the sales meeting (an homage to the Myth of Motivation), all is "can-do," and any doubts are the signs of character flaws. The idea here is to say as many positive words as possible and appear motivated. Nay-sayers, or even critical thinkers, need not apply.

Competitors know that some meetings are for participation, where you're expected to share your ideas. Others are merely for attendance—being there and lending the weight of your presence to whatever is going on. At other meetings, Competitors break the rules—ask bold questions and put forth new ideas. They know whether it's time to shut up or put up, to nod silently or to make a statement.

Like all Competitors' activities, the rules here are subtle. You need to know how to size up a meeting. If you don't know what's going on, you watch other Competitors and see what they do before you open your mouth. This isn't quite as simple as it sounds. (Nothing Competitors do is.) When you're checking other Competitors, you have to be sure that they are at the same status level as your own before you start acting as they do.

Before he learned how to play the game, Howard was invited to the board of directors meeting, to represent his section. This was a ritualistic honor. Everybody at the meeting knew that Howard's role was to sit quietly and, when asked, to take no more than three minutes to introduce himself and recite the latest accomplishment of his department. That is, everyone but Howard knew. He let the honor go to his head. The poor clown thought he'd been invited to participate as an equal.

So Howard spoke right up—several times:

". . . Well, that's one possibility, of course, but I think we should consider a higher-profile stance. I mean, why not go for it all? I know I encourage my own guys to think big and, I hate to toot my own horn, but our department record's not too shabby. What I'd do here is. . . ."

". . . That reminds me of a cute story. There were two personnel directors marooned on a desert island with a duck and . . ."

"I'd second that, Nate. . . ." (Everybody else was calling J. Nathaniel Billingsworth, the first VP, by his nickname—but everybody else belonged there.)

As the meeting adjourned, Howard chummily blocked the CEO's exit to tell him there was a great sale on suits at Macy's.

Being invited to a meeting is *not* the same as being asked to join the group. A Competitor who is not acutely aware of differences in status can lose big-time.

The Presentation to Management

Lesley goes into the meeting expecting that the upper managers will listen closely to what she says, ask piercing questions, and take notes—just as her professors did when she defended her master's thesis. She is prepared for anything—except what she gets. Apathy. A couple of people get up and leave. Some talk among themselves (and there will always be some guy in the front row, "listening" with his eyes closed). Many other Believers (including Lesley a few months ago) would have forgotten their lines, dropped overhead slides, and forgotten to hand out reports—so astounding is the difference between the expectation and the reality. Not Lesley (at

least not Lesley *now*). Lesley feels crushed, but she realizes that there is something she needs to learn.

Competitors delight in pointing out differences in status level by being, well, rude. You have to demonstrate that you can take it without blinking.

Lesley keeps her cool and goes on like a trouper. To herself, she says, "This is just the kind of thing Dana was talking about. They're *not* going to see *me* sweat!"

Competitors-to-be are often invited to staff meetings to make presentations. If nobody listens (and usually nobody does until they hear the numbers), then *why* does management keep having these meetings, anyway?

This ritual is a test of a Competitor-in-training's knowledge of form and presence under duress. The purpose of such a presentation is *not* to give information to the upper-level managers in the meeting. Nobody really cares what you say (except what you say about the numbers). They just want to be sure that you know the drill. Like reciting the multiplication tables, you have to be able to show you can do it. Management will leave knowing Lesley's name and that she did well. That's usually enough.

You have to know how presentations are done in your company: Do presenters use overhead transparencies or electronic blackboards? Should your report be bound or unbound? How many copies should you make, and what color paper should you use? How many times should "excellent" or "excellence" appear?

This can be a way for you to show that you can do hard work, by preparing many things that show: lots of handouts that people probably won't read and several overhead transparencies that they won't pay attention to. They *will* pay attention to the fact that you had all that stuff, but the content itself is nearly irrelevant.

If you want to call further attention to content (and to yourself), you can use the same thing that flusters Believers—the unexpected. Explain the numbers, as expected, line by line, on the graph. Right in the middle of your litany, though, switch off the overhead and stand quietly in front of the group for a few moments longer than is comfortable—then, based on the work you've done, make a specific prediction about something that will happen within the next six months. If the prediction comes true, people will remember—but it had better be correct.

Making *positive* predictions is an excellent way to call attention to yourself. Management tends to see negative predictions as evidence of a bad attitude. Persian kings used to behead the bearers of bad news.

Ritual of Combat: Let's Make a Deal

The making of deals is what being a Competitor is all about. It is the ritual combat for which these corporate warriors have been trained. The great lesson of deal-making is that nothing is as it seems, that all the important information is communicated by nuance.

Let's look in on a traditional scene for deal-making: the Strategic Lunch.

In an exclusive private club, two people of power have taken their places across a luncheon table. What they agree to will be binding on their companies. Jack James has donned his power suit—the very cut of which (the more Savile Row, the better), like heraldic crests and horned helmets, is intended to make the enemy feel inadequate and shabby.

Each has done extensive research on the other person and his company, but they act as if this is just a getting-to-know-you meeting. Safely camouflaged behind the "How're the wife and kids?" and "Went skiing at Steamboat two weeks ago. Ever been?" small talk, each is looking for twitches, hesitations, insecurities. Each is waiting for the other to bring up

"The Deal." Mentioning business first is a sign of greater need, a weakness to be exploited.

Jack's most highly guarded secret is the limits of his authority. This is what the other combatant must discover—just how far can this guy go without calling home? Jack realizes that, once you know the limits, then you know where to push.

Even though he'd like to sit down and say, "These are our terms. Take 'em or leave 'em," he won't. (He knows, of course, that the other guy is over a barrel and will have to take 'em.) This would be adding humiliation to defeat, though, so Jack won't do it. (He considers this a "Bronson Tactic," which he regards as more suitable for organized crime than for business.) You never know when you're going to be on the same side at some point down the road. (Also, if you wipe the floor with too many guys, eventually they'll dry off and come looking for you.)

No, Jack is cool, smooth as the imported silk of his tie— especially after the other guy got up and went to the men's room right after Jack ever-so-casually mentioned some terms that might fly. (Ever notice that the rest rooms and the phones at fancy places are always next to each other?)

Other, less smooth Competitors might let on that they knew the guy was backed up close to a wall. (You never get much extra authority from a phone call.) Because his casual reference to "321K" had sent the other guy to the rest room, Jack knew this meant that he had exceeded the upper price that the other guy was authorized to pay, but not by enough to have him call off negotiations then and there. (Master stroke. Jack had used 321K because even numbers sound negotiable; 300 sounds ballpark, but 321 sounds firm.)

Of course, there's no paper on the table; it's an unwritten rule not to. That doesn't matter, though. All Competitors need to be adept at doing math in their heads. (Ever notice how they always know exactly what to tip?)

Never mind that many deals could be made more directly, or even less competitively. This is what Competitors *do*. Each

participant goes back and tells tales of his or her prowess—
"The other guy thinks *he* took *us,* but *we* took *him!*"

When you've made enough deals, perhaps you can write
your own romantic legends, telling in glorious detail about all
of your deals, so that aspiring Competitors will hang on your
every word. Can't you see the title now? Just your last name
and an exclamation point. Valhalla—warriors' heaven.

The Joining of Clubs

In the Competitors' world, you're judged by the company you
keep. Competitors know that there are clubs, and there are
clubs. Some organizations have nothing to do with work and
are exactly what they seem—reflections of people's interests.
Some are service-oriented, some are for dining, and some are
for golf or tennis.

Other groups and gatherings are for self-improvement. If
you can just sign up and go, Competitors probably won't. They
would already know the kind of material that would be presented there. However, if the program is very expensive, and
admission is very selective, *then* you'll see Competitors signing up. Even then, there may be problems if the curriculum is
too factual. Competitors have a lot invested in knowing the
facts, but Competitors' training programs are more often about
Vision, Leadership, Mission, and other Cult of Winning intangibles.

Very competitive business simulations are also big with big
shots. Who you meet at such training programs is as important
as what you learn.

Corporate climbers will join nearly any organization that
has Competitors as members. Members know why they're
there, but ostensibly everybody is there to serve the goals of
the club, or to "get away from business" and not to promote
yourself. Each club has its own goals, purposes, and culture.
As a Competitor, you know how to discern immediately how a
respected member acts. In most of these clubs, it is bad form to
talk business without being specifically asked to do so.

When you are invited (or apply) to join a civic organization, there is the clear understanding that you're joining the club as a representative of your company and that your purpose in joining is to improve the company's image (and probably to get more business). Another reason for joining is to present the company as being highly involved in the community.

Using the membership list for cold calls will brand you as someone unfit for the company of Competitors. Your status is about the same as a student guest at a Rotary Club. The group may treat you well, but you're not initiated as a member.

Many Competitors enjoy these clubs (and some of them actually forget about business while they're there). Because you can't really make friends in your own company if you're the boss or first VP, a club can have many purposes (not the least of which is demonstrating that you're the sort of person who could get into this particular club).

Membership tips off other members that you are roughly of the same social status as they are. They don't have to waste time checking up on you; the membership committee already did. Your job is just to be there and to be a regular person—while never forgetting to form contacts with people who might send you business. (Like most other things Competitors do, they pretend that making contacts really isn't the club system's purpose. If you don't admit it, it isn't so.)

The Warrior's Code of Silence

In all warrior cultures, you have to conceal your pain and your vulnerability. This is especially true among Competitors. Rebels gripe all the time about everything. Believers try to hold it in, but eventually, when they can no longer take it, their complaints and misgivings spill out all over the place. Among Competitors, however, you keep your feelings to yourself.

It was reorganization time at Neander-Tek. What it really meant was laying off important people who would be hard to replace, to save a few bucks on this quarter's bottom line.

Dana had fought against it and called it "short-sighted." She had opposed this kind of management from the beginning, but now it had been decided.

Dana will help the people who are leaving as much as she can. She will sympathize with those who are staying and those whose workloads will double. But she will never tell her subordinates how stupid she thinks the reorganization is.

* * *

Stu's boss stood, smiling, in the doorway of Ken's office next door. The boss pointed a finger at Ken and said, with mock severity, "Pack it in *now*, Kenneth. We're late! You know how eager Katherine is to see your lovely Diane and the kids again." Ken made a great show of shoving his unfinished report into his desk and scrambling into his jacket. The boss looked in and smiled politely at Stu.

"Don't work too long now, Stu," the boss tossed over his shoulder as he and Ken started down the carpeted hallway together.

Stu felt as if he'd been kicked in the gut. Not once, in the four years he'd worked for the guy, had the boss ever invited Stu and Nancy to his house for dinner. This is the second time for Ken. Ken and the boss. Old buddy-buddies. There it is—as plain as if he'd put up a billboard—the Old Man has chosen his successor.

But Stu forced cheer into his voice as he called out a "Good night, y'all!" with false jauntiness, loudly enough for the two to hear him.

He'd just keep smiling until he found another job. He imagined his boss's feigned surprise when he turned in his resignation. "Why, Stuart? Why are you leaving us?" the old phony would ask. Stu would just smile and say, "It's time for new challenges." At Stu's level, things are very civilized.

* * *

The contract talks were a big success. Dana was amazed at Jack James's negotiating skill. (No wonder people called him "El Tigre.") Dana also knew that the company's future depended on this contract—and it had appeared to be hanging by a thread more than once. Dana had been terrified and was dying to find out how El Tigre felt.

Over lunch, she finally asked, "Weren't you ever scared? Did you ever doubt we'd do it? Did you ever think about what would happen if this contract didn't go through?"

"Sure," El Tigre answered. "So what?"

The Worship of the Bottom Line

The one thing that is always apparent and completely measurable to the world of business is the Bottom Line. It is the single fixed star in a universe of ambiguity. No wonder Competitors worship it. They know that a good bottom line buys everything important in the corporate world. The Bottom Line is a jealous and demanding god who insists upon sacrifice.

It's the end of the quarter, and things seem to be looking up for Carl and the rest of Bronson's department. Carl wants to attend a conference in San Francisco; another staffer is excited about a new software program, and someone else wants to hire an assistant to work on a dynamite project. When Carl and the others bring their budget requests to Bronson, he looks at them as if they're crazy. Do they think this company is made of money?

No matter how well things are going, toward the end of the quarter, Bronson cuts travel budgets and doesn't fill positions. He knows that you can't be too rich or too thin, or have a bottom line that is too high.

Competitor managers are famous for ignoring the long run in favor of improving this quarter's numbers. Whatever they want to do can be justified by the ceremonial Invocation against Evil: "If we keep performing at this level, we'll be ripe for a hostile takeover."

On the face of it, this ritual incantation makes sense. If earnings are down, stock prices go down, and some unscrupulous raider can offer the pension funds that own the stock an attractive price. There you have it—the end of the world as Competitors know it. That is something to fear.

The Hostile Takeover is only the latest of evils that lurk in the corporate woods. The usual strategies for avoiding it typically involve short-term belt-tightening, acquisition of debt, poison pills, and other more arcane methods. Companies that have been historically most resistant to hostile takeover have long-term good relationships with their employees and communities, although budget-cutting and poison pills *are* easier.

In a larger sense, takeovers are juust the latest of Competitors' justifications for doing what they've always done, then saying, "Hey, it was our only choice." If hostile takeovers didn't exist, Competitors would have to invent them.

Competitors have intricate rituals and codes of conduct. Really, they are just as obsessed with rules as Believers, but their rules are seldom spoken and never written down. Competitors learn their rules by careful observation. If you can't learn what you're supposed to do by watching, the world of Competitors is not for you. It will drive you crazy.

Does Your Savvy Cost More Than You Think? Is There Too Much of the Competitor in You?

Which of the following are true of you?

1. I sometimes use humorous names for people ("rubes," "bleeding hearts," "pencil-pushers") who are naïve or don't know what's really going on.

You tend to listen to the opinions of the people who count most. Good. This may also mean that you don't listen to 80 percent of the people in your company. Not good. In fact, no good leader disdains the people he or she leads (the Jim Bakker syndrome.) Maybe they know something you don't (even though the Management Mystique says, "Impossible").

2. I don't think about how much sick leave or vacation time I have. I don't see why others should.

Usually, you'll have the time off you need. If not, you can negotiate. However, you may forget that other people have to pay closer attention to what's due them. It is not a sign of weakness to take all the sick leave you're due. Especially if you're sick.

3. In the past five years, I have been significantly promoted at least twice.

You know how to advance, but your competitiveness may lead you to focus more on how to get ahead than on how to do the job well. Also beware of the tendency to assume that the next person in your position will clean up your mess. It worked for Ronald Reagan, but unless your promotions proceed exactly on schedule, oversights have a way of catching up.

4. I play to win. Period.

Way to go! This is a religious requirement in the Cult of Winning. However, if you see everything as a competition, you'll go through life clobbering people—making many enemies and few friends. (The Bronson syndrome.) The friends you have may end up doing to you what Julius Caesar's did to him.

5. Rules for most situations at work are relative to so many factors that any attempt to specify what they are will be incomplete.

Though this is true, there have to be some rules that everybody obeys. If you want to get the best from the people you lead, you'll need to level with them about which rules really count. (Also, not everything is relative.)

6. I have taken no training courses in the past year (although I may have considered a course in economics).

Self-reliance is the way of the Management Mystique. However, if you're perfect, you never learn *anything*—and there *are* things other people can teach you. Sign up for the next human relations course that your company offers, and during the class, keep your eyes open and do the role plays. Most of the people you work with are Believers. If you want to be effective with them, you have to learn their language and customs. Passing them off as Neanderthals can cost you in employee turnover, personality clashes, and time spent tearing out your hair.

7. **There is nothing more important than a good bottom line.**

You may have a good business sense, but you may sacrifice values for expediency. This attitude can foster a short-run view of gain and loss, which can cost big money in the long run. (Ask Detroit.)

8. **I have names for large groups of people whose opinions don't really matter or only matter as a group (peons, the troops, labor).**

You will probably get ahead. You may have a realistic sense of what is expedient. Your attitude, however, is a bit elitist, don't you think? You may miss a good idea that could make you look good if you ignore everything that comes from a peon. The Japanese say, "We will beat you because you think workers are good only for turning screwdrivers." If two heads are better than one, what about two-thousand heads? Can you afford to throw away that many ideas?

9. **My subordinates sometimes think I'm insensitive.**

It's lonely at the top. Good management decisions are sometimes unpopular. On the other hand, your subordinates' opinions are often important. (How about loyalty and trust?) Where do you draw the line? Do you know how much distrust costs you?

10. **OK—I've read the book, I've taken the quizzes—and I figured it out: *I'm* the Neanderthal who's driving *them* crazy!**

In the immortal words of Elvis Presley (who, like many kings, thought he was winning when he was losing), the authors say, "Thank you . . . thank you very much. . . ." Now read the rest of this book to see what you can do to change.

If You Are an Ultra-Competitor

If five or more of the preceding statements are true of you, you are likely to think or behave as a Competitor at work. You probably know how to get things done, how to get ahead, and how to figure out what is rewarded at your company. However, you and your company may be paying more than you realize for your political savvy and commitment to personal excellence. You're probably not as good at encouraging teamwork or perhaps inspiring loyalty and trust in others.

Many companies don't even track turnover. (They consider it a motivation problem in the people who leave, rather than anything management can control.) The companies that do track turnover, however, find that it costs much more than anyone had guessed. They are finding that the main reasons that people leave have nothing to do with how much they are paid or are given in benefits.

As the skills required to do most jobs increase and the trained population decreases, Competitors are beginning to discover that to remain competitive, companies must hold onto their skilled employees. Inspiring the loyalty and trust of Believers and Rebels suddenly has a major dollars-and-cents value. Competitors, ever pragmatic, will be looking for ways to make people really feel a part of the team.

Real teamwork—not the Cargo Cult version practiced in many companies, where *teamwork* means "doing just what the Captain tells you"—begins at home, with loyalty and trust. That means that teamwork has to start with you. This may not be as difficult as it might seem. Like most Competitors, you probably are not a Bronson clone. You want to be a better person and a more effective leader, but some of your beliefs may get in your way. You'll have to learn to trust and value other people, instead of thinking of the workplace as a battlefield and other employees as soldiers or enemies. Here are some ideas to help you remove some of your psychological battle gear.

1. **Ask yourself which team you're a part of.** A *team*, by our definition, is a group of people whose collective goals are more important than the goals of any one person on the team. If there's no group at work whom you trust and whose interests you would place above your own, you probably need to take a page (or an entire chapter) from the Believers' section.

2. **If you manage people, try to put yourself in their shoes.** Make an effort to understand things the way they do. For each person on your staff, list whatever he or she likes most and least about the job. Write down what each wants from the job and from you. Then check out your list with your employees. (If trust is already a problem in your department, you could ask people to write anonymously what they like and don't like, and see how close you come in general terms.)

Pay attention to what you say in memos and written work that you send to your team. Be able to distinguish what you say to give people information and what you say for effect. When you do say something for effect, make it a conscious choice instead of an automatic habit.

3. **If you are a manager, make a special effort to spend time with the people you manage.** Your boss will probably make many other demands on you, but in the end, you may best meet those demands by having a team that is loyal.

4. **Be aware of the Competitors' tendency toward Cargo Cult thinking.** This is the tendency to talk about what you *wish* were true as if it *were* true. Competitors sometimes have a hard time seeing what's in front of them instead of what they want to see. The more you listen to Rebels and Believers on your team, the clearer your vision will become.

5. **Know your own priorities.** It is too easy for Competitors to believe that whatever is in their own best interest is in everyone's best interest and that anyone who disagrees has an attitude problem. (What's good for General Motors is good for America.)

6. **Find a Believer for a mentor.** Run some of your ideas by this person and see what the reaction is. If your actions can

pass the Believer's scrutiny, and you've been honest, then you're apt to be ethical and effective. Trust the Believers you know to tell you what you need to work on.

7. **List the things that you don't tell anybody.** You can do this in your head because, if you're like most Competitors, you'd be uncomfortable about putting them down on paper. Then ask yourself why you can't tell anybody these things. You may be surprised at how little of yourself you feel safe in revealing.

8. **Work on getting around the typical Competitor's short-sightedness.** With every decision you make, practice asking yourself what will be the result ten years down the road. Force yourself to think in terms of the long run, even though there will be demands on you to think short-term.

9. **Do something every day that runs counter to your own self-interest and is good for somebody else—and never tell anybody that you did it.** Try it for awhile and see if it changes your perspective.

(**A note to Believers and Rebels:** Competitors are not savage Neanderthals. Their moral sense is as highly developed as either of the other personality types. Their values are different. If you're thinking, "Competitors don't have any values or ethics," then you know firsthand what Neanderthal thinking feels like. Try going to lunch with a Competitor this week.)

If You Manage Competitors

If you're a Competitor yourself, it's easiest for you to think in terms of individual effort and only one winner. Recognize that if you don't reward teamwork, there will be no team play in a department heavy with Competitors. Here are some ideas for bringing out the best in the Competitors you manage.

1. **Develop an explicit ratings system, and stick to it.** Let the Competitors know what you value, and surprise them by

being consistent with your system. A part of your rating system should be finding out how their subordinates rate them and letting them know that those ratings are as important as how *you* rate them.

2. **Maneuver them into team-playing situations.** Make sure that their important goals rely on teamwork. If one member stands out from the team, don't be so hasty in seeing this person as the most capable member. His or her major skill might be in attracting your attention and pleasing you. You will have to decide whether that is what you want to reward or whether the company requires other skills.

3. **Check the day-to-day aspects of their jobs.** Competitors tend to pay attention to the flashy stuff and sometimes let the day-to-day things slide. This usually doesn't catch up with them for a long time. Realize that Competitors will figure out right away what's important to you and what you value. You will have to work to make your values, goals, and rewards consistent with the company's.

If You Work for a Competitor

That's what most of this book is about. Your boss probably is a Competitor, and it is to your benefit to learn his or her language by paying particular attention to the next part of this book. Here is a summary of our suggestions so far for working more effectively with a Competitor boss.

1. **Demand priorities.** Ask for clarification of goals.

2. **Don't rely on your boss's memory.** Keep a file on what you've been told to do and what you've accomplished. Update it monthly. Promote yourself even to your boss.

3. **Don't expect your boss to follow your standards of fairness.** If you do, you're apt to be disappointed.

4. **Develop your own sources of information.** Your boss is supposed to be the person who supplies you with what you need to know—but Competitors think you should already

know what you don't know. You have to ask. Develop other reliable sources of information besides your boss.

5. **Demand regular meetings for which you set the agenda.** This is the time for close study of the Competitor you work for. These sessions will give you the chance to ask questions and gather specifics from your boss. Like most Competitors, he or she is probably hard to pin down. Use these meetings to update your boss on your work—and don't miss the obvious opportunity to promote yourself.

6. **Don't nickel-and-dime your boss to death.** Go to the wall for the issues that are important, but also develop the capacity for letting some things slide. Assume you're allowed one complaint a year—and choose it wisely.

7. **Take risks, take the initiative, and take the heat if you're wrong.**

8. **Allow your boss to criticize you without your going off the deep end.** Accept criticism quietly and with dignity.

9. **Don't demand constant reassurance.** There is nothing Competitors dislike more than overly dependent employees.

10. **Make your boss look good.**

PART FIVE

The Rules of the Game

13

Ogres in the Front Office

"I Don't Have Any Problem with Authority in General. It's Just That My Boss Is an Incompetent, Petty Horse's Rear End."

Check out the parking lot of almost any business. You can probably pick out the Rebels' vehicles by looking for the bumper stickers that say, "Happiness is seeing your boss's picture on a milk carton."

Hating your job and your boss is so common that people actually make big money on bumper stickers that proclaim this feeling. Rebels let their hostility hang right out there. If they think their boss is jerk, they'll stick the message on their car for everybody to see. Also, more often than not, they *do* think their boss is a jerk.

Believers and Competitors may have the same negative feelings toward the boss, but they show their dislike in subtler ways. A Believer (such as Frank in the following example) might go upstairs to let upper management know "what's really going on down here."

In the general manager's office, Frank began tentatively, "I just had to see you, sir. You said your door is always open. . . . Well, maybe you don't know that morale is at an all-time low in accounting. People are sick a lot. One guy left, as you know, and there are at least three more who are thinking of leaving. . . . You see, it's Bronson. He just doesn't seem to know how to run a department. . . ."

Competitors, on the other hand, subtly imply that their superior's intelligence or competence is not quite what it should be.

Franklin, the division head, has taken over the meeting again with his prognostications. More ideas about what the economy is going to do and how the company can turn a real profit by making the right financial moves. Blah, blah, blah. . . .
Dana turns to Jack James and rolls her eyes. Jack knows exactly what Dana means: Here he goes again; we'll be here another 45 minutes, at least.

There are two basic reasons for this widespread dislike of the boss. The first is that, below our professional facades, many of us still carry around inner Rebels: Our inner Rebels haven't resolved our teenage authority issues and still get angry when people tell us what to do.

These inner Rebels show up in the vehemence and immediacy with which we get upset over anything the boss does that restricts our freedom. It's a reflex that flares up; the boss may have to answer not only for whatever he or she did, but also for many of the unavenged wrongs of our *parents* as well.

"I know he was right," Marie said to her husband that night. "But when he criticized me in that soft voice, he re-

minded me so much of my father. Daddy was such a perfectionist—nothing I did was right. I could never please him. Why did I have to get a boss who's so much like him?"

Marie's husband wondered, but would never say out loud, why her last three bosses—all very different people—reminded her so much of her father.

Sometimes, dislike of the boss has nothing to do with who the boss is or what the boss does. At other times, though, the problem arises exactly because of the things bosses do. Most bosses are Competitors, and many people don't like the typical behaviors and attitudes of the Competitor culture.

On the other hand, Competitors tend to disregard and underestimate non-Competitors. Because they believe in self-selection, they often give an edited version of the truth, believing that if people have what it takes, they'll figure out the whole truth, based on the little bits they can put together. If they don't have what it takes, then they don't matter anyway. Though most Competitors want to be effective leaders, their Competitor beliefs sometimes keep them from being as effective as they could be.

Usually, in companies run by Competitors, being tough is valued, and being liked by subordinates is a very low priority. The important part of managers' jobs is pleasing people at their own level or higher. Managers get no particular rewards for instilling loyalty into their staffs—just for keeping them quiet and producing a good bottom line. The one place in which Competitors never compete is in a popularity contest with the people who work for them. This can, of course, lead to excesses—indulging one's own need for status by taking advantage of those below. The power trip.

Bronson isn't what anybody would call a people person. Once a year—at the office picnic—he says people are important, but the rest of the time his focus is on the product. He tends to run roughshod over employees.

People have told him for years that he's a tough S.O.B. to work with, and Bronson takes pride in that. He pays little attention to other people's feelings and has never concentrated on trying to motivate or understand them. His approach has been to tell people, *"Do It."* If they didn't do it, he got rid of them.

His idea of a motivational talk is to bring people in and rake them over the coals for 45 minutes, just to let 'em know who's boss (as if they didn't know).

He delights in calling his managers at any time, even at home, and asking at the spur of the moment for a detailed rundown on the most complicated projects. If somebody's not up to the minute on an area, that's the one Bronson hammers away at, suggesting that the manager has no idea what's going on in her or his department.

His philosophy of motivation can be summed up in one word—fear.

Bronson seems the archetypical Boss from Hell. While Competitor culture does not encourage people to act like him, it doesn't discourage it, either. Our "inner Rebel" expects such an abuse of power from any authority figure. When employees detect even the slightest hint of this kind of behavior, most of them will react strongly. Rebels will start making mistakes and having accidents. Believers will develop stress symptoms (which they conspicuously ignore) and then run to a higher authority. Competitors will begin intrigues and start covering their rear ends.

All of these reactions will make the boss angrier and confirm everyone's view of the situation.

Dealing with Ogres in Power

Some people (such as Bronson) just can't handle the responsibility that goes with power. They can't resist the temptation to push around their subordinates, and they seem to take perverse delight in the discomfort of others. They don't care about the feelings of the people who work for them. They hand out precious little praise, but plenty of criticism—especially when everybody is watching. Unlike a mere intimidator, who uses the threat of aggressive action as an attempt to control other people, the hard-core ogres usually have no goal in mind, other than indulging their own sadistic desires.

What do you do if you report to one of these corporate dictators? Obviously, the first and best answer is to look for another job, but if you don't want to choose this option, then consider making the best of a bad situation.

To deal with a tyrannical boss effectively, your head has to win out over your heart. If you respond emotionally to a petty tyrant, you will at least be miserable, and you risk being fired. You have to _plan_, not merely react. Your own beliefs can kill you. Ogres are not playing by your rules—or by any non-Competitor's rules or codes of honor.

The most dangerous strategy is to go over your boss's head and hope the big boss will side with you. This is as risky as trying to corner a wounded wolverine. To go over the head of this kind of boss, you need a case that's strong enough to ensure that the beast will be banished forever—because a wounded ogre is the most dangerous animal in the corporate jungle.

Sara actually has a tape recording of Bronson chewing her out, acting like a maniac. She knew it was coming and turned on her microcassette. _Now_ the big boss will listen. Bronson was running true to form, cursing, raving, making no sense. For once, Sara almost enjoyed it, knowing that she had proof.

She took the tape to Franklin, Bronson's boss—but he wouldn't even listen to it. He was angry because of what he called Sara's "sneaky tactics." Now Sara is sitting at her desk, sweating, because she knows Franklin will tell Bronson. Then what?

Unfortunately, few cases of abuse are strong enough to motivate big bosses to fire their petty tyrant underlings. Ogres such as Bronson often do quite well with the bottom line, so their bosses tend to give them quite a bit of leeway. If you plan to attack from above, realize it's a kill-or-be-killed situation. If you're not ready for combat, the following suggestions might help.

- _Don't expect the ogre to change._ Be realistic. Accept what your boss is like, and don't expect him or her to start acting differently. Don't be disappointed; be prepared.

Dee keeps hoping Bronson will change. Every day she goes to him with reasonable requests and comments. Sometimes, he answers reasonably, but most of the time he just blows up. Dee never learns.

- _Don't wave a red flag in front of the bull._ When someone in authority is unreasonable, most of us feel like doing the very things that get under his or her skin. For example, if the boss is a lunatic about punctuality, coming in two or three minutes late or taking a longer lunch may be temporarily satisfying, but it will leave the boss with a score to settle with you. Follow the rules, no matter how arbitrary.
- _If possible, develop competence in an area in which your boss is unfamiliar._ This will make you more indispensable and may lead to giving you some latitude because your skills are so important.

Griff knows the regulations cold. He knows what the government says you can and cannot do in every area. Griff doesn't make the mistake of being the champion of the government; he never shouts, "You can't do that!" Nonetheless, when Bronson asks, Griff can recite chapter and verse. He knows the rules, and he knows which ones are enforced. Griff can get away with a lot because Bronson needs him.

- _Transcend temper._ Most ogres delight in criticizing their employees in front of others. When this happens to you, meet it quietly and with dignity. Maintain eye contact, and resist the temptation to explain. Your best strategy is to listen to what the boss has to say, ask what he or she wants you to do, and get out of the situation as quickly as possible.

Here it comes again, Sara thought, her stomach tightening, as Bronson came charging down the hall, brandishing Sara's report. She had been through this so many times before—being chewed out for a minor error in front of everyone.

Many office tyrants say that they want employees who will stand up to them. We have never known any that would tolerate it, especially in front of an audience.

- _Know what's going on in your department._ Be ready at all times to cite facts and figures. Ogres love to get their information by cross-examining their employees—at the ogre's beck and call—_not_ by listening to their employees' presentations.
- _Warn your family._ Let your family know that your boss may ask you to do things at inconvenient times, such as the middle of the night or two days into your vacation. Make sure your family recognizes that you'd rather be with them than toiling for the ogre.

    Resist the temptation to treat your family the way your boss treats you, letting the abuse flow downhill on the path of least resistance. Also, don't turn your boss into the family villain with daily tales about the awful things he or she did. It will only make you feel worse, and there will be pressure (though it may be subtle) from home for you to "stand up to the idiot."
- _Avoid the temptation to blame._ There's nothing more tempting than getting together with fellow employees and talking about atrocities. This feels good while it's happening, but it makes the situation harder to live with in the long run. The more you talk about how bad things are, the worse you will feel.

- *Keep records of what you're asked to do.* When you're told to do something, make sure that what you're asked to do is clear. Revise your MBO form, and send it for initialing. Log conversations and directives. You may need to refer to them later. This does not mean keeping a list of infractions. Nobody will read it but you and your cosufferers. (Despite how important the list is to you, your CEO probably won't care.) All it will do is keep the coals of anger burning in your heart. you already have enough of that, don't you think?

  The other person who might read the list is your lawyer. One of the most destructive fantasies in these situations is the vague idea that some day, you'll sue the ogre's pants off. Before you go further with any idea of a lawsuit, *consult a lawyer to find out whether you have a case.* If your lawyer asks you to keep a list, fine. If you aren't represented by counsel, the list will only harm you.

- *Develop the ability to assess your own performance.* Ogres are quick to blame and slow to praise. To keep your own sanity, you have to be able to know how well you're doing without being told. Pay close attention to your goals and objectives and to how well you meet them. This is partly a way to defend yourself, but it's also a way to convince yourself that you're doing a good job, even if you're unappreciated.

Linda keeps her ducks in a row. She knows how she stacks up against others in her field. Even though Bronson does nothing but criticize, Linda knows that she's as fast and as knowledgeable as anybody else in this company—or others.

Linda attends professional conferences and knows, despite what Bronson says, that she's good. She's just waiting for a chance to transfer. The company is great. It's just Bronson who's the problem.

- *Demand top dollar.* Many ogres are willing to pay for the privilege of pushing their employees around. If you're going to stand firm in any area, it probably should be salary. Make a coherent case, and don't be afraid to push. This is one area in which your boss is likely to understand your view and will probably be willing to pay for his or her self-indulgence. One person's salary is "small potatoes" to the ogre, especially if no one else is willing to fill the position. Expect to negotiate, however—so start high.

Maybe you've read these suggestions and are saying to yourself, "Well, you're right that my boss is an ogre, but I can't do any of the things you've written about." If this is the case, however impossible you think it is to change jobs, _this_ job is probably costing you too much.

The Laundry-Hoop Approach

Most bosses are not as ogrelike as Bronson. Our rebellious side expects behavior like his and can detect it at levels of one or two parts per million. What we usually see is more subtle. Competitors are often undone by their own belief systems. The unwritten management code—the Management Mystique— requires managers to be smarter than those they manage. If you think you're smarter, there's often a temptation to try to trick people into doing what you want them to do.

An item on the market—a laundry bag attached to a toy basketball hoop—illustrates the kinds of mistakes managers make when they try to trick people. The laundry hoop is marketed as a way to get children to pick up their dirty clothes and put them in the laundry basket—because it will be so much fun! Any child with more intelligence than an unwashed sock will realize in 10 seconds that this is a trick.

Leaving laundry on the floor gives a child a certain amount of control and power, a way to fight back against parents. No self-respecting child is going to give that up for the sake of shooting a pair of grass-stained jeans through the plastic circle. If parents are serious about getting their children to pick up the laundry, the parents are going to have to do some serious negotiating. The price for having the laundry picked up is acknowledging the limits of parental authority—and this is as it should be.

Let's look at an example of the "laundry-hoop" approach at work:

A large bank designed an incentive system for its clerical staff. In announcing the system's adoption, the CEO said, "When a position comes open, you won't even want it filled! You'll want the work for yourself!" More work, more money.

The equation was simple, but the employees weren't. Very quickly, they learned how to maximize their gain by doing simple, easily completed tasks. The more difficult jobs went begging. Over time, less and less work was done, because people started hoarding the information needed to do the easier jobs. What had begun as a simple trick to increase productivity almost ground the bank's operation to a halt. The bank ended up having to create two new positions to clean up the mess.

You can't trick people into doing more work. People will beat the system every time. The real trick would have been to include some of the staff members who would be working under the incentive system in the planning. They would have seen in a minute how to beat it.

Unfortunately, hard-core Competitor managers have to see themselves as omniscient, so they don't ask other people's opinions—it would spoil the trick. The incentive system disregarded what the clerical people considered important and valuable about themselves. Instead, management substituted a naïve competitive system that was based on their own thinking: "If Competitors like us had to do boring, repetitive work like this, what would make us do more of it?" With enough knowledge and planning, the bank could have made its system work. The problem was management's apparent belief that they were so much smarter than their employees that they could easily manipulate them.

The laundry-hoop approach was intended as a motivational tool to trick Believers and Rebels into doing what management wanted. It ended up tossing out several important motivators for the other groups—pride in doing a structured job well and having their own duties; being a part of an organized team—and put in a single, less effective motivator: money. Management assumed, as many Competitors do, that competition is more effective than teamwork. (Competitors have a very tough time believing in teamwork.)

The bank management also assumed that the clerical work was so unimportant that it required little coordination—just get more of it done by fewer people. The whole system implied that people were not working hard enough. Neither Believers nor Rebels are trying to get out of working. Believers especially pride themselves on working as hard as they can. When that was not acknowledged, the Believers saw it as a declaration of war. Because of the conflict (which was based on Competitors' misperceptions), the bank had to pay the price in lower morale and decreased productivity. For the Rebels, the situation was nothing new—just another day at the battlefront.

Competitors' underestimation of non-Competitors can sometimes be a fatal flaw. How many expense-account Competitors do you think are in trouble now because they thought they could outsmart that most Believer of institutions—the IRS? At this moment, how many are desperately hoping they don't get audited?

What If You're a Boss?

Dana's first management position, a promotion to department head, was a real shock to her. The people she had worked with the day before were now reporting to her. She thought their relationship would continue as it had—friendship, trust, camaraderie, and all that. Was she wrong!

Her coworkers had always liked her good ideas, but when she became their boss, every change brought mutters that it

was better the old way and maybe Dana didn't know what she was doing.

She was conscientious about giving praise, but the first time she had to reprimand one of her old colleagues—even though she did it word for word out of *The One-Minute Manager*—he acted as if she had no right to comment on his work! Then for the next week, the conversations in the coffee room stopped abruptly when Dana walked in. What was going on? Those people were her friends. Weren't they?

Most new managers discover, as Dana did, that when you're the boss, people react more to *what* you are than to *who* you are. What do your employees think of you as a boss? Do they think you're competent, fair, and honest? Do they feel appreciated and valued? Or do their bumper stickers proclaim variations of "Take my boss . . . Please!"

National polls suggest that a significant number of American employees think their bosses are not particularly competent—and are definitely unethical. In fact, so many people give their bosses low marks that this society doesn't even like people who like their bosses. They're labeled "yes men" or "brown-nosers"—and it's not just the Rebels who do the labeling.

Rebels—and most of us still have a little bit of the Rebel inside us—believe that "Nobody can tell me what to do. People in authority don't know what they're doing. They're out for themselves, not for me."

Being a boss is hard enough without having to contend with people's leftover authority problems. Unfortunately, if you want to be successful as a manager, that's exactly what you have to do.

How do you cope with the "I hate my boss" attitude if you're a manager? First, realize that some of the authority-related problems you're dealing with are not your fault. Many employees simply have problems accepting any kind of control. If you, as their boss, start getting bent out of shape every time you meet resistance, you're in for a lot of difficulty. Resistance to authority is a fact of life—in the boardroom as well as on the shop floor. (On the shop floor, they admit it.)

No matter who you are as an individual, most people have certain internal expectations about bosses. Their "inner Rebels" tell them that bosses are out for Numero Uno, that they don't care what their employees think or feel, and that their main concern is wringing as much work as possible out of their people, no matter what the personal cost.

Most of the time, they don't really believe it, and they can evaluate you objectively, but if you do anything, intentionally or not, that fits the negative stereotype, you'll create a setback in the relationship with your Believers.

Real Rebels probably will behave the same way toward you, no matter how fair you are. They respond more to the authority figure in their head than to the real boss in the office down the hall. They need structure and external contingencies to function best. (Actually, there are some steps you can take to manage Rebels more effectively, described in our section on Rebels.)

If you're the boss, everything you say and do will be taken out of context and out of proportion. There will be times when the slightest criticism will make you an enemy for life, and the smallest bending of the rules will have people spreading rumors that you are incompetent and corrupt. If you've ever been through this kind of situation, you know how demoralizing it can be. The relationship between superiors and subordinates, like the one between parents and children, is seldom rational.

Many managers take the irrational behavior of their employees as evidence that there is indeed a war on. There *is* a real discrepancy in attitudes and value systems among Rebels, Believers, and Competitors. They don't approve of each other, so they don't listen to each other. They can often justify hostile actions because they firmly believe that *they* are *right* and the *other guy* is *wrong*. Unless you make a concerted effort to avoid it, this conflict is inevitable.

What kind of effort do you make? What can help you? That's where the science of management comes in. Amidst all the theories, there are certain basic principles that come up again and again:

- *Persuade and cajole, rather than give direct orders.*
- *Take the time to listen.*
- *Delegate power.*
- *Back your people's decisions.*
- *Use more praise than punishment.*
- *Play by the rules.*

Everybody knows these principles, and everybody forgets them. It's much easier to perpetuate the conflict than to avoid it. All we have to do is what comes naturally. All that's left, boss, is you alone in the dark with your own personal values— and one simple guarantee: If you respect your employees, they (even some of the Rebels) will respect you.

American business is beginning to realize the high cost of managing money instead of people. All of a sudden, Competitors are dusting off their management textbooks because they are seeing that those "Neanderthal" theories have a real dollars-and-cents value in today's marketplace.

14

The Manager as Professor and King

Dealing with Benevolent Dictators and Corporate Royalty

Trickery isn't always the only way that bosses make subordinates feel resentful because the bosses believe themselves to be smarter than their subordinates.

In Bronson's folder was yet another consultant's brochure and cover letter. (Don't they ever learn?) This one offered "management training" for all the supervisory people in the department.

At the staff meeting, Bronson waved the brochure in the air. "I have nothing against this proposal. I just don't see why you want *management* training.

"Management is the easiest thing in the world," he said with the kind of smirk that meant he thought he was making a self-deprecating joke (a technique the last consultant had suggested). "All it takes is telling other people what to do!"

Nobody laughed.

Bronson was right. Management *is* easy to do—badly. Bronson thinks he is the teacher; he does *not* think that *he* needs to be taught.

The Kindly Dictator

Do you ever have the feeling at work that you're still in school, because your boss's management style reminds you of the professor you had in Sociology 202? If you work for this kind of person, you probably have been made to understand that there is only one professor in charge of this "class," and he or she has *all* the power. When a manager's training or a company's culture doesn't offer any clear models for leadership, people tend to use the models they already know. For most managers, aside from their own families, the classroom is the organizational structure they know best.

Robin J. Johnston, Ph.D., CPA, runs the finance department at American Excellence & Quality. Dr. J. was an A+ accountant—still is, when he gets to work with spreadsheets. As an administrator, though, he leaves a bit to be desired.

He says he doesn't believe in bureaucratic red tape and that he likes to keep his operation simple. Everybody with an MBA is the head of something in his department. This means that the lines of authority are so blurry that they're meaningless. Dr. J. really runs everything to suit himself.

In some areas, such as employee relations or budget management for his department, he couldn't care less. He has Jerry Smith for that. In issues involving other people's spreadsheets and profit-and-loss statements, however, no detail is small enough to escape his scrutiny. Dr. J. demands accurate, comprehensive printouts on *all* departments—whenever, however, and wherever he needs or wants them.

This up-to-the-minute knowledge of everyone's bottom line (usually before they know it) is the cornerstone of his power in the organization. If he needs figures right away, he will get someone from his staff to access another department's data program to get what he needs. Nobody knows how much data has been dumped because of this procedure, which Dr. J. calls "cross training." Everybody else calls it "screwing up my

work." (There are other names as well.) He will also access people's work in progress and send "helpful hints" to them through computer mail.

Even though he has people in supervisory positions, he will often take aside their subordinates and lecture them on the way they *should* be doing their jobs. Dr. J. is often right, but the damage he does to the chain of command is nowhere near being offset by the educational value of his lessons. His meddling drives everyone crazy.

Everybody knows he's a nice man and that he means well, but he's so hard to work for. He cares little about formal management, so he doesn't require that his program managers provide for their staffs' supervisory needs. The managers don't have much power to do so, anyway.

Dr. J. says, "We're just one big happy family here." This means that he's Dad, and he gets to meddle in everybody else's business—for their own good, of course.

At least Dr. J. means well, but not everyone says that about Jerry Smith. When Dr. J. became department director, Smitty recognized a power vacuum when he saw it and got himself appointed Assistant Director because he understood "personnel issues." Smitty takes care of money and schedules, and he actually runs the department.

People who please Dr. J. and Smitty always have all the resources and people they need. Those who disagree end up finding their particular part of the operation "restructured" so they have to share office space, secretaries, and even printers. That drives people nearly to homicidal frenzy, but if the money isn't there, what can Smitty do? (If you go to Dr. J. with a complaint, he'll say, "Ask Smitty." Smitty's job is to protect Dr. J. from such trivial issues.)

Both Dr. J. and Smitty like to have intimate "collegial" discussions with people in their department. This means that the two bosses try to corner people and find out what they really think about the rest of the staff. They maintain their power by knowing all the gossip. If you tell them something, it will come back to haunt you.

These "classroom" organizations usually are headed by a benevolent dictator who is strongly identified with the company. The professor's value is based on the performance of the entire organization or division (the class). No detail is too small, and nothing is too private.

Often, the professor is supported by a sidekick, a corporate "second banana" such as Smitty, who has seen an opportunity for power by accepting a role as adviser or troubleshooter for the boss. The second banana's real function is to justify whatever the professor wants to do and to handle all the messy financial or personnel-related details.

The professor clearly recognizes his or her responsibility to the "students" and frequently makes reassuring comments such as "Everybody's ideas are important," "My door is always open," or "We're all one big happy family here." (Within this family, the teacher always gets to be Dad or Mom.)

Dr. J. doesn't have much good to say about formal corporate structure. His comments make him sound like a liberal, but the real reason he doesn't like structure is that it implies the sharing of power. It's not that he's unwilling to share power, really. . . . He's just waiting until people can handle it as well as he can—after they "graduate," for instance.

Dr. J. really doesn't understand typical organizational structure. Instead, he tends to set up administrative nightmares, such as two research directors for the same project, or a "quality control" panel (with no supervisor) that functions like a seminar, endlessly discussing the issues, rather than making any decisions. Structure doesn't really matter to Dr. J. It doesn't make any difference what the organizational chart says, because *he* will always make all the meaningful decisions, anyway.

Professors don't realize that at the top of the hierarchy, they are supposed to give directions downward to the people at the next level, who direct the next level, and so on. These professor—managers consider it their duty to be all over the classroom, helping everyone solve problems. They never realize that this management style causes more problems than it solves, because, for them, practicality and efficiency are less important than "doing it right."

These professors are usually very bright people. Many of their professional decisions may be sound, but the organization as a whole is only as good as the boss's judgment on a particular day. They never realize that they are wasting vast resources and causing great inefficiency by not allowing other people to make decisions. When the professor is out of town, for example, people might as well not come to class because nothing gets done.

In classroom-type organizations, there is usually a marked division in status between professionals and nonprofessionals. The professionals at least are asked what they think before the professor does what he or she wants to.

Dr. J. thinks of secretaries as, well, servants, rather than as members of the department in their own right. If a dispute arises between anybody and a secretary, Dr. J. asks the secretary to make allowances for "professional temperament"— which means that he expects the secretary to give in.

Decisions about hiring, firing, promotion, and, especially, salaries are as arbitrary as the grading was in many of your college classes. It's not that these professor—managers are consciously trying to exploit people or to keep control of all the power. Usually, they just haven't thought about how else things might be run. They usually are such perfectionists that they assume that they can do everything better than anyone else. Mistakes are very difficult for them personally, so they never give anybody else a chance to make them.

Professor—managers are often overly involved with how people feel about their jobs and how people feel about them.

It hurts Dr. J. deeply to be told he is unfair or in any way difficult to deal with. He will say, "My door is always open,"

but nobody ever uses the open-door policy to talk about real feelings, for fear of hurting Dr. J.'s feelings—and for fear of getting the equivalent of a "D." Nobody really gets fired, but when grades drop below "C" level, it is expected that people should decide on their own to drop out—or Smitty might discover that there is not enough money to pay them full time.

When a group of "professors" is running a business, expect strong conflicts over minor issues, turf battles, power trips, and, often, the sacrifice of the slow learners.

If this sounds like the organization where *you* work, the first thing to do is to recognize what the structure really is. Understand that, whatever the chart says, *to make the grade, you have to please the teacher.* The following tips may help you to do this.

- *Ask questions; don't give opinions.* Realize that the person in charge sees the manager's role as being the provider of knowledge *and* tends to confuse knowledge and authority. If you seem to have *"too much knowledge,"* the professor might think of you as a threat—just as in school.

  You can get professor—managers to change a bit, but you have to do it within their own frames of reference. Get the professor to teach you about such things as what the organizational chart really means, how certain kinds of decisions are made, what must be done when the teacher is out of town, or, perhaps, how other, similar companies are managed. Professors learn best when they have something—or someone—to teach.

  Some professors will be willing to follow an organizational chart and share power as an exercise or experiment. They probably won't react well if you tell them there are other ways to manage, but if you *ask them* what those ways might be, they might discover for themselves that they are running a very inefficient operation. They are usually pretty bright, but often, like Sherlock Holmes (who never realized that the earth revolved around the sun), they are totally ignorant of matters outside their specialty.

- *Avoid any kind of attack.* Professor—managers usually have oversized egos and will fall apart and become quite irrational if they are attacked, especially in front of a group. They also will tend to respond irrationally to any attacks against their sidekick. Professors have to be right. They can learn new things and change their opinion based on new knowledge, but they can never be wrong.

- *Resist the temptation to participate in evaluating other "students."* Professors will often engage you in conversations about how other people perform, and they will just as often repeat the information you give them. They think of it as research.

It's possible to get along quite well in a classroom-structured business, especially if you're interested in pursuing your own work with a minimum of disturbance. You will be most likely to rise to the top of the class if you remember not to argue with the teacher, to follow instructions carefully, and to get your work in on time. (Neatness counts.)

CEOs as Royalty

Arthur Cole is the chairman of the board, but everyone calls him "The King." He lives in a castle on the bluff across the river—you can just see the turret from the parking lot. He calls himself "the general," loves military metaphors, and calls meetings "to address the troops."

The company may be having its problems, but King Arthur is still pulling down a million per year, plus who knows how much in perqs.

Last week, he closed one of the smaller plants in Riverdale. "Another battle in the war against protected manufacturing overseas," he decreed. "Another strategic retreat."

King Arthur and his upper management court don't seem to feel the effects of battle. *Their* jobs (and their bonuses) are secure. In contrast, a lot of the workers nearer to the battlefield know there's a war going on. The King's memos advocate companywide belt-tightening as a way to fight back, but nobody has noticed that *his* belt is getting any tighter.

When he was interviewed by a major business mag, Arthur spoke gravely of his responsibilities to the organization and his plans for bringing it through the difficult time ahead. He said he knew his people were behind him, and things were just beginning to turn around. The stock was climbing back up in response to his new no-nonsense approach to cost cutting.

Then the King and his court announced the sale of the company to a West-German-based conglomerate. Arthur had engineered a sweet deal for the stockholders and himself. He floated away on his golden parachute, a hero to his courtiers but a villain to the employees he had sold down the river.

This King Arthur, of course, is an extreme case, but it drives employees in many companies crazy when they wonder whether their CEOs and upper management think they were born to royalty. Employees know that their upper management can do exactly as Arthur did; they aren't bound to protect employees. One thing non-Competitors do know is that when Competitors say "the company," they often mean themselves and the stockholders.

Competitors love to set up hierarchies. From the playground to the boardroom, there's always a top dog and an underdog. Throughout history, most people have loved and respected their royalty and believed that the monarchs deserved special treatment. The hatred of kings is historically a very new concept and limited mostly to countries that were once colonies.

Few of us have any quarrel with the honor accorded to the great heroic kings and queens of the past, Arthur (the other one), David, and Victoria. We Americans can even understand and condone it when some of our politicians, and certainly our great sports figures and entertainers, act like royalty— because we see them as really representing us. We do, however, resent CEOs acting like royalty because not only are they not really monarchs, but also *we* aren't really their subjects.

Real monarchs have a mythic bond with their subjects. Quite literally, they would die for each other. Monarchs pledge to protect and care for their subjects, who offer love and honor in return for that protection.

In business, there is no bond of mutual protection or representation. In most companies, the real subjects are the stockholders. They're the ones whom the CEO pledges to protect. The Believers and Competitors who do the king's work are mercenaries, the hired soldiers. Even though they have some value, they can be sacrificed for the good of the real subjects. When the war is over, the soldiers just go back where they came from or are left, bleeding, on the battlefield.

CEOs aren't really monarchs, but they have taken on the trappings of a mythic role that isn't theirs. They are pretenders to the throne, and it is the pretense that makes us resent them. A mercenary may respect his general, not because he is the symbolic leader, but because the general shares the risks of the battlefield and lives as the soldiers live.

Many modern CEOs have problems with mixing their metaphors—giving themselves the title of general, but taking the privileges of kings. Respected generals never had golden parachutes, nor did they typically switch from one army to another. They were in the battle with their soldiers, and the swords could kill *them* just as easily.

It is hard for Competitors to pay attention to the needs of the people below them. Their mythology and values subtly push them toward seeing management as taking better care of the company's financial resources—its numbers—than of its biggest investment—its people. Managing people can be an afterthought. The Competitors who become responsive managers do so because this is important to them—not because anyone is making them develop their "people skills." The others, like Bronson, tend to do what comes naturally—drive people crazy.

15

The Language
of Management

Why do Rebels, Believers, and Competitors have so much trouble communicating with one another?

The governor reclines on his chaise, absently plucking at his lyre (they were all the rage on his last visit to Rome). "What next?" he asks his chamberlain in a voice that resonates with the right balance of decisiveness and boredom (also big in Rome).

"Some ambassadors from the mountain provinces, your excellency."

The ambassadors are ushered into the chamber. (Where do they get those outfits?) They stand silently, shifting from foot to foot.

"Get on with it. . . . I'm listening," the governor says with a hint of pique.

"They don't speak Latin, your excellency," says the chamberlain. "We have an interpreter."

The governor rolls his eyes skyward. "If they don't speak Latin, surely they don't expect to talk to *me.*"

In the Roman Empire, all important business was conducted in Latin. If you didn't learn Latin, it was proof you weren't management material. Today, Competitors who are obsessed with winning and conquest tend to handle the communications problem with the same flair and finesse that conquerors always have. To them, it's a perfect self-selection device: If you don't know how to ask for it, you don't get it.

People in business speak several different languages. To understand your coworkers, you need to know which language they're speaking and how to translate it. If you can't or don't, you'll never figure out the moans and groans of these Neanderthals. The first language you need to recognize and learn to translate is the code that Competitors use when speaking to outsiders, either to those outside the company or to non-Competitors in-house.

The Language of the Press Release

At the Competitors' level, it is recognized that this language has many meanings, but those meanings are carried more in nuance and choice of words than in literal content. This is the language Competitors speak to people they don't have to level with.

Read the following press release, to see whether you already have some fluency in this language.

—PRESS RELEASE—

John Charles Doe III, vice chairman of Worldwide Corp. and president of its Worldwide American Co. subsidiary, said today that he would retire in May, seven months short of his 65th birthday.

Worldwide also announced that from now until his retirement, Doe will undertake a study of Worldwide's changing business environment to help it set its future direction.

To free Doe for his new assignment, Worldwide said several of his principal administrative responsibilities would be reassigned to other executives.

Were you able to read the real message? If so, you may be management material (i.e., Competitor-speak may be your native tongue). At the very least, you may be able to translate for your less fluent fellow non-Competitors. (*Translation:* "This guy is senile, and we have to get rid of him.")

The language of the press release—the words that are on the record—has three simple rules:

1. Everything (even criticism) is presented in varying shades of positive.
2. Everything you say about yourself and the company indicates that your actions are motivated by the noblest of reasons.
3. You don't accept blame for anything negative because nothing negative has been said.

This language needs to be scanned to find out what's really going on, rather in the way that news articles in the Chinese press are scanned, not so much for content as for nuance and deviation from the norm.

For example, let's look at the typical comments about performance that most managers use, then at the real meaning behind what they say:

What They Say:	*What They Mean:*
"I'm giving you a project with more responsibility. . . ."	"You did the last project as well as I would have done it."
"Excellent. . . ."	"Adequate; I could do it better."
"Good. . . ."	"Needs improvement."
"Fair. . . ."	"Do this a couple more times, and you'll be on probation"
"This is a can-do company. We expect and get excellence at every level. This reorganization will make it possible for us to maintain our customary excellence at a more competitive level."	"More work—fewer people, fewer resources."
"George Smith has been transferred to the home office, where his skills and years of experience can be better used as vice president of com-	"Out to pasture."

munication, market analysis, and training."	
"Your work has been satisfactory, but you need to develop better skills for interfacing with others in your work group and with management."	"You're a pain in the butt."
"You need to work on leadership skills."	"You don't know what's going on. Figure out The System on your own, or stay put."

No Negatives Never!

When Competitors speak their language among themselves, no insult is implied. Communication, like everything else, is a game that can be won or lost. Competitors are used to playing their cards close to their vests and rarely really level with anyone about how they really feel. (Ask their families.)

An element of magic is evident here, related to the Management Mystique: To admit any doubts, faults, or misgivings is somehow to make them more real. Denial in this context is more or less institutionalized as a job requirement at this level.

Yes, there are Competitors such as Bronson who blow up and chew out their underlings. Usually, this kind of self-indulgence never occurs when other Competitors are around. It is viewed in most companies in much the same way as a manager's weekend drinking binges were viewed a generation ago—what managers do in the privacy of their own departments is their business. The company doesn't approve but probably will not stop the situation. It is merely bad form to be negative in private. Being negative in public is a crime.

Your boss, if he or she is a Competitor, will seldom let you in on negative feelings about his or her boss. The most you'll get might be quickly rolled eyes, or a "Well . . ." and a pause, where a more positive phrase should be used; or perhaps a slight shrug that says, "You know what he's like."

Among friends, such a gesture or comment would usually be followed by your probing, "Well, what *is* he like?" and the sharing of more intimate thoughts. In the corporate world, this kind of intimacy is almost illicit. It is either an expression of great trust or poor judgment on the part of the boss. Companies differ in their tolerance for this kind of behavior, but it is always bad business to give away too much information. People who expect a regular candid conversation are regularly driven crazy.

"Rapport talk" versus "Report Talk"

It is in the use of language that the tradeoffs of power are most clearly visible. In return for power, Competitors trade away emotional closeness and the direct expression of thoughts and feelings. It is indeed lonely at the top.

A Competitor who reads this, might say, "Well, that isn't such a big loss. A manager doesn't have to be so cold-hearted that he loses all capacity for intimacy. We're just talking about losing verbal intimacy—and that's a pretty small price to pay for more power."

We used the pronoun *he* deliberately in the preceding paragraph. Business is definitely set up along male preferences. Generally, men are more often intimate shoulder to shoulder, doing "guy stuff" like The Deal, the War Council, or the Company Softball Team. In such situations, talking about doubts and misgivings may erode a male Competitor's courage and cause him to let down his brothers-in-arms—a fate worse than death.

Every member of the team has a responsibility to keep motivation high. Sitting down and sharing feelings of fear—or any other feeling than enthusiasm or aggression—before battle have no place in the male Competitor's world.

Women, however, generally are more accustomed to being intimate face to face, to talking about things, to admitting to the confusing inner world of mixed feelings. A current business theory suggests that women tend to communicate by using "rapport talk," while men's tendency is a more fact-focused style called "report talk."

Another way to look at this is to consider the "female" (and non-Competitor) communication style as saying, "You and I have similar feelings and vulnerabilities, so we have a common bond. We try to understand one another in order to come closer to one another and to like one another more." The "male" (and Competitor) communication style says, "We aren't equals—I'm one up, and you're one down. I don't show you my vulnerability because that might jeopardize my ability to win (and to make you lose). I try to understand you in order to find a weak spot that I can use for beating you." Business needs *both* styles of communication. Most of us use only one or the other and often don't realize that important information may be conveyed in another way than the one we use most.

Damning with Hearty Praise

A good example of this complexity and the need to be fluent in more than one language style is in the use of praise. For a Competitor, praising someone in all but the most ritualistic ways (usually, as on the playing field, by phony criticism— "You're a mean old S.O.B.") is really almost an insult because it implies that the praise is needed or wanted. Real Competitors have what they need to motivate themselves inside. Give them money or power—even criticism—but don't demean them with praise. Praise is for the weak.

On the other hand, when Believer managers say, "Your work is always excellent; your contribution to the XP-75 project was especially helpful, and your team spirit is an inspiration to us all," they probably mean it. They are following the dictum (true) that managers should praise their employees. (All the studies show that praise works well in motivating most employees to be more productive.)

When Competitors say the same words, they, too, mean what they say—*but* they also mean to say, "You are at a level low enough that you *need* this kind of comment. I don't begrudge it (*too* much), but it means that you aren't leadership material."

Often, Competitors *don't* praise the people they really respect because they think those people are fellow Competitors who don't need the verbal pat on the back.

For most people, however, praise *is* important. How many times have you heard competent, valuable people complaining that their bosses never praises them (maybe you've made the same complaint)—without realizing that sometimes this lack of praise is a compliment?

In general, Believer managers are better able to communicate with their subordinates (who are probably fellow Believers), and Competitors are better able to communicate with their superiors (who—you guessed it—probably speak the same language: Competitor-speak). Managers are not really warriors; they are *managers*, which *does* require the ability to communicate downward. Believers tend to make better managers for other Believers and Rebels, but nearly always are ineffective as managers of Competitors.

The ability to communicate downward—though touted as the essence of leadership—is valued about as much in most Competitor-run companies (aren't most of them?) as the ability to teach (compared to getting grants and publishing) is valued in most big, research-oriented universities. It's considered a skill for amateurs. This lack of concern for the people below their station represents a crucial blind spot for Competitors. It is a belief related to the Cult of Winning, which says that a manager must be a conqueror rather than a caregiver.

This blind spot is especially evident when Competitors talk about "teamwork." They're all for it, of course, but if you listen closely, you can hear that they don't really consider themselves a part of the team. They are captains, coaches, teachers, or kings and, as such, are playing a different game. Teamwork, like training, is for underlings.

Asking for a Raise

The business world is run by (and perhaps for) Competitors. You don't necessarily have to be one to get ahead, but you do have to learn their language or you'll be in for untold problems. One language-related problem involves asking for a raise. Competitors know that you don't actually *ask* for a raise; you *negotiate* for it or even *demand* it (not because you deserve it or need it, but because you want it.) In addition, Competitors recognize that the money itself is not the important issue. It's what the money means—its value in the eyes of the company.

Competitors see clearly that using any kind of personal appeal in this situation ("My bills are high." "I'm getting a divorce" or the like) shows that you haven't mastered the vocabulary. Never assume that the boss is likely to feel obligated by your need for a raise (such as, "Tommy's gotta get braces.")

Another unsuccessful method assumes that you have already met your obligation (for instance, getting a raise by saying that your responsibilities exceed those stated in your job description). To give you a raise for this reason, a boss would have to admit to robbing from you before.

In contrast, successful ways of getting a raise most often recognize that the raise is something your boss gives you, which leaves you with some obligation—staying, producing more—to him or her. Here are examples of successful ways to ask for a raise:

"If I do x, y, and z, I can save the company $20,000 per year. I'd like a third of that."

"What do I have to do to get a 10% raise?" followed by **negotiating specific changes in responsibilities.**

These examples show an understanding that a raise costs money, so, to get one, you need to generate money. The manager needs to have some justification for giving you the raise. One way is to give your boss the justification in exactly the form your boss will give to his or her superior.

Another alternative that sometimes works is to give a simple demand: *"I want 10K more a year"*. The implication is that, if you get turned down too many times (probably twice), you will move on. You may, of course, bluff (Competitors do that). However, if your bluff is called, you can't back down without losing status as a Competitor in your boss's eyes.

You can't get a raise, or anything else in business, until you know how to translate and how to transact.

"What Did He Say? What Did He Mean?"

When people go to their bosses with problems, the bosses will react as if they were posting their answers on the company bulletin board. (The issue, by the way, should not be a personal problem unless you're literally talking life or death.) The boss's communication will be designed to convey as much information as possible, but also to limit and, especially, to clarify the commitments that the company is *not* willing to make. Don't read your boss's lips—or even the words. Read between the lines.

Competitor language is particularly distinctive regarding mistakes, requests, and tattling.

Mistakes. Most of the time, the big boss cannot tell people that their department head made a mistake. By saying what he offers to do to help, the boss will be letting people know the limits of the company's liability for rectifying the mistake.

Requests. The boss will usually give a "yes" or "no" answer if people ask for something *specific*. If you give your boss vague or abstract requests, such as wanting "fairness" or "justice," these words might have very different meanings for the two of you. You may end up having your boss grant your request—but still not get what you want.

Tattling. When employees tattle, the boss will say, "Very interesting," or something equally noncommittal. If you get this kind of response to what you thought was the exposé of the decade, it's a sign that what you're doing may be driving the boss crazy. Proceed with caution.

You have to learn what to ask for and to understand what the boss can and cannot grant. For example, nonunion companies that set up a formal grievance procedure usually back up the supervisor. The boss needs to uphold the chain of command and should not undercut a subordinate who is a supervisor. Undercutting is worse than most crimes a supervisor might commit.

Figuring out the Real Message

Let's look at the situation of an engineer of an electronics firm who did not understand the language of management.

Hal worked in a division that was being closed down. Although his company had elaborate transfer procedures, Hal's boss (a notoriously ruthless manager) took Hal into his office and told Hal that he had to transfer to a job that he didn't particularly want, in a location he hated, or he would be out on his ear.

Hal wasn't stupid; he had advanced degrees in engineering, but he was naïve as to corporate procedures. He believed what his boss had told him, and he transferred. He should have fought the battle then.

Believers drive Competitors particularly crazy when they make a deal and, after finally realizing what they've agreed to—maybe a month or so later—want out because the deal "isn't fair." In the world of Competitors, the time to assess the fairness of the deal is *before* you agree. (This interpretation of the rules of fairness, of course, drives Believers crazy.)

His company had a rule that required transferees to stay in their new positions for at least two years, so here was Hal, stuck in a town he and his family hated. His depression deepened until he told Kikanza, his department's Human Resources person, what had happened.

Kikanza was aghast that Hal's boss had not followed the proper transfer procedures, and assured Hal that "Oh, we will certainly take care of this for you." As she began going through channels for him, she told Hal to visit the plant in the city where he wanted to be transferred, to check out possible openings. She also had him write a long letter to the division head, focusing on the deviation from the transfer procedure, accompanied by a long letter of her own, explaining what the procedure should have been.

At the plant where he wanted to work, department heads told Hal that only a division head could open a position for him before the next fiscal year when, coincidentally, his two

years were up. (He didn't realize it, but they were talking about the two-year rule. They also were waffling due to their concern about hiring somebody who had tried to get around the rules and thereby enraged upper management.)

When Kikanza arranged an audience for him with the division head, Hal expected that person to gush all over him, as she had done, and to say, "Oh, we made a big mistake, and here's what we'll do to fix the situation for you."

Instead, Hal's interview lasted all of three minutes. He came in, briefly outlined his case, then heard the division head say, "Well, it looks like you made your choice, but if you can get somebody in Podunk [the city where Hal wanted to be transferred] to take you on, I won't stop you." End of interview.

Hal went away, more deeply depressed than ever. His interpretation was that the division head had not even read his letter, had just glanced at it, and had given him no information. Kikanza felt the same way, but she was a long way from the center of power.

(In most companies, the Human Resources department is just about as far away from the center of power as anyone can be. It doesn't add a lot to the company's bottom line, so you can guess how important it would be to the Competitors in the executive suite. The HR people are the keepers of the rules; their function is to see that procedures are followed for hiring, transfers, helping with interpersonal difficulties and the like. They usually have no power, other than some counseling skills and their winning personalities.)

Kikanza was preparing to write another long letter, pointing out that the rules had been broken, but at that point, Hal decided to meet with a business consultant. Hal and his wife were both depressed and wanted advice about what they should do in a situation that looked hopeless to them.

After hearing Hal's description of the meeting, the consultant pointed out that the division head had actually made a very definitive statement.

Let's look at the way the consultant translated the manager's language for Hal:

When the division head said, "Looks like you made your choice," he was acknowledging that the time to deal with the impropriety would have been when it happened. Because Hal hadn't spoken out right away, the division head did not consider the impropriety itself the issue now. So his essential message at first was,

"You don't have any case with me."

However, when the division head said, "If you can get somebody in Podunk to take you on, I won't stop you," he meant,

"I won't invoke the two-year rule."

He was clearly suggesting that, while he wasn't going to intervene to open a position for Hal, he wouldn't stand in the way of it, either. His real message was,

"Hal, you're free to go to the other plant and see whether you can get someone to take you on. I'll let them know in Podunk that the two-year rule has been waived."

In his language, the division head had acknowledged some culpability on the company's part for what had happened, but he certainly was not going to tell this engineer (who was nowhere near being his peer) that the company had messed up. Instead, he *offered* Hal a *settlement*, but Hal hadn't realized that that was what it was.

There also seemed to be another, more subtle message to Hal from the division head:

"Hal, if you can effect this early transfer, under your own steam, it won't hurt your career with the company. Selling yourself to me and to the folks in Podunk might mitigate your earlier naïvete."

This, of course, would not be the case in many companies, where junior employees who started invoking rules and playing me-against-the-company could damage their careers.

In situations like Hal's, the time to raise hell is before it happens. Standing up to a ruthless boss is much more acceptable than buckling and then going to a higher authority. The very idea of this turns most Believer hearts to ice. Nevertheless, this engineer didn't realize what was going on or what he was being offered. Until he got outside help, he was still looking at his situation as impossible to change until the two-year rule expired for him. He also felt that his company didn't care about him. It drove him crazy.

Hal didn't realize that upper management cannot speak to underlings as peers and that anything the division head said to him would be a policy statement. Instead of admitting that the company had done anything wrong, the division head instead, very quickly and abruptly, told Hal, "Here's what I offer," and Hal had missed it.

Once Hal realized what he really had been told, and he had checked it out with a few people in the know, who agreed with the consultant's interpretation, he felt that he had been dealt with more fairly.

Speaking to Peers

In contrast to the formal, read-between-the-lines language of upper management to those below, the language that Competitors speak to professional peers should be more direct. To Competitor peers, you can talk about disagreements and mistakes. In fact, if you start spouting the party line at a meeting of peers, they will probably look at you as if you need to change your light bulb. Yet you do have to appear motivated and with the program.

Even in meetings with colleagues, however, there are a few topics to avoid. Avoid name-calling, personal blame, or suggesting that anybody is operating unethically. These will come back to haunt you and are the kinds of things you can talk about only with people who are intimate and trusted. Likewise, reserve for intimates your discussion of your own feelings, your self-doubts, or the internal workings of your own reasoning process.

Company cultures differ as to what is appropriate to say—especially regarding conflict and disagreement. There's no substitute for listening and figuring out the rules by observing them in practice. Wherever you are in the corporate hierarchy, you must realize that other people at other levels may speak a different language from yours.

Why Don't People Talk Directly?

As a manager, it may be to your advantage to translate so your subordinates understand you—and to know how to translate for colleagues who are having trouble communicating. Getting people to talk directly to each other about problems is one of the toughest jobs in management, but it is absolutely necessary—the report of facts, rapport among equals, and the one-up/one-down style of communicating. We'd like to share a neat trick here, learned from a manager friend, for getting people to communicate directly.

When a colleague would call Frances, the manager, to complain about another person in the organization, Frances would put the caller on hold. She'd then get the other person on a "conference" call and arrange to be called away from the phone. By the time Frances got back on the line, the two people usually would have settled their problem.

Why is it so difficult for people to say what they need directly to the people who are involved? Most people who communicate about their problems indirectly aren't trying to take Machiavellian control of the kingdom. They're simply avoiding something they fear: the consequences of talking directly. Usually, the immediate consequences are negative, even if the long-run effects turn out to be positive.

It's safer to talk to the people who will tell you what you want to hear, with no fear of reprisals—talking to your secretary, for example, when you should be telling your boss. This kind of indirect communication has an added—but mixed—blessing.

Other people tend to talk about what they hear, and eventually your message—in whatever distorted form its journey along the grapevine has transformed it—will reach the person who needed to hear it. Unfortunately, the message usually comes with information about who originally said it. Also, being talked about behind one's back drives almost everyone crazy.

Think of the last time you had something important—and negative—to tell someone. What did the person do? Deny it? Act hurt? Attack your character? The incident probably was nearly as unpleasant for you as it was for the other person. Unless someone is feeling very strong and confident, it's difficult to accept a negative comment merely as information. It's taken as a personal attack, and the tendency to respond personally is tough to ignore.

People have to be *taught* to deal with each other directly and to be supported for doing so. That's real management. Anybody can complain about rumors. Unfortunately, a manager can't really put every warring faction on conference call, so let's look at other ways to encourage your staff to communicate directly, by recognizing and dealing with the reasons that people don't talk directly.

1. **They're afraid they'll get in trouble.** The main reason that people don't talk directly is that they fear negative consequences: a reprimand, a grilling, a parental lecture, a long-winded denial. If your culture punishes people for what they say, they fear being punished for saying it. They might also worry about punishments other than reprimands, such as the fear of becoming the object of too much attention or the fear of hurting someone's feelings.

If you want people to talk directly to you, remember to take what they say as *information*, rather than as attack. When someone criticizes you or says something negative about you, a good strategy is to try on the message for a day. Think about it, and tell the person you'll respond tomorrow. Avoid the immediate urge to fight back.

2. **They assume you won't care.** If, in the past, you ignored—or dismissed as "unimportant," "petty," or "trivial"—an issue that was important to other people, they will avoid

coming to you directly next time. You will have to earn back their trust by listening when they talk to you, writing down their concerns, and following through on requests. We're not saying that you have to agree with every opinion or to grant every request; we *are* saying it's important to pay attention. It takes skill and wisdom to listen, at any level.

3. **They assume it's somebody else's responsibility to speak up.** Maybe they're inarticulate or they don't think it's their place to give you the word. In any case, the remedy is *active listening*: paying closer attention to what people tell you, paraphrasing their statements, and asking them whether your rephrasings show an understanding of what they mean.

If you want things to be different in your department, you have to work hard to make them change. You can have the most effect at the point when people come to you directly, either by following the preceding guidelines—or by stepping out of the way. Sometimes it's all right to be a sounding board, but you'll seldom gain an advantage by being a messenger service.

4. **You assume that state secrets should be kept from employees.** "State secrets" are merely another form of indirect communication. It's awfully tempting to use national security as a reason to withhold anything embarrassing to people in power. This says very clearly, "Disclosure requirements are different for me. When I mess up or bend the rules, it's classified." Managers who believe that there are lots of things that their employees shouldn't know won't be told much by their employees. Believers especially assume that the things that are kept secret are things people are ashamed of.

Direct communication is fragile, easily destroyed as soon as people give in to the impulse to avoid saying something because of what might happen if they did. In every company, it is communication problems that most often drive people crazy. Most "communications problems" we run across are really language problems. It's not so much that people don't speak to one another; it's that they don't understand that whatever people say or do conveys information. Even in silence, you can't *not* communicate.

16

Losing Your Corporate Innocence

Understanding the Six Mysteries

The luckiest day in Lesley's life was the day she met Dana. Lesley, the highly motivated Believer, was interviewing managers about child care, and Dana, the manager in Marketing, seemed to take a real interest in the project and in Lesley's ideas. She really listened.

They had coffee a couple of times, and a few lunches. One day over chef's salad, Dana asked Lesley, "Would you be terribly offended if I told you that you were going about everything in the wrong way?"

Lesley was offended, but she tried not to show it, and she trusted Dana enough to work hard to get past it, to listen to what Dana had to say.

Nothing was ever the same after that.

Mystery #1: Everything Has a Price Tag.

Dana pushed her salad plate aside, signaled to the waiter for coffee and eyed Lesley. "I told you that you were going about

236

everything all wrong. Let's start with the proposal your committee's working on for child care. You have people from several departments 'volunteering' to handle scheduling and other details, right?"

Lesley nodded. "Right."

Dana shook her head. "But what about the cost of their time, Lesley? When they're working on child care, they're not working for *us*. Any manager looking at your proposal is going to add on those people's time—which means that the price is really higher than the one you quote."

Lesley looked worried.

"That's OK," Dana said quickly. "But you need to demonstrate what management is going to get for the money. There's nothing in your proposal about that."

"But child care is good for employees," Lesley argued.

Dana smiled. "Sure, it is, but that isn't enough to motivate management. You have to show them that it will pay. Let's see some numbers from other companies—lower turnover, less sick time, that kind of stuff."

"I can do that. Sure. No problem," Lesley said. "But why do you guys need all those numbers? I think the proposal would be a lot stronger if we appealed to management's ethical side. I mean, funding child care is the right thing to do, Dana."

Dana started craning her neck in an exaggerated search across the restaurant.

"What are you looking for, Dana?"

Dana smiled at the younger woman. "The turnip truck you just fell off, kid. Listen. The first thing I learned when I moved up was to *remember the numbers. Everything has a price tag.* Everything has to be supported by numbers. Don't tug at our heart strings. We're talkin' purse strings. If you want to get it done, show us the numbers."

Playing by the numbers is the Competitors' most sacred ritual. For management to spend money, there has to be some way they will make money or save money. They will never even read Lesley's proposal (although Dana doesn't have the heart to tell her so.) They'll just flip to the tables, numbers, and graphs. If the numbers aren't there, management will say, "Surely this isn't for us. Where are the numbers?"

True, numbers can be "cooked," and they often are. At best, they're somebody's opinion rather than facts, but they still have to be there. (When you use numbers, make every effort to be sure they're accurate—don't "cook" them. You never know when some Competitor knows the same recipe.)

Mystery #2: Nobody Will Tell You the Mysteries of Your Company.

Lesley frowned, concentrating. "How do you know all this stuff, Dana? You're smart, you're not a sleaze, and . . . I'm not sure how to describe it . . . you know how to act. I feel like such a child around here sometimes—and you know what? I'm too old to feel like that!"

Dana nodded. She knew exactly how Lesley felt. In fact, she still felt like an innocent herself sometimes when she was in a roomful of veteran managers. Despite her empathy, though, Dana would have jumped out her high-rise office window rather than admit her insecurity. She was touched that Lesley felt she could trust her with such a politically risky admission.

"It's the Eleventh Commandment," Dana said.

Lesley blinked. "Excuse me?"

"The Eleventh Commandment," Dana repeated slowly, "is that nobody will tell you your company's first 10."

Lesley smiled tentatively. "I get it. I think. . . . But why, Dana? Why don't people tell you? Luke says it's a conspiracy, a bunch of good old boys sitting around, deciding who's going to make it. Is that what you guys do—tell us to work hard and follow the rules, when all the time you're making up secret codes?"

Dana laughed. "No, Les, we don't have any secret signs. It's just recognizing that certain people know how to act; they

**know what's important. . . . It's all kinds of little details that
are hard to explain. . . ."**

It's difficult to get a boss to talk with an employee about
these things. Competitors are expected to spend most of their
time dealing with other Competitors in meetings and doing
what Competitors define as running the company. Actually
doing the work and managing the people who do the work
seem to get squeezed in between making the deals, putting
together the proposals, and meeting with upper management.

Competitors can't identify with Believers' innocence and
ignorance of The System. To a Competitor, the most important thing is having enough sophistication and knowledge—
learned on your own—to be able to work within The System.
Competitors often see their own Believer attitudes and doubts
as weaknesses, to be covered over and denied.

In fact, most of what Competitors will tell you may be the
opposite of the way things really work. The whole point of the
Competitors' initiation is that you have to look at each new
situation and figure out what the rules are for yourself.

Mystery #3: Neither Merit nor Hard Work Can Be Measured.

**Dana planted both elbows on the table. "I remember when I
was where you are. I worked my tail off, always did more
than my share and waited for somebody in management to
notice and promote me. Well, my boss noticed, sure. My ratings were always 'Consistently Exceeds Standards.' But promotion? No way."**

**Lesley said bitterly, "_My_ ratings are great, too. I worked
like a mule to learn new software on my own in two weeks—
and, if I do say so myself, our inventory came off without a
hitch. But _then_ Jack asked me if I was really ready for a
promotion! Can you believe that?"**

"Yes." Dana was firm. Then, before Lesley could interrupt, she went on. "Let me tell you what I finally figured out. Working hard is *not* the winning ticket. It doesn't qualify you for the grand prize. To get that, you have to do something more."

"Work *harder?*" Lesley was shocked.

"Nope. Work smarter," Dana said. "Figure out *what kind of work* gets rewarded around here—and what kind of behavior gets you noticed by the people who count."

Believers trust that those performance rating sheets actually measure something important (how hard and how well they work) and that decisions about their future will be based on what is written on that paper—wrong on all counts. Rating forms are mostly for leaving a paper trail to justify decisions that have already been made. Nearly every important business decision actually is subjective. Merely working hard at a task that you think is important may not get you anything but a lot of 5s on a rating sheet. It's like rubles. Who cares how many you have if you can't buy anything with them?

"Besides," Dana went on, "you can't expect management to know what you do. You have to *promote yourself*—let people know that your actions have saved a certain amount of money, or brought in new business, or contributed in other ways that count—and that you want a promotion."

In every company, particular behaviors and results are important. If you attend to those, you can ignore a lot of other things, but you *must* attend to those.

"Take Howard, for instance," Dana said.

Lesley wrinkled her nose. "That sleaze?"

Dana smiled. "Well, he is a little obvious, but he's on the right track. Howard has it figured out. To get anywhere in this company, you have to be known. He never misses a chance to do things with upper management. He goes to every meeting possible. He joins task forces, special project teams—and he even took tennis lessons."

Lesley groaned, but Dana shook her head. "Don't laugh. Howard knows that the people who get promoted are the people that management knows will act appropriately and project the company image. He's good at that. He's come a long way from the time when he pretended to *be* an upper manager. Now he's a lot smoother—respectful when he needs to be, a firecracker with ideas when that's called for.

"He's a real political animal now—that's where all the perqs are." Dana smiled tolerantly.

"But, Dana," Lesley protested, "the people in his office call Howard 'The Seagull'—he flies in, dumps work on them, and flies away again. They hate him—but you're telling me that Howard has figured out the way to get ahead! Won't anybody ever check with his employees to see what kind of job he's doing?"

Dana shook her head. "Unless there are big productivity problems in his department, probably not. I can't say I like it, or that Howard doesn't abuse The System, but he does know what The System is."

Lesley sighed. "I see what you're saying about image. It just seems like a waste to me. Howard's department runs fine without any support from him. Think how much better they could do if he were actually managing."

Dana paused over a sip of coffee. "You have a point, Lesley. You really do," she said. Inside, she was thinking, "Lesley may be naïve, but she does have a way of pointing out obvious problems that we sometimes overlook."

In every company, there are certain behaviors that are rewarded—such as spending time with high-level Competitors in Howard's company. If you're a Competitor, you need to know what passes for merit where you live. You can probably bet it doesn't have to do with how much support you give your employees or how hard you work. Chances are, nobody really cares, as long as your product gets out and the numbers look good.

Most of the time, people considering you for promotion don't even know *that* much. They do know how you look, how you act and whether you fit in. (If they *don't* know that, then you haven't been doing your job.) In other companies, the competition is strictly "Who has the best bottom line?"; it's the numbers that talk.

Believers miss the point on this. They think that the busier they are, the better. Even when promoted to management, they're always shuffling papers around. Much of the important work managers do leaves no visible wake. Sometimes, the most productive work they do is staring at the wall, thinking through a tough problem (although they would have a hard time doing it openly in most companies—too many Believers about).

Dana shifted gears. "Think about your desk for a minute."

Lesley laughed. "Do I have to? It's so cluttered I can hardly find it!"

"Exactly," Dana said. "'See Lesley's cluttered desk! Look at all the work she has to do! See how important she is! She's so busy that she can never even find her desktop.'"

Lesley pouted. "You're making fun of me."

"Sure. But there's a point. Pay attention. 'Now see Lesley flying down the hall at an aerobic pace? She's on her way to a very important meeting. She has to run that fast because she's so busy that she can't slow down! Now there she is, hunched over her desk again as the clock strikes midnight. See how hard Lesley works?'"

Lesley was steamed. "Damn it, Dana, what's your point?"

"It's coming." It was a good sign that the kid had sworn at her, Dana thought. Maybe she had what it took after all. "Now let's picture *my* desk. Clear. No clutter. And I don't have to sprint to meetings, either. Does this mean I work less hard than you? Does this mean I'm less productive than you? No.

"It means that I don't have to look 'busy' to get results. My ducks are in a row, Lesley. I know what the big guys consider priorities, and that's how I structure my time." Dana paused. "But at the company where my husband is a manager, looking 'busy' is part of the act, so that's what he does. Do you see what I'm saying?"

"It's getting clearer all the time," Lesley muttered.

"Good!" Dana laughed.

"Notice I didn't say anything about leaving work at 5, though. This isn't a total fairytale!"

If people are naïve enough to ask their boss for step-by-step instructions to get a raise or a promotion, the boss will probably say, "Work harder." Maybe they'll start coming in earlier and staying later, and then feel extremely frustrated when their colleagues snub them and management "rewards" them by raising their quotas. They feel cheated, but they don't realize they're cheating themselves. To get a raise, you have to negotiate. Give the boss something he or she wants. This usually doesn't simply mean working harder. It means doing something that will make the boss look good.

Lesley took the straw out of her soft drink glass and started folding it between her fingers. "What you said about your husband made me think of mine. Don's a sales rep in a telecommunications company, but he isn't doing all that well. His company spouts slogans like 'Service Is Job One,' and Don takes them seriously. What he really likes to do is to help people get their equipment set up and make sure they know how to operate it and are satisfied with it.

"Well, this means that Don doesn't spend as much of his time on the other part of his job: selling. His sales totals are always lower than some of the more hard-nosed salespeople's. In sales meetings, they say, 'We give service so that people will become repeat customers.' But the truth is, when service gets in the way of sales, then service goes.

"It just drives Don crazy," Lesley said. "To me, it seems like Don's company is really saying, 'Forget customer service. Just meet your quotas.' It's just so *cold*, Dana."

Dana sighed. "It's not cold or hot, right or wrong, Les. It's just *the way it is* at Don's company—and at most companies. If Don wants to get ahead, he has to focus on what his company considers the blue-chip tasks. If Don wants to do extra service-related work on his own time, that's fine. But first he has to show he can meet—and exceed—his quotas. If he can't do that, it doesn't matter how good his relationships with customers are."

Lesley asked angrily, "But if that's the way it is, why do they pretend service is so important?"

"Because they would like it to be," Dana answered patiently. "They hope that slogans like that will motivate people like Don to meet his quotas *and* give good service."

Lesley nodded in disgust. "And that's why it drives him crazy—they say one thing and do another. I don't see why they have to do that. . . ."

Dana had an idea. "That button you have pinned on your baseball cap, Lesley. What does it say?"

"Huh?" Lesley blinked, then checked her cap. "Oh, it says, 'We're Number One.' It's kind of our team slogan. I got buttons for everybody."

"Are you really number one?" Dana asked.

"Well, not exactly . . . ," Lesley said. "We're tied for ninth in our league. . . ."

Dana just looked at her.

Lesley said defensively, "But this is the *softball team*, Dana. We're not taking advantage of anybody. It's not the same thing at all. . . . Is it?"

Competitors quickly learn that management values certain behaviors more highly than others, no matter what the slogans say. Those who spend time doing the blue-chip tasks are the ones who get the perqs, promotions, and pay raises. The slogans and rhetoric point to the *goal* that people are trying to reach. The Competitor's job is to know what the priorities really are—what needs to be done first.

"In a nutshell, Lesley, here's what it takes to succeed here (and it's a good bet it's the same at Don's company): Pay attention to your bottom line, and do the things that the most successful people in the company do—whatever those things are.

"Sure, making presentations with lots of AV aids, wearing Brooks Brothers suits, having lunch with upper managers— these won't be the kinds of things that show up on rating sheets," Dana said, "but you'd better believe they define 'merit' in the hearts and minds of the people who have a big say in your future."

Mystery #4: Image Is More Important than Reality.

The waiter came to take dessert orders. Lesley ordered a chocolate brownie royale. Dana asked for a coffee refill, then studied Lesley across the table. Shiny, shoulder-length hair, neat little navy suit and white blouse. No accessories, if you didn't count the company-logo softball cap, which Lesley had placed on the table next to the empty soft-drink glass, and the oversized purse on the floor at her feet. Dana sighed. *Vogue* magazine, where are you when we need you?

She took a deep breath. "There's something else. It's called 'image.'"

Lesley cut her short. "I know about image. It means being phony—like Howard. I don't care, Dana, I just can't stoop that low."

"The original 'I Gotta Be Me' kid, huh?" Dana said. "Well, before you write off Image, let's take a look at yours. What image do you project, right now, Lesley?"

"Well, a hard-working, motivated employee. . . ."

"That's right," Dana agreed. "Hard-working, motivated, doing great, *right at the level you are.* To be considered management material, you have to act like a manager—and, Les, you have to dress like a manager."

"Oh, gosh, do I have a spot on my blouse?" Lesley anxiously checked her front.

Dana sighed again. "It's not the blouse. . . . exactly. It's the whole look. Neat, responsible, safe, and . . . innocent."

Lesley's eyes flashed. "What do you mean? I bought this suit in the Executive Career Woman department at Bergstrom's! Thanks a lot, Dana."

Dana decided to cut to the chase. "The baseball cap has to go, Les. It makes management think you're not a player. (Excuse the pun.)"

"But I manage the team!" Lesley cried. "It's good for morale if they see me wearing the cap on game days!"

Dana figured any jury would acquit her if she strangled this kid. "Let's let the team worry about its own morale," she said patiently. "Let's talk about you. Here's what it takes to pass as management material:

"Dress like a manager. That means that the occasional pinstripes won't hurt—yes, even for women. Forget the purse, and carry an attaché. Accessorize the suit—scarf, cuff bracelet, lizard belt. Get your hair styled."

"Oh, gosh," Lesley whispered.

"Look, Lesley, in an organization the size of ours—heck, in any place that's bigger than 10 employees—most people won't know you very well. They'll just know your image— what you look like, who you associate with, what your attitude seems to be—not who you really are.

"Sure, I'm suggesting that you need to do some politicking, be like everybody else and dress for success—enough to show there's nothing wrong with you. Think of your image as a long-lasting version of a first impression, and maybe that'll help you recognize how important it is."

Lesley stuffed the baseball cap deep into her purse and sat up straighter. "What else?"

Dana laughed. The kid was finally getting into it. "Well, next is to get an M.B.A."

"I've got one! I've got my M.B.A.!" Lesley shouted with glee.

"Congratulations," Dana said dryly. "OK, then: Never miss a chance to spend time with those above you—like *moi,* for instance. Go to meetings, sit on committees—the *right* committees, the ones that the big guys notice. Join the right organizations. What organizations do you belong to now?"

"Executive Women in Management," Lesley said proudly. "They let me join, even though I'm not a manager yet. We have motivational speakers and training seminars, and we meet for an early breakfast the second Thursday of every month."

Dana could feel herself getting a headache. "Most real managers would not be caught dead in any organization that offers management training or includes the word *executive* in its title. Call us cynical, but that's how it is. We just have a hard time publicly admitting there's anything we don't know—especially about business."

(Business clubs for real Competitors are usually called "social clubs.")

Dana's list continued. "Also, read the right stuff. Forget the editorial commentary; turn to the market statistics and the big stories about corporate management. Read about the numbers and the money."

(One area a real Competitor cannot fake is knowing investments. You need to know about stocks, bonds, commodities, mutual funds, and money markets. In the world of Competitors, the ultimate management is not of people, but of money. You need to know how this is done, even if you don't do it yourself.)

"And know how to speak the language," Dana said. "Know our management buzz-words, and use them."

"That resonates with me, motivation-wise," Lesley said solemnly.

"What? Yeah. Oh—" Dana grinned. "Exactly."

(Nothing brands you as a Believer more quickly than using an English phrase when you could use a management buzz-word or a noun that's been "-ized" into a verb instead.)

"Beyond that," Dana went on, "there's also name recognition; having a few higher-ups who trust you; name recognition; appearing to work hard at the things upper management values; name recognition; having people owe you favors; name recognition; being associated with moneymaking projects, and name recognition. Are you getting my drift?"

"Gotcha," Lesley said.

Dana nodded her approval and signaled for the check. "I'm glad you're not raging now about 'playing games and not being myself' because—trust me, Lesley—the higher you go, the more senior managers are going to put you into a lot of tense situations. You'll have to figure out what you're supposed to do—and look good while doing it—so you won't let the company down. That's what this whole 'initiation' is really about. Once you've proved you can do what's needed, then you can worry about being yourself."

Mystery #5: Keep Your Doubts to Yourself.

Lesley studied her new mentor in awe. "How can you be so confident, Dana?"

Dana laughed. "Let me tell you something. This is just for you. One of our best-kept secrets is that inside each of us is a 10-year-old kid, playing at being an adult.

"Remember when you were 10, and you thought that, when you became an adult, you'd know everything? Surprise! Now you realize that you're often no more sure of yourself than you were then—but now you have to take actions that count. Here's the secret: *Keep your doubts to yourself.*"

In the corporate world, there is no one more disdained than the indecisive, overly dependent person who needs continuing support and always has to be told that he or she is doing a good job.

Managers may talk about positive reinforcement, but real Competitors need to generate their own positives from within themselves. If you keep demanding that your boss give you a pat on the back, or complaining that management only talks about the bad things you do, then you don't understand the real rules.

A manager can mean just the opposite when he or she says, "You're doing a good job." The meaning might actually be, "You're doing a good job *but* there's a problem here. You're too needy. You demand too much attention, too many pats on the head. You're too insecure."

We all need praise, and we are all insecure and indecisive at times, but the Competitors' code states that we only reveal this to the people who are closest to us, and that's it.

Mystery #6: It's *All* Political.

Dana picked up the check and started to get up from the table, then stopped. "I almost forgot the final mystery, the Big Truth about office politics: It's *all* personal, Lesley. You have to know people.

"When managers are facing a hiring or promotion decision, most of us would rather choose a known and acceptable person—somebody who knows the form and won't embarrass the company. We don't want to have to search out a newcomer who might have top skills but whose behavior is unknown and unpredictable."

Lesley thought for a minute. "It's all personal—and it's *all political.* That's what it's really all about, isn't it, Dana?"

"That's exactly what it's all about," Dana said heartily.

As the two women headed back to the office, Lesley said thoughtfully, "It all makes sense when you tell it, Dana. Be tough, know the rules, put the job first to get ahead, play politics. But you're a mom, too. How does all this fit with what you teach your kids about how the world is supposed to be?"

Dana stopped short. How could she talk about her own personal struggle with a young colleague who had not yet fought the toughest battles? She knew there was a very thin line between being a winner and making everyone else a loser. She had seen more than one of her colleagues cross that line. (Bronson, for one.) Sometimes, she wondered how close she was getting, herself.

Lesley deserved an answer, but Dana couldn't give her the real one. What *did* she believe in? Instead, with a silent thank-you for her liberal arts education, Dana came up with a quotation. "It's like Winston Churchill said, Les. ' . . . It has been said that democracy is the worst form of government, except all those other forms that have been tried from time to time.'"

Lesley looked at her dubiously, but Dana smiled and kept walking. She would have to think about her personal answer in private.

17

The Competitors' Ten Commandments— Plus One

Dana stared pensively out her office window at the city below. (Finally, she thought with a melancholy smile, not only a room of one's own, but a room with a view). She knew how her former colleagues saw her. Since her promotion upstairs to a real management position, they thought she had it all: title, office, power, and salary. They didn't understand the tugging and pushing she felt from above and below. Everybody she talked to or met with wanted her to do something— and nobody wanted her to do the same thing.

Her new peers in management were not only necessary allies; they were also potential rivals for the next promotion or the bigger piece of the boss's time and attention. The people in upper management never let up: Produce, produce, produce. Not to mention how split she felt at having to work even longer hours than she'd put in before. "Once you've proved you can do what's needed, then you can worry about being yourself." She'd said that to Lesley, but what she hadn't said was that the proving never ends.

Lesley's question, "How did playing to win at work fit with

what she told her kids about the way the world ought to be?" had shaken her. Maybe this weekend, she'd reintroduce herself to her husband and kids. . . .

I almost didn't say anything to Lesley at lunch today, Dana mused. Where do I get off, giving advice? Anyway, I was sure Lesley would just get offended—and end up being buried in that stupid baseball hat. Then I thought, isn't that the kind of thinking that I would have called "male chauvinist" back in my own Dark Ages? Now I'm a Good Old Boy and a mentor! Not bad.

Lesley made some good points, though. Even though I had some pretty glib answers, she raised some issues that I'm nowhere near resolving for myself.

. . . The truth is that I was more like Lesley than I want to admit. Talking with her brought back a lot of memories. Maybe eight or nine years ago, I felt the same as she did about a *lot* of things—not softball, thank God—but blundering like she is. Doing things I was sure everybody would think were great, then feeling crushed when I realized nobody gave a damn.

. . . I don't get crushed any more. Until I talked with her, I'd forgotten that. It's not just a matter of being slicker and more devious (though I bet that's what Lesley thinks.) I'm different now. I've made it through a lot of pain and fear. I am really stronger. There are so many things I thought I could never do, and now I do 'em every day.

. . . It's not just the money and the room with a view. I like what's happened to me. I'm proud of myself. It's just that sometimes it's a little harder to keep track of who I am. I know how The System works—and it's usually a lot easier just to do what The System demands, instead of asking myself what *I* really want. Sometimes it drives me crazy—to keep asking myself what I really believe, what's really important in my life. . . . But if I don't ask, well, there are worse things than being driven crazy. . . .

Dana recognizes that in some ways, she has less power over her own life than she had before she became a Competitor. She is starting to realize that her new definition of a good day is a day when she doesn't get surprised by any of the tugs and pushes—and a great day is when she can direct some of the force. The realization that she has *less* will give her the chance to gain *more*. You can't learn anything until you realize there's something you don't know.

With the passing of the melancholy sometimes comes a feeling of dread, even terror. New Competitors begin to realize that, no matter how much pressure they're under, whatever happens to them will be a result of their own choices. They're on; there's nobody to blame but themselves.

Then, somehow, the energy of fear is diverted into a positive force: acceptance, action, excitement, anticipation. In plain English, this is called "having your act together."

There will always be questions to drive you crazy with fear, anger, and doubt. When you stop questioning yourself, though, you stop learning, and your career can take on a life of its own. At that point, you run the risk of becoming a caricature like Bronson, our battle-obsessed Competitor, or Howard the "Seagull," our corporate gamesman.

When you can turn your fear, anger, and doubt into the energy of action and accomplishment, you know you've got it right. That's when you know you're ready to wear the pinstripes. You realize the Competitor's truth: You are in control of your life.

So what do you have to do to be a Competitor?

1. A Competitor Is Decisive.

Dana remembered . . . I used to make decisions by writing down the pros on one side of the paper and the cons on the other. Somehow, I thought that would give me the answer. I'd stare at that paper for hours. Then I'd finally *do* something.

One of the things I've learned is it's not so much what you decide. It's what you do *after* you decide that's important. That's what makes it into the right or wrong decision.

Nonetheless, when I have a tough choice to make, I still list the pros and cons on a sheet of paper. . . .

Some managers become paralyzed with their decision-making rituals and can't act.

"Get me more data!" the division head demands. "How can you expect me to make such a tough decision when I don't have enough data? We'll meet again in two weeks."

To be decisive, a Competitor has to master the urge to run away or become immobilized. "Getting more data" can be a disguised form of running away. As a Believer, you learned that you need to do your homework—to gather the data. A Competitor learns how to *act* on the data. A successful Competitor knows how much and what kind of information he or she will need to make a decision—and then makes the decision.

You can use your own favorite rituals to help you have more confidence in your decisions. Maybe you consult the Council of Economic Advisers, or the statistical projections of next month's sales, or maybe the weathercaster on Channel 10. You might run the figures through the computer or simply call a meeting—or use whatever ritual is meaningful to you and helps you face uncertainty.

Give up trying to predict the future, though; you will never have all the information you need. To make a place for yourself as a Competitor, first you have to be able to choose a road, then to follow it and *make whatever you decided the right choice.*

Being decisive has its dark side, Dana mused. You get good at not seeing alternatives—at drawing the curtain over other possibilities. I know you reach a point where you have to, or you'd never get anything done. But sometimes it's so easy just to ignore other points of view.

Lesley is naïve; there are things she doesn't know about how things are done. That doesn't make her stupid, though— or wrong. Most of the people in this company think like Lesley, and they have to spend a lot of time worrying about

what we in management think. Yet we don't pay much attention to how *they* think.

They're the people we're supposed to be leading. It's like Lesley said about Howard's department. Maybe they could accomplish so much more if we were listening to them. Because sometimes they're right. . . .

2. A Competitor Doesn't Ask for Permission.

In school, you had to raise your hand to get permission to do anything; there were rules, structures, and grades. In the world of work, if you have to ask, then somebody is probably going to tell you, "No, you can't do it." Sometimes, you will need to make positive use of your aggressive tendencies to make your own rules.

Mike is the new guy in Info Systems. His job, and that of the whole department, is to help people with their computers— fix problems, advise them on better ways to use the system, consult on new equipment.

The department has a reputation for being unresponsive. Some people have said it might be better to let all departments have direct contact with vendors to arrange for their own computer information and service. Mike's boss talks endlessly to his own people about accuracy, courtesy, and timely response, but he does little to get that message out to other departments.

Mike sees that the department needs to go out actively and improve its image. On his own, he starts making cold calls: dropping in on departments that use computers, leaving the latest computer cartoons on people's desks, and offering an idea or two about making the system work better. Mike leaves his card and says, "If you have any questions, call." (He also makes more formal calls on department heads.)

Within a month, his boss's boss is hearing, "You need more guys like Mike."

Mike sized up the situation and acted. His boss probably would have suggested that he stay in his office and work on programs, but Mike made positive name-recognition for himself and his department his top priority. When advancement time came, he was the first person at his level to get a promotion.

Sometimes, you have to be able to take action without anybody's permission. To do this, you will have to accept that not everybody is going to agree with what you do. (If you're smart, however, you'll learn whose approval is most important.)

Dana knew it was time. There were several career options on the horizon, and she wanted her boss's opinion about which way she should go. She made herself comfortable in the club chair in his office and sketched a couple of possibilities.

Franklin wasn't a shady guy, but when Dana asked for his feedback, he suddenly sounded like somebody from Human Resources. "Sure, that one's a good idea. The job in Marketing looks like a solid position. Now, the Sales Department has points going for it, too."

The position she didn't mention was the Division Manager. Dana's agenda was to see whether Franklin would suggest it to her. She had thought about bringing it up herself and asking whether he thought she was ready, then decided to let him make the first move.

She went away deflated when he didn't mention it. The next day, the thought struck her that the way she would get that position was to announce to Franklin that she was going for it and to lobby for his support. He wasn't going to give it to her without her taking a risk in reaching out to grab for it.

When she saw him later that day, Dana announced that she was putting her hat in the ring for Division Manager.

"Do you think you're ready for it?" he asked.

Dana looked him in the eye. "You bet I am!"

"Well, you've got my support," Franklin said. "You know how to keep your people on course and your budget on target.

You're a motivator and a leader. You've had the guts to stand up for your department and for yourself when it counted. You've won a lot of big ones. You've lost a few, too, but when you lost, you handled yourself with class. That counts around here.

"And nobody has forgotten the way you handled the Nielson project—man, you picked up the ball at the one-yard line and took it all the way downfield for the touchdown! That campaign put this whole company in the game, Dana.

Franklin smiled. "Do I think you're ready for Division Manager? Hell, yes. I'm just relieved you're not going after *my* job!" He put out his hand for a shake.

The penchant for self-selection can lead to typical Competitor disdain for people who don't make the grade. Their attitude is, "Let them do it the hard way, the way I did." If you have to ask permission, you don't have the right stuff. You have to be able to get it for yourself.

Competitors get what they get the hard way. They have to take personal risks—and to know when the time is right to take a risk. Dana's strategy of guts and nerve paid off for her because she was ready for the promotion, and her boss knew she was competent. Her decision to go for the big one could have been disastrous if she had relied on nerve alone.

". . . That's when I really went for it," Dana remembered. "It was one of the hardest things I've ever done. I had to do it. I'm an achievement junkie; I admit it. To feel good, I need to push myself, see how far I can go.

"But everybody isn't like that—at least, below the thirtieth floor, they aren't. It's easy to look down on people who are happy where they are. One of the reasons I like Lesley is that she has drive. She's going for a promotion—that's motivation I can understand.

"People like Luke are harder for me to figure out. Promotions don't interest him. He just wants to work on computers and have as few hassles as possible. I don't think he even cares if we pay him. Every time I hear about his latest heroics with our systems, I think, 'With a mind like his, he could go *so* far.' That's right, Dana. Assume that if people are any good, they're just like you!

"Well, not everybody wants a promotion. They want to do a good job, have some stability and security, and enjoy the other parts of their lives. I've caught myself wondering what's wrong with them—how can they settle for second best? Of course, they probably think there's something wrong with *me*.

"And how am I supposed to feel when I've climbed as high as I can reach? Nope—stay away from that one, girl—that's like thinking about death. I'll worry about it when the time comes."

---

3. A Competitor Learns the Unwritten Rules.

"That Lesley," Dana came back to her office, shaking her head, after another lunchtime pep talk. Every time somebody doesn't play by what Lesley *thinks* are the rules, she takes it so personally.

"It's hard to tell what the real rules are," Dana thought, remembering. ". . . I guess I learned by joking around. Years ago, Jack James made a comment at a meeting: 'The main rule here is, "You can do whatever you can get away with."' We all laughed, but that stuck in my mind. He was right! There were rules beyond what they told us. We just had to figure them out for ourselves.

"That was the day I started trying to figure out The System, instead of getting mad at it. . . ."

The Competitor's great skill is the ability to read and operate within The System. To be a Competitor, you must develop the ability to figure out the real rules—the unwritten ones. (The written rules are there usually as a showpiece for Believers so they have something to believe in.)

What are the 10 commandments where you work? What would happen if they were miraculously engraved above the company logo at the front door?

In some companies, there aren't 10 commandments; there is only one: *"I am thy bottom line. Thou shalt have no other priorities above me."* In others, there are qualities and behaviors that are valued above profitability, but even those will not allow you to lose money indefinitely.

Most companies have unwritten rules about the following:

Productivity: "Thou art thy bottom line: Thou shalt show a profit in all cost centers. They who meeteth not the quotas shall find no shelter in the Promised Land."

Pace: "Thou shalt be busy"—or—"Thou shalt be punctual and prompt in meeting thy deadlines"—or—"By yesterday thou shalt have it done"—or—"Thou shalt take thy time and get it right."

Primacy of work: "Thy company shall come first in word and deed; such other commitments as ye may have shall not keep thee from thy appointed work. If thou canst not stand the heat, get thee out of the kitchen"—or—"Thou shalt be a balanced individual: job, family, and community shalt thou have."

Accuracy: "Thy figures shall tally even to the eighth decimal place"—or—"Close enough for government work shall suffice."

Reverence: "This is the company that pays thy wages; love it or leave it."

Attitude toward authority: "Fault not thy betters, for the ways of management are beyond the comprehension of mere mortals."

Ethics: "Thou shalt be honest"—or—"Thou shalt look honest"—or—"Think only on thy most sacred Commandment 'Love thy bottom line as thyself' (All other commandments are negotiable.)"

Accountability: "Screw up not, for thy transgressions shall come home to roost."—or—"Thine errors are between thee and heaven, for in this world, thou shalt not be checked." "Rules 2 through 10 do not apply above the 12th floor."

Demeanor: "Positive, Professional, and Managerial shall be thy dress, thy word, thy thought, and thy deed"—*or*—"If thou art a star, thou shalt do whatever thou wilt."

Secrecy: "Display not thy company's dirty laundry in public." "Thy thoughts on all matters shall be shared on a need-to-know basis." "Thou shalt not upset the Believers."

Creativity: "By thine ideas shalt thou be judged; let 'em rip"—*or*—"Thou shalt not be *too* different."

Toughness: "Thou shalt not be pushed around"—*or*—"If someone above thee smiteth thee, turn the other cheek."

Employee relations: "A satisfied team shalt thou lead." "Thou shalt maintain the respect of thy people"—*or*—"The nice guy finisheth last; team players shalt have fewer digits on their salary checks."

Public relations: "He that createth bad press shall be banished from Jerusalem."

Responsibility to employees: "On the laurels of past battles may thou rest in thine old age"—*or*—"What hast thou done for us lately?"

Obviously, it is important to understand *your* company's unwritten commandments. You might want to ask several trusted colleagues to help you come up with a list. Another possibility is to make this a companywide exercise, with lists compiled by different divisions and employee-management levels. Usually there will be agreement on most of the unwritten rules—but you can learn quite a bit about your company by the few "commandments" on which there is disagreement.

"What are the real rules around here?" Dana wondered. "One of them surely is 'Spend thy time with those above you.' Could I just get up in front of my department and list the real commandments? What would they think?

"It's so easy to get cynical and think, 'What do they know?' and just give them a half-explanation. I've done it a thousand times with my people. Of course, I'm usually concealing the

stuff that's embarrassing, to me or the company, and trying to keep my staff satisfied and quiet.

"When Lesley and I talked, I tried to level with her. I told her some things I *never* talk about. What would happen if she took that information back to Jack James or, God forbid, the chairman of the board, and said, 'Dana told me this is how things are really done around here'?

"I could see myself getting a good lecture from Franklin. He's always talking about playing your cards close to your vest. This whole company depends on having people like Lesley believe that their hard work will be rewarded—when the fact is that we managers are sometimes too busy with each other even to notice it.

"Another of the commandments here is, 'A manager gets to do what she wants in her own department—if the bottom line looks good.' Well, it's up to me to know what my people are doing and what they want—and to show them the connection. To lead them for what they are, instead of assuming that, if they were any good, they'd be like me. . . . I don't imagine I'll get in too much trouble for that. . . ."

4. A Competitor Must Face Down the Fear of Failure.

Adopt a strategy of maximizing success, rather than minimizing failure. Let's look at the difference:

Carl doesn't ever like to get his hopes up too high, because then he won't be disappointed. Go for that promotion? No way. He'd never get it anyway, so why put himself out there and risk getting shot down in front of everybody?

Disappointment is the worst feeling for people like Carl, and they will do nearly anything to avoid it. In the process, these failure-minimizers tend to undervalue themselves, often preferring to remain in the safety of the Believers rather than risk getting "shot down" among the Competitors.

Teri, Carl's former officemate, describes herself as a real "go-for-it" type. When a promotion opportunity was posted in her department, Teri would go for it, even if she was under-qualified. Several times, she didn't even make the first cut, but that didn't stop her from trying again. She knew she'd make it the next time and, several "next times" later, she did.

Maximizers such as Teri are sometimes disappointed, but they end up achieving more in the long run. To be an effective Competitor, you need to know which decisions are important enough to warrant taking a risk. You also have to develop ways of talking to yourself about setbacks.

Imagine a cow in a pasture bounded by an electric fence. If she has been shocked two or three times, the cow will never get close enough again to check whether there's any current. After a while, you could put a string where the fence was, and the string would have the same effect as the fence.

Failure-avoidance is hard to unlearn because, like the cow, you never check. You never experience the pain of failure, so you never develop any skills to handle it. If you fail at something, you're devastated. Although your abilities develop, you tend to avoid all the things you've always avoided. You tend to replay the old tapes in your head, internal messages such as "It would be so embarrassing to fail," or "Watch out—don't take a chance."

Success-maximizers, on the other hand, tend to think optimistically:

"Now I know what I need to do it right next time."
"Nothing ventured, nothing gained."
"It hurts now, but I'll heal."

They try, and fail, and thus learn to accept failure as specific and temporary. They never say, "I am a failure." They develop a loaded arsenal of thoughts and behaviors to deal with setbacks. The only way to do that is to have setbacks to deal with.

5. A Competitor Must Abandon the Need for Praise.

Dana checked her messages and found the summons from her boss: "See me today." Her neck muscles tightened, and her stomach churned. She had no idea what she'd done to make him mad, but she'd better find out and get it over with. She headed down the corridor to the boss's suite.

His secretary waved her in, and Dana, pale-faced, said, "You wanted to see me, Franklin?" She made sure to keep her voice steady.

Her boss looked up, nodded curtly, then reached into the drawer of his rosewood desk. "Here." He handed her two tickets. "Think you and your hubby can use these Thursday night?"

Dana stared at the tickets. The Bulls game. Center court. Sold out for months. "We love basketball," she said, smiling. "Thanks, Franklin! Thanks a lot!"

"Don't mention it," her boss said.

Competitors don't believe in praise and especially don't see the need to praise other Competitors. Often, Competitors will *not* praise someone they particularly respect because they think the person is like them and doesn't need it. They might, however, use other ways to show their approval, as Dana's boss did.

Though all the studies show that praise *is* important, Competitors (i.e., most bosses) just don't think to praise their subordinates. What's more, they consider anyone who wants (or obviously enjoys) praise to be beneath their status and definitely *not* management material. (If a Competitor *does* tell you you're doing a good job, this can be a signal that he doesn't think you're a real Competitor.) You have to rate your performance yourself. Have a clear idea of what you're good at—and what you're not so good at. You need to know objectively where you stand among your fellow Competitors. Nobody can be completely objective, of course, but you need to have an accurate idea of your own strengths and weaknesses.

Here is where the Myth of Motivation can deceive you. When you repeat 100 times, "I'm Number One!" to overcome your doubts, you will also be blinded to your weaknesses. You have to be able to say, "I'm better than anybody in my league" but still know which league you're in.

Don't rely on other people's evaluations of you, especially your company's annual evaluation. It is designed to protect the company over questions of impropriety in giving raises or firing people; its purpose is not really to give you a clear idea of how you're doing.

"The Bulls tickets were a nice touch," Dana thought. "It's part of Franklin's style never to let you know where you stand. He'll go months without a word one way or the other, then all of a sudden do something like this. He loves to keep people off balance. It drives me crazy sometimes.

"I can't expect him to tell me I'm doing a good job because he really doesn't know much about what I do. Well, I can handle it. As I told Lesley, that's just the way it is.

"That *doesn't* mean I have to play the same game with *my* team, though. Everybody needs a little praise now and then. More than that, they need accurate feedback. I can't just say, 'Great job,' without really knowing what they did. They'd catch me on that one for sure."

6. A Competitor Does It *Now.*

"I used to put things off," Dana admits. "I still do, but now when I notice I'm avoiding a task, I ask myself, 'What are you afraid of? Who are you ticked off at?' I made some headway when I stopped calling it 'procrastination' and started seeing it as a message to myself about my own fears or my need to say 'No' to somebody.

* * *

Paul was promoted to department head, and suddenly he developed a time-management problem. His reports were always late; he missed meetings, and even the simplest task seemed to take weeks.

* * *

Maggie's boss was domineering and pushy. Somehow, the more demanding the boss became, the slower and more forgetful Maggie became.

* * *

Bob is so agreeable. Whatever you ask him to do, he always says, "Sure." Of course, that's usually the last you hear of it. He's made so many promises, he can't possibly keep them all.

* * *

Cheryl knows that the only way to sell insurance is to make cold calls, but every time she looks at the telephone, she thinks of a hundred other things that need to be done.

If you asked them, each of these people would say that their problem was procrastination. They probably have attended a seminar or two on time management and were surprised when the techniques didn't work. They didn't work because procrastination itself is not the problem—it's actually what protects them from the problem.

Paul's procrastination protects him from his doubts about his ability to perform his new job; Maggie's protects her from confronting her boss directly; Bob's keeps him from having to say 'No'; and Cheryl's protects her from the rejection of prospective clients. For all four, procrastination is an expensive and inefficient way of self-protection.

7. A Competitor Avoids Martyrdom.

One day, over coffee, Dana told Lesley, "I used to bust my behind, covering for Rowan, my former boss in Purchasing. I

thought for sure everybody would be so grateful. Was I ever wrong about that one!

"It was only when I stood back and let Rowan's mistakes show that his boss did anything about the situation."

Get rid of the notion that taking on more than your share is your way to the top. It's all right to help out other people sometimes, but you'll never be rewarded for regularly doing the job for an incompetent boss or for protecting a sloppy colleague. (Of course, doing the occasional favor, if asked in advance, can be helpful to your career.) Even though you need to work hard, you definitely do not need to become a martyr.

8. A Competitor Ignores Personal Limitations.

"I've done so many things I never thought I could do," Dana thought as she flipped back through her century-at-a-swoop calendar. "Presentations, negotiations, conferences all over the world—and a lot of hours just staying here until the job was finished. . . ."

Competitors learn they can do more than they thought they could. The essence of a classical warrior is doing heroic tasks. Most often, in the Competitor's world, the heroism lies in working as many hours as it takes to get the job done—doing what needs to be done even if you're afraid or you don't want to or you don't think you can do it. It's you and the task until it's done. You surprise yourself at how much strength and endurance you have.

The other part is the heroic deeds you do for show. For most Competitors, that means putting in long hours. In the 1950s, business Competitors were proud of their ulcers. In the 1990s, the 60-hour week is the badge of honor. In most companies, the number of hours is more important than the amount of work. Hard work is not measurable or visible. Long hours are. Being together at midnight while sweating out a deal forms a powerful bond between brothers- and sisters-in-arms. It's like leaving home and going to war. The purpose of the long hours is the ritual sacrifice for the job.

9. A Competitor Abandons Family?

"If Lesley ever asks me what the hardest part of my job is, my answer's ready," Dana thought, rubbing her neck in exhaustion. "It's balancing these killer hours at work with our family life. There's never as much time as I want at home."

Abandon family? Not really—but it feels like it. There is almost no way to have a responsible management position without putting in the long hours. This is what the "wife of the '50s" made possible. Now she has a job, too. How many times have you heard two-career couples wail, "What we really need is a wife!"?

Being a two-career family implies a certain amount of equality. If that equality is not there, or it's unclear to one of the partners what the rules are, they need to sit down and discuss it. Now. In your family, if you don't have a clear agreement on whose job-related responsibilities come first, and when, you'll probably soon be spending your time and money on marriage counseling or attorney fees.

If there is one secret to making a two-career family work, it's *communication*: talking, scheduling, planning, deciding when and how you're going to do the things you want and have to do. Sometimes, though, you have to make tough choices.

Dana looked anxiously at the clock on her desk. Her son's school basketball team was in the finals—and she'd promised him that she'd be there for the opening tip-off. To make it on time, Dana would have to leave right now.

Of course, Franklin *would* call an emergency meeting. She felt her stomach churning again with anger and worry. It should be so simple to decide: Skip the game, or skip the meeting.

The logical choice was to miss the game, of course. When Franklin called an emergency meeting, he expected everybody upstairs in the War Room, on the double. Her son would understand. He always did. It wasn't as if these were the NBA finals; her boy was only fourteen years old. He'd have years of basketball games still to come. She wouldn't always be this busy, would she?

What would Lesley say? Another zinger about what do you tell your kids?

"It's just a basketball game," Dana tried to tell herself. But she was hearing another, louder message: "It's just another meeting."

10. A Competitor Abandons Self-importance.

As a Competitor, you're always having to prove something. Especially in the early days, life is just one initiation ritual after another. "Hell Week" goes on forever, or at least it seems that way. You have to show that you have what it takes. You don't rely on the Believers' naïve view of fairness to get you through. You can stand or fall on your own merits. You put the group ahead of yourself. (Later, there will be plenty of time to see to self-interest.)

Competitors are a very judgmental group. You may have developed all the qualities we describe in this chapter, but you still have to prove yourself.

What you usually have to sacrifice to get into the group is your self-importance. You will have to accept teasing, defer to other people's opinions, and, most of all, to *listen when you feel like speaking.* If you can't recognize what is demanded of you, everybody else will know that they won't be able to rely on you to take care of the group, and you'll never really be an insider.

The other purpose of initiation rituals is to establish your place in the pecking order. That's important, too, as many management books will tell you. However, before you start engaging in power struggles with people who are already members of the group, you first will have to show you can be trusted as a fellow Competitor.

Be very careful. What you do in the first six months of your new job can determine how you will be perceived throughout most of the rest of your career at the company:

Don't rely on your boss, your job description, or your professional training to get you respect. This is something you have to do by yourself, and it has to do with your own personality, rather than formal rules. In the first six months, you probably don't understand what's going on if you think the answer to a difficult situation is (a) getting your boss to intervene, or (b) acquainting the offending party with your educational credentials or your job's responsibilities.

The Competitors above you are setting up a situation to see how you'll react. It's all personal, and these rituals are very important to them.

Show you can listen. The best way to show deference to a group is to show interest. Listen to people. Ask about the way they do things. Ask for advice and take it. You're not allowed to apply the Management Mystique to colleagues' advice until you're really accepted in the group.

Many people believe that the way to be successful on a new job is to dazzle people with your brilliance. Actually, during the initiation time, they care very little about your brilliance. They want you to show them that you value the experience and knowledge of the group. *Under no circumstances should you tell them how to do their jobs.* (Sure, you learned it differently in business school, but this is neither the time nor the place; trust us.)

When people in the group begin asking you for your opinion, that's a sign that they regard you as an insider. Don't give opinions until you're seriously asked. Then the Management Mystique will work for you, too.

Demonstrate that you can take teasing and can give it back. Teasing, another common initiation ritual, occurs most often on shop floors, but it happens in boardrooms, too. The style and content differs from company to company, but the purpose is the same. You have to show that you can take it and give it back with equanimity.

If you get angry or appeal to an authority, you lose. Certainly, there are situations when teasing exceeds the bounds of propriety, especially those that involve racism, sexism, and the like. But before you accuse people of prejudice, though, make sure that that's what you're seeing. If you're a Competitor, it might be worthwhile even to put up with these things in order to win. Remember that, through teasing, you're being asked to sacrifice a little of your personal dignity to the group. *The less seriously you take yourself, the more quickly you'll be accepted.*

Make allies. Do favors for the people who can help you win. Find out what they need from your position, and let them know that you can supply it (if you can). Sell yourself. You have to find out where they think your position fits in and how you can help the group. You have to *sell* changes, rather than having your boss decree them.

It can be helpful to find a mentor, someone who's a part of the group. Usually, your boss won't do for this purpose. You need somebody who is willing to be your guide and sponsor and will interpret for you the meaning of some of the situations you meet—someone to help you understand and fit into the company culture.

If you're lucky enough to find a person like this, *do what he or she tells you.* This person is offering a bond that may last throughout your career. The price of that bond is accepting that the mentor is the knowledgeable one and deserves to be listened to—It's not okay to compete with your mentor.

Abandon your own way of doing things for the company way. Whether it's a high-tech company or a primitive tribe in the Amazon, the basic initiation rules are the same. You have to go through a few difficulties without complaining to become a member of the tribe. Before you will be allowed to be creative or to have a chance to do it your way, you first will have to demonstrate that you can play by the rules. The real rules. The initiation is tough, but the prize is full membership as a Competitor.

"Talking with Lesley has brought back a lot of memories for me," Dana mused. "I remember how frustrated and angry I used to feel because everything seemed so unfair, like a personal slap in the face. I can't believe I used to be that naïve. Now, come to think of it, things still seem unfair and frustrating, but for different reasons. I guess there's still a lot I don't know. . . . The company way. My way. Where do I draw the line?"

The phone on her desk buzzed, and Dana picked up. Her boss was on the line, telling her everybody was waiting for her in the War Room.

"Franklin, I can't come to the meeting," Dana said. "I have a previous commitment. I'll be in early tomorrow, and we can go over the details."

18

A Happy Ending for a Business Book? How It Could Happen

The 1990s are being promoted as the decade of teamwork and partnership. Unless Competitors learn to work with and value Rebels and Believers, the "theme of the decade" will be just another corporate slogan, papering over business as usual. Competitors have been talking about teamwork for years.

Teamwork is the American way, right? Actually, *talking* about teamwork, but doing what's best for *you* is more consistent with the values and beliefs of the Competitors. Even when they do more than talk about it, their idea of teamwork means the team's uncomplaining acceptance of whatever the captain tells them to do.

We believe that Competitors have prevented teamwork and cooperation—until now that the Good Guys are falling behind in the global marketplace. These high stakes may be what finally compels Competitors actually to use the human resources at their disposal to pull ahead and win.

Can Competitors rise to the challenge? They can—if they realize that this battle won't be fought in boardrooms, but in the hearts and minds of individual Competitors. Teamwork cannot be created by decree. If you try it that way, all you get is another slogan.

There is help available, but it will come from the most un- likely place—the minds of Rebels and Believers. The big ques- tion is the same as it has always been—will the Competitors listen? We think the companies that learn to use all their re- sources by cooperating will be the ones that come out on top at the end of the decade.

To illustrate the possibilities of real teamwork and coopera- tion, we take a final look at our Rebel, Believer, and Competi- tor characters a few years later into the '90s.

Dana and Luke Find a Way

Bronson has had a heart attack. Even he'd have to admit he'd been asking for it. During his recuperation, Dana has moved in to take care of his division. (It took some heavy-duty politi- cal maneuvering, but she pulled it off. She's keeping her per- sonal perspective, too. Her son's team is in the finals again, and she'll be there, no matter what.)

Soon after she accepted her new assignment, Dana discov- ered that some departments—those that Bronson considered important to the bottom line—were running smoothly. On the other hand, the computer department was among the major disaster areas. Dana immediately recognized this department as a great resource and saw Luke as its shining star. So she did what any Competitor would do with someone valuable— she promoted Luke within the department.

Luke accepted, though not without some hesitation. He knew Dana was a straight shooter, though, and he'd always said that if *he* ran things, they'd be different. At first, the promotion was a disaster, however. Luke refused to accept any responsibility for the department. He would regularly help people out, as he always had, but the things he wasn't interested in—paperwork was at the top of that list—just wouldn't get done.

Dana called him in several times to tell him that he *had* to get it together, but Luke ignored her. He privately thought, "She's just like a boss. She doesn't even know what we do in the department. She's obsessed over the little stuff we're *not* doing."

Luke didn't say what he was thinking, though. (He may be a Rebel, but he's not crazy.) He just went ahead and did things his own way and didn't talk about it. Dana finally lost her patience and threatened him with demotion. Then Luke's pride and rebelliousness took over. He became a Captain Bligh, cracking the whip and demanding that the paperwork come in letter-perfect and on time. If not, heads would roll. The work came in, but Luke's staff was threatening mutiny. Luke was suffering, too. He used to be one of the guys. Now he was one of *them*.

Finally, Luke burst into Dana's office and exploded. "You don't have to demote me! I quit! I told you I didn't want to be a boss, and now you know why! I'm going to find someplace to work where they'll just let me do my job and leave me alone!"

You'd think Rebels would make good, sensitive bosses, but people with authority problems often make the worst authority figures. They're always rebelling against authority so they don't figure out what it really is. To them, it looks like pushing people around, so that's what they do when they get the job.

Dana refused to accept Luke's resignation. She realized that something was very wrong. People with Luke's level of computer skills were one in a million, and she would not lose him over something like this. There had to be an answer. She thought a minute and asked, "What job would you like to be left alone to do?" Luke started to answer, but Dana stopped him. "Don't tell me. Show me." I'll clear my calendar, and I'll spend all day Wednesday with you, seeing exactly what you do, so I can get a clearer picture of what the problem is. Do we have a deal?"

Luke grinned. "Deal."

Dana's day with Luke showed her that he loved his computer work but showed little interest in the details of management. The meetings, the organizing, the details, and the planning bored him stiff. Dana decided to get him an executive assistant, Bill, who was new to Neander-Tek—eager to prove himself but basically a Believer. Bill's job would be to help keep Luke organized and to free Luke to do the work he liked best—the work so crucial to the company's bottom line.

Dana's solution worked. Luke's paperwork doesn't drive him crazy any more. He has Bill to take care of those cursed forms. Luke can spend his time leading the "assault teams" that solve problems, create new software, and limit down time to the bare minimum. Computer reliability in Dana's division is the envy of the rest of the company.

When Competitors take Rebels and Believers seriously, everybody can win. Unfortunately, not all Rebels are as lucky as Luke. His luck was having a skill that had a very high dollar value—*and* having a boss—Dana—recognize it. If you are a Rebel, make sure that you're paying particular attention to the parts of your job that save costs or make money for your company. If you do that, you can buy yourself a lot of freedom.

Carl Rises from the Ashes

When Dana took over Bronson's division, she also inherited Carl, the embattled assistant manager who had written the policies and procedures manual. As Dana looked over Carl's personnel file, she shook her head and thought, "This man is really burned out," and was ready to cross him off as not having anything valuable to contribute. "Let him stay in his back office and keep out of people's way." Fortunately for Carl, though, Dana read parts of Carl's manual, in which she recognized Carl's first-rate organizing ability.

Dana was particularly on the lookout for this skill, because

Bronson hadn't paid much attention to day-to-day opera-
tions. He had gone for the glory and made the deals, leaving
other parts of his division in shambles. Maybe Carl had what
it takes to get people back on track. Dana decided to meet
with Carl to find out.

Carl sat across from her, arms crossed, eyes narrowed sus-
piciously as Dana began to speak. Nonetheless, Carl slowly
thawed as Dana asked questions about his job and referred
positively to sections of his manual. Dana had actually read it
and was interested in his work! Carl let down his guard
enough to complain in Dana's presence.

Dana doesn't like complainers any more than most Competitors, but she recognized that before she could build a good
working relationship with Carl, she would have to listen to
some of his complaints and take them seriously. So she listened attentively but did not try to jump in and solve Carl's
problems.

Finally, when Carl's list ended, Dana said, "Well, Carl, what
do you want? What would make you happy?" Nobody at
Neander-Tek had ever asked Carl what it would take to make
him happy. He had to stop and think for a minute. When he
answered, he spoke with quiet dignity: "What I want is to be
respected for what I do well. I want some recognition. I don't
want to move up—I want to keep doing what I've been doing—
but I want to feel that I have some value to this company. I
haven't felt that way in a long time."

Dana looked at him with new respect. "I have a deal for
you," she said. "There's absolutely no reason for you to trust
me right now, but here's what I'm offering. See what you think
of it. You want to be respected. I want to look good in how I
run this division. I need somebody who can help me get
things organized and standardized. I've seen your manual
and know you have a talent for that. Let's get it out and talk
about how we're going to get procedures standardized around
here."

Dana spent some time over the next few weeks going over the manual with Carl, section by section, helping him to eliminate unnecessary steps and streamline the rules so that they were easy to follow and required less paperwork. When Carl balked, Dana was ready. "The guys down in the computer department will never fill out all these forms. What can we do to make it easier for them? Their main job is working on computers, not filling out forms. We need to meet their needs, not the other way around."

Dana was amazed at Carl's grasp of the intricacies of running the division. Dana learned that some of the rules and policies that at first had seemed like quirks were actually the most efficient ways of getting difficult jobs done. Carl won her over on several of these procedures, and Dana made sure to tell him he had won. "Carl, you're right about this. This *is* the best way to do it, but it's hard to understand. You and I are going to have to sell it to people."

Dana helped Carl understand how to be more effective, rather than a stickler for rules. She gained Carl's respect by listening to him, taking him seriously, and being honest with him about the manual's strengths and weaknesses. A little gentle teasing didn't hurt, either. What Carl wanted most was to be respected—and liked.

Soon people were talking about Carl's new attitude and how much less crabby he had become. His status rose dramatically because of his new value to Dana and because he was finally learning how to cooperate.

Dana knew that all the admonishment in the world would not make Carl more cooperative. Instead, she worked to figure out what would prevent Carl from engaging in his most florid uncooperative behavior. Dana also reminded Carl that lording his new authority over other people or demanding that they

follow the rules to the letter would not make Dana look good—
which was to be Carl's top priority. Dana made it clear that
when there was a compliance problem, Carl should come directly to her.

Carl, who had never been stupid, recognized the value of
this new approach. He changed, too. He blossomed into one of
the most valuable employees in the division, firmly loyal to
Dana and to the company. He didn't want to be promoted, but
he got what he wanted: People respect him. They go to him for
information. They ask him questions. Most of all, they follow
his new streamlined policies and procedures manual and recognize its value in making the division more efficient. They
also like him.

"El Tigre" Goes Global

**Jack James has successfully lobbied the Neander-Tek board to
do some cooperative projects with Japanese and European
companies. After he got the go-ahead, he spent much of the
next year out of the country, setting up negotiations and laying groundwork for deals with his customary skill.**

**When he returned, he reported his preliminary success to
an enthusiastic board, which saw Jack's work as the wave of
the future. There was immediate talk of a publicity campaign
built around a new slogan for the twenty-first century: "Neander-Tek—Hands around the Globe Pulling to Win."**

**But Jack held up a hand. "Wait a minute. One thing I
learned this year is that there are other cultures out there that
seem to have a longer-term view of things. Before we take
credit for this stuff, let's see what happens. Let's take it slowly.
The fact is, some of these deals may not work out. We've got
time."**

Jack has always been good at learning what he needs to
learn. Competitor that he is, he quickly figured out what his
peers in other cultures valued—cooperation. Back at his own
company, Jack started searching out people who were good at

team play and sensitive to other cultures. These were the executives he wanted on his new team.

Before long, some of Jack's international ventures had paid off big-time. *Forbes* magazine interviewed him for a flattering profile on the man and his deals. Suddenly, El Tigre was global—the man to watch, not only in his own company, but also all over the world.

Through the 1990s, Jack kept rising at Neander-Tek—more promotions and a great deal of personal glory. As he did so, he gradually realized that his greatest satisfaction was the international team he had created. During his climb to the top, Jack had taken the time for another look at his own values and his contribution to something beyond himself.

The Mellowing of Bronson

Bronson (you didn't think we'd get rid of him so easily, did you?) is recovering from a heart attack. He knows he will have to change his ways to win this battle. If it takes mellowing out to beat the Reaper, that's what he'll do. He quit smoking last year, and he listens to relaxation tapes. (He got them at a stress-management seminar. Would you believe it?)

Back at work in a different division, Bronson heard the legendary tales of Jack James's international ventures and knew that was where he wanted to be now. He went directly to Jack and said, "You're riding the wave, and I want to be on it too. How about if we team up on this?"

Jack gave him a straight answer. "Bronson, you're a bright guy and a real Competitor, but I wonder about your ability to handle people. I don't know whether you can cut the mustard in terms of cooperation."

Bronson, who always rose to a challenge, recognized that this fit in with what he had been trying to do for himself. He'd been trying to work on relaxing, seeing other people's point of view, and mellowing out. Now there was more to gain than just a healthy heart. He could win big again. He grinned at Jack and clapped him on the back. "I might surprise you, buddy. I just might. . . ."

Bronson had run into Carl a few times and was amazed at what he had seen. "You must be some kind of magician," he told Dana. "I thought good old Carl was just about out the door, but he's really changed. He's got what it takes after all."

Dana said, "Don't tell *me*, Bronson. Tell Carl."

He did—and read Carl's manual cover to cover. (He had never bothered to read it when he was Carl's boss.) "It's a real solid piece of work," he told Carl, who relished seeing the respect in Bronson's eyes. Carl knew Bronson wanted something. Bronson did, but he knew he'd have to make some real changes to get it.

Bronson's new goal was to get involved in Jack James's high-profile international projects. He knew that to be on that team, he'd have to pay more attention to detail and become more of a people person. This chance to move up depended on getting some help with the day-to-day work. He surprised Dana by asking her to transfer Carl temporarily to his division to help him do a policies and procedures manual. The *really* big surprise came when Carl told Dana he'd go. Later, Dana overheard Carl telling a colleague, "You know, that Bronson isn't really such a bad guy . . ."

Bronson worked on making his division a showplace of co-operation. At first, this was just a tactical move to make him look good in Jack's eyes. It wasn't too long, though (he *is* smart) before he saw some real advantages to working with people. He looked at what was going on in his old division under Dana's leadership and realized that in some areas, her style was more effective than his. He decided to spend a couple of lunch hours talking with her, even though she was his junior.

He also made a note to sign up for a course in Japanese. Heck, it couldn't hurt. . . .

Bronson clearly hasn't lost his ability to pick a winner. He has chosen well in trying to learn from Jack, Carl, and Dana. Now, he is finally triumphing over the Management Mystique by realizing that there still *are* things he can learn.

Lesley Moves Up

Lesley has been promoted; she's a full-fledged manager now. (You knew she'd do it.) She did it by leading a campaign for an issue close to her heart: child care. Armed with facts and figures—and strong support from Dana *(Remember*—criticism in private, support in public)—Lesley convinced upper management that establishing a child care program would save the company money and give them a competitive edge. Neander-Tek would be keeping and attracting the services of trained employees with small children. The Competitors in charge paid attention to Lesley's bottom-line approach and placed her in charge of a small pilot program. Its success convinced them to set up companywide child care—and earned Lesley the promotion she craved. (On the day her promotion was announced, Dana sent her a bottle of champagne, topped with a baseball cap that said, "I'm Number One!")

Her conversations with Dana gave Lesley a much clearer idea of what is rewarded in their company. She wants to keep moving up, so she pays major attention to the bottom line. She knows how her work affects her department's profits and losses, and she can produce facts and figures to show exactly how much her work is worth in dollars and cents.

Now Lesley is heading a multidepartmental task force on recruiting technical employees. The task force has raised a number of issues about the image of the company and the

changing characteristics of the work force. Through Lesley's efforts, everyone can see that more technical people are coming aboard. (Quite a few of them are women who like the company's child care program.) This is quite a change from the days when it was difficult to fill those slots.

Lesley has become better at promoting herself. Her presentations on the task force's success have earned her name recognition with upper management. She hasn't changed completely, though. She's still managing the company softball team because that will always be important to her—but now she wears the cap only at games.

At the quarterly management meeting, Lesley ran into Bronson, whom she hadn't seen for awhile. She had heard about his heart attack and said she was glad to see him looking so healthy.

Bronson smiled. "I've heard about *you*. You're the head bounty hunter now."

Lesley frowned and stifled a defensive rush of explanation. The task force work was serious, and she wanted to tell him exactly what they were doing—but then it dawned on her. Bronson's joke was a *compliment.* Calling her a bounty hunter was Bronson's way of acknowledging that she was doing a good job. By comparing her to a Wild West character, Bronson, the ultimate Competitor, was praising her.

Meanwhile Bronson was thinking, "Oops, there I go again. She takes that work pretty seriously. I bet I offended her." He put his hand on her jacket sleeve and said, "Hey, I know you're not a bounty hunter, Les. I was just joking."

But Lesley just grinned. "No, Bronson. That's OK. I like the sound of it."

She went to her seat thinking, "My attitudes have really changed. There was a time when I would have missed that compliment completely."

Bronson watched her walk away and thought, "I must be

mellowing out. It never would have mattered to me before that somebody might take offense."

During a break in the morning session, Lesley met Jack James at the coffee urn. She was just about to compliment him on his international ventures and his recent profile in *Forbes* when it struck her. Direct praise isn't the way it's done here, she realized. How would Bronson say it?

Lesley put out her hand and said heartily, "Jack! Good to see you. Though I hear they're calling you Tiger-san now."

The slight smile on Jack's face told her that she had done it right. Even the old Tiger lapped up the praise, just like everyone else. When Jack mentioned her recruitment task force, Lesley said, "I'm beginning to like the life of a bounty hunter."

Jack's smile grew wider, and they talked a bit about the old department. "Jack," Lesley asked, "what would you advise a new employee about how to get ahead at Neander-Tek?"

Jack thought for about three seconds. "Work hard and play by the rules. With the right kind of motivation, you'll make it."

"Just out of curiosity, Jack, what would you advise *me?*" Lesley asked.

He looked her over, smiled and said, "It doesn't look as if I need to tell *you* anything."

Index

Alexander the Great, 149

Believers, xv, 7–10, 91–146
  and authority figures, 113–24
  and bureaucracy, 123–24
  and burnout, 96
  and conflict with Competitors,
    8, 124
  as corporate innocents, xv, 10
  and illness, 134
  and job interviews, 34–37
  and luck, 62–65
  management of, 144–45
  as managers, 55
  and motivation, 64, 94–97
  responsibility of, 17
  and The System, 95–96
  and teamwork, 18
  as watchdogs, 122–23
  work ethic of, 91–92, 93
  working as, 142–43
  working for, 145–46
  and work rituals, 33
Boone, Daniel, 47
Bottom-line thinking, 83, 141,
  186–87
Bronson syndrome, 188
Burnout, 125–39
  avoidance of, 139
  versus exhaustion, 136
  myth of, 129–31
  pattern of, 133
  responses to, 133–36
  symptoms of, 130

Campbell, Joseph, 74
Cargo Cult thinking, 41–44, 98
  and corporate slogans, 44

Carter, Jimmy, 158
Catch-22, corporate, 101
Communication
  with peers, 232–33
  press-release, 221–25
  of problems, 233–34
  roadblocks to, 234–35
Competitors, xv, 10–13, 66, 149–
  94
  and the Bottom Line, 186–87
  and business meetings, 176–79
  and club membership, 183–84
  code of silence and, 184–86
  commandments of, 251–71
  and deal-making, 181–83
  independence of, 17–18
  and job interviews, 37–41
  and luck, 64–65
  management of, 192–93
  as managers, 12–13, 54
  and office politics, 11
  and presentations, 179–81
  and promotion, 11
  and rewards, 17
  and The System, 95
  and teamwork, 18, 111, 154–55,
    190, 191, 193, 226
  working as, 190–92
  working for, 193–94
  and work rituals, 33, 41
Conflict, 13
Conspiracy Theory, 65–66
Corporate innocence, guidelines
  for losing of, 236–50
Crockett, Davy, 47
Cult of the Brown Bag, 105–6
Cult of Cool, 6, 7, 69–74
  and Baby Boomers, 162–63
  M*A*S*H-style, 73–74
  as protection, 72–73